MAINE

*Bird's Eye View of Saco and Biddeford, Maine.
Color Lithograph by J. H. Bufford, from a sketch by
J. B. Bachelder, circa 1850–1870. Courtesy, Library
of Congress*

American Historical Press
Sun Valley, California

MAINE

DOWNEAST AND DIFFERENT

AN ILLUSTRATED HISTORY

NEIL ROLDE

Library of Congress Catalogue Card Number: 2006935071
ISBN 13: 978-1-892724-50-2
ISBN 10: 1-892724-50-2

Bibliography: p. 280
Includes Index

CONTENTS

Pemaquid Point, the extreme tip of the peninsula, is marked by Pemaquid Light.

PREFACE

Maine is the 23rd state and was only admitted to the Union in March 1820 after its separation from Massachusetts. But, in point of fact, it is one of the most historic sites of settlement in the United States. A would-be colony from England set foot on what is now Maine soil thirteen years before the Pilgrims stepped onto Plymouth Rock. We Mainers proudly declare that the first Thanksgiving feast was actually held at Popham Beach in our mid-coast region. Our off-shore islands were occupied by English sailors even prior to that occurrence. Captain John Smith, following a stay on our Monhegan Island, coined the term "New England" and constant reference to the "main" or "mainland" by such seafarers led to the eventual adoption of our state's name. There was a Province of Maine as early as the 1640s. Furthermore, Maine Indians helped the Plymouth Pilgrims survive financially by trading them furs they could sell in England to pay off their creditors.

Writing about Maine history is thus a journey into the deepest routes of the American past. Those same Maine Indians who were here to help the Pilgrims called themselves "People of the Dawn" because they lived where the sun first sends its rays to illuminate our continent. The settlers who followed were also among the first to start the adventure that ended in the creation of the United States. While Maine has only been one of those states since 1820, its antecedents are far more ancient and so the story of the Pine Tree state is a fascinating one to tell.

As a former politician as well as an author, I used to forego individual thanks for help in my books, fearful I would forget someone and thereby lose a vote. Since ending my active seeking of office in 1990, that hasn't been a problem. In this case I've already thanked many—if not all—of the folks at Maine libraries who've been so helpful in educating me on our state's history. These institutions include the Portland Public Library, the Maine Historical Society Library, the State Library, the Legislative Law Library, the Fogler Library at the University of Maine, the Bangor Public Library, the Maine State Archives, the Old York Historical Society Library and the Baxter Library in Gorham, Maine. This is not an exhaustive list.

In addition, I do have to proffer thanks to three individuals who have guided me through the perils of employing a word processor and computer in my work and, even more daunting, showing me how to transmit manuscripts electronically, which I still consider a form of black magic. These guys are Jeffrey Wilford, Craig Annis and Mark Annis. The first two are my sons-in-law and the third, my son-in-law's brother,

Also, special thanks to Amber Avines, a most helpful and enthusiastic editor.

Neil Rolde

To those authors who have written books about Maine.
These are almost always works of love, not commerce, devoted
to all aspects of this remarkable state of ours.

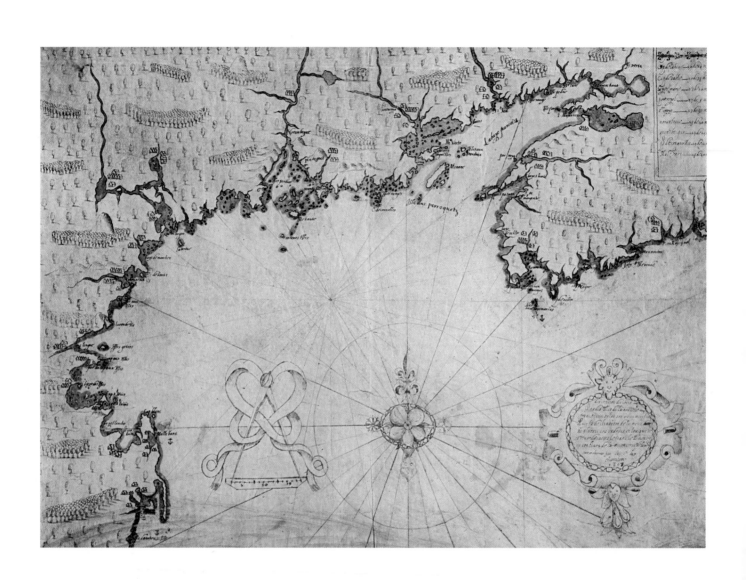

1

BEGINNINGS
PRE-HISTORY–1689

This extract from Samuel de Champlain's 1607 map of New France, shows the Penobscot River as the Pentagoet and the Kennebec River as the Quinebague. Looking for the fabled Norumbega, Champlain left a detailed cartographic record of the area that shows settlements already beginning on the waterways of Maine. Courtesy, Library of Congress

THE NATIVE AMERICANS

First, there was the land. The path of the bedrock of Maine can be traced around the globe. Once, the land that is now the Pine Tree State was located five degrees from the Equator. The new geologic science of plate tectonics can trace the journey of this earth matter from the beginning to billions of years later when it was lodged in its present location on the northeastern shores of the western Atlantic. When this earth mass occupied its current location, a series of glaciers covered the land, repeatedly melting and returning—shaping its topography. The last of these mile thick ice caps only vanished from "Downeast" about 14,000 years ago.

Next, there were the people. They often call themselves the first people but are known as paleo Indians to anthropologists and archaeologists (paleo meaning old in Greek). The terrain they occupied twelve millennia ago took eons to reach the geological and geographic environment in which they formed their society. The land evolved from arctic tundra to boreal forest, thick with magnificent pines and spruces and firs, bordering majestic rivers and shiny lakes. A cold land, but for paleo Indian hunters and fishermen, it was a land of plenty. The people called themselves Wabanakiak, often shortened to Abenaki—people of the dawn—for they intuited that they were the first on the continent to see the sun rise.

Their legends, told at campfires generation after generation, explained how Gluskap, their hero-god, had created them on the spot from arrows he shot into willow trees, how he made rivers flow and how he broke the back of Oglabamu, the giant frog who had sucked up all the available water.

Along the rivers, the Indian peoples formed into tribes. In the days before the white man arrived, these waterways were the principal roads. The Penobscot, Kennebec, Androscoggin, Saco, St. Croix and St. John—these are the liquid backbones of Maine. The invention of the birch bark canoe

GLOOSKAP AND KEANKE SPEARING THE WHALE.

Providing life, education and sometimes humor, Gluskap, or Glooskap, is a central figure in Algonquin creation stories. From Algonquin Legends of New England *or* Myths and Folklore of the MicMac, Passamaquoddy and Penobscot Tribes *by Charles Leland, 1884. Courtesy, Maine Historical Society*

The Wabanaki people refer to the Abenaki, Micmac, Maliseet, Penobscot and Passmaquoddy Indian tribes. The Passamaquoddy, like the porpoise hunters shown here, share a cultural heritage with the other groups. While both words mean "people of the dawnland" and sound very much alike, Wabanaki and Abenaki are not the same thing. The Wabanaki Confederacy is a political alliance and regional group that shares many cultural, linguistic and historical connections, and the Abenaki are a band of tribal groups within the Wabanaki Confederacy. From, Scribner's Monthly, *October 1880*

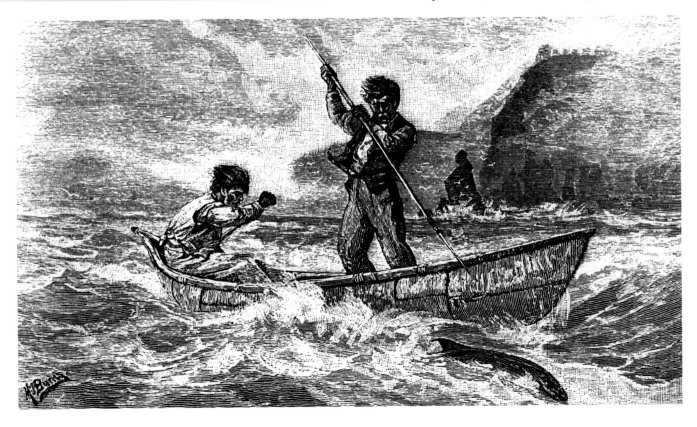

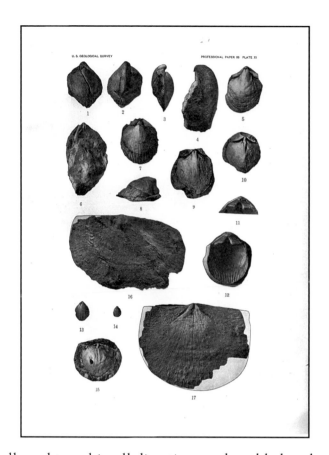

This a plate showing fossils found during a U.S. Geological Survey in Chapman Township, Aroostook County near Presque Isle Stream. Brachiopods likes these are the most common fossil found in Maine. Like clams or mollusks, brachiopods are bivalve marine animals. They can be distinguished from the clams we know because the shells have lines running vertically to the hinge rather than horizontally. The Maine state fossil is Pertica quadrifaria, a Devonian Era plant that lived 390 million years ago. From The Fauna of the Chapman Sandstone of Maine by Henry Shaler Williams, United States Professional Paper, 1916

allowed travel in all directions and enabled trade with a wide variety of native people. Artifacts unearthed in Maine have shown a provenance from as far north as the Eskimos to as far south as the Susquehannas in Pennsylvania. One startling item unearthed in the 1950s was an ancient Norse coin. For a thrilling moment, this was seen as proof that the elusive region Leif Erikson called Vinland had been located in the state. However, experts concluded it was a trade item, swapped with Indians from Newfoundland where recent excavations have uncovered a Viking community.

Hints of these ancient days emerge in the Abenaki myths. The mention of ivory-tipped weapons reflects the tusked mammoths that were known as game animals to their ancestors. The bones of elephant relatives in Maine have surfaced during excavations. The most ancient find, the dig at Lake Azicohos in the northwest corner of the state, revealed an 11,500 year-old "killing ground" where great herds of caribou, their major food source, were slaughtered. Moose and white-tailed deer replaced the caribou as the climate gradually warmed and in time established a pattern of life for the bands of nomads roaming the enormous north woods. Each group had its hunting territories; each had its villages along the rivers; each traveled to the coast in the summer. These groups ventured out to sea to spear swordfish, porpoises, and seals and, once ashore, feasted on clams and lobsters. This seemingly idyllic existence was fraught with dangers, including periodic raids by the fierce, cannibalistic Mohawks out of the west, internecine wars between the Maine tribes and harsh winters made worse by a lack of stored food.

Yet, the worst threats to the Native American peoples of Maine—the Penobscots, Passamaquoddies, Micmacs, Maliseets (the present-day survivors) and the now extinct Kennebecs, Androscoggins, Sacos, Sokokis, Wawenocs and Piquackets of yore—were nothing they could ever have imagined, even in their most blood-curdling tales. It would come from across the Atlantic in Europe, at the end of the 15th century, where the notion of exploration was taking hold.

THE EARLY VOYAGES

The Portuguese and the Spanish led the pack. Indeed, soon after Columbus' discoveries, the two Iberian nations had the effrontery to divide up the entire world between themselves in a pact know as the Treaty of Tordesillas—a unilateral action that also was endorsed by the Pope. But other Catholic monarchs, like Francois I of France, refused to recognize the *fait accompli*. "I

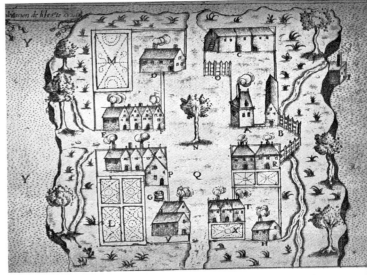

know of nothing in Adam's will that allows of such an inheritance," he declared and sent out ships to the New World to stake his claims. The English, having divorced themselves from the Church of Rome under Henry VIII, had no compunctions whatsoever about entering into the race for overseas territory.

Maine was caught in the crossfire of conflicting "discoveries." The French based their possession on the stopover in 1524 of Giovanni Verrazzano. An Italian sailing under the French flag, he went ashore on the Maine coast with a party of armed men. Another Italian, twenty-seven years previously, his name anglicized to John Cabot, had reached Newfoundland or Nova Scotia and given the English a reason to say they owned North America all the way down to Florida. Later on, in 1583 Sir Humphrey Gilbert, a half-brother of Sir Walter Raleigh, took possession of Newfoundland in the name of Queen Elizabeth I. Since she was known as the "Virgin Queen, the eastern American stretch of land north to south was called Virginia.

It had a name, but it was still an unknown territory to Europeans, even though the French had named the country *L'Acadie* (Acadia). Expeditions were mounted to gather information, to bring settlers and to substantiate verbal claims of ownership.

In this regard, the French were a step ahead of the English. The year was 1604. Henri IV was King of France, and one of his noblemen courtiers, Pierre du Guast, the Sieur de Monts, received royal permission to outfit ships and crews and establish a foothold on what was to become the Maine coast. It was an unusual period in French history. The vicious hostility between Catholics and Protestants in France since the start of the Reformation had ended in a temporary truce thanks to the king— born a Protestant who converted to Catholicism. The de Monts trip was meant to illustrate that brief concord. Sieur de Monts was a Protestant Huguenot, and his navigator and second-in-command, Samuel de Champlain, who was destined to become far more famous, a devout Catholic.

Sieur de Monts had obtained fur trading rights in the St. Croix River region of New France and traveled there in 1603 to form a short-lived colony. He left after an arduous winter killed half of the settlers, and the colony was abandoned. Samuel de Champlain traveled with Sieur de Monts as a representative of King Henry IV and made detailed maps of the region. This view is Champlain's map of Sieur de Monts colony. From Habitasion de L'Isle Ste. Croix *in* Les Voyages, *1613*

Italian explorer, Giovanni da Verrazano (circa 1485– 1528), visited the Maine coast for the first time in 1524 while looking for a passage to the Orient for the King of France. He and his crew received a chilly reception from the native peoples. Unwilling to meet or even trade, the Indians mooned Verrazano and crew from the cliffs above the water. From A Pictorial Field- Book of the Revolution *by Benjamin Lossing, 1851*

Thus, it was not sectarians that made this Gallic maiden attempt to populate Maine a failure. For reasons best known to them, the two leaders chose a poor location too far north and isolated, on which to disembark and set up a colony. Today, it is an International Historical Site protected by the United States National Park Service, midway between Maine and New Brunswick, Canada, in the St. Croix River. Also referred to as Dochet Island, the setting was one of tragedy for the eighty arriving Frenchmen who encountered a murderous winter for which they were ill prepared. Half of them died horribly of scurvy. Inexplicably, when Champlain guided the survivors south in the spring, they passed up magnificent harbors at Portland, Boston, Plymouth and Cape Cod, electing instead to stay even farther in the north at Port Royal on the upper shore of Nova Scotia.

The following year, 1605, an English vessel reconnoitering in the region, captained by George Waymouth, achieved dubious fame by kidnapping five local Indians and shanghaiing them to England. Their enforced incarceration, though, was not traumatic. They boarded with noblemen, were

Samuel de Champlain (1567–1635), the French explorer and mapmaker, made twelve trips to New France from 1603 to 1635. He explored Acadia and the Atlantic Coast, making the first detailed maps of the region. His maps show early habitations and travel routes, leaving us with an important documentation of early European exploration. From Harper's Popular Cyclopaedia of United States History, *volume 1, by Benjamin Lossing, 1893.*

treated kindly and were pumped for information. Learning English as they went, these canny "exotics" told their interrogators exactly what they wanted to hear—that, yes, Maine was full of treasures—hoping that their captors would return them to their land, which they eventually did.

Their hosts were Sir John Popham, the chief justice of England, and Sir Ferdinando Gorges, a rich military man who commanded the city fortress in Plymouth—the dominant port in that distinct section of the British Isles colloquially dubbed "The West Country." Sir John and Sir Ferdinando were business partners. They believed immense fortunes could be made in the New World and that England needed to compete with the other imperialistic powers. They were both close to King James I and had no trouble receiving a sizeable grant of land in America from him. Money was raised from wealthy investors and two companies resulted, one to colonize North Virginia and one South Virginia.

Therefore, two expeditions left England in 1607. One arrived in Jamestown and settled permanently. The other, as fleeting a venture as the French on St. Croix Island, stopped in Maine. What defeated the Popham Beach "adventure" was neither the weather, nor illness, nor Indian hostility as some historians maintain, but bad luck and lack of leadership. One of the co-commanders, Sir John Popham's nephew, died, and the other, Sir Humphrey Gilbert's son, was called home on family matters.

Gone in a twinkling were the visions of fabulous gold and silver mines that the Indian captives had described. The Maine Indians, too, had been brought back as interpreters and once among their own people, they never left. Sir Ferdinando Gorges described the failure of the Popham colony as "a blow to all our hopes." Yet he did not give up his stubborn, some may say quixotic, dreams of finding glorious success across the ocean. Fixated to the day of his death with English overseas expansion, he, if anyone, bears the title of "The Father of Maine."

Credited as being one of the founders of Biddeford and Saco, Richard Vines was sent to explore the region by Sir Ferdinando Gorges who had obtained a patent to the area. Vines spent the winter of 1616 at the mouth of the Saco River—a most important achievement because it proved that Europeans could survive a winter here and this was of interest to Gorges who wanted to entice settlers to move to his land. The area where Vines spent that winter in the Biddeford Pool area was known for a long time as "Winter Harbor." From A Popular History of the United States *by William Cullen Bryant and Sydney Howard Gay, volume II, 1878*

The McIntyre Garrison House was built circa 1707 in a section of York called Scotland. While it has the traditional overhanging second story of a garrisoned structure, it's not known to have housed any troops. It is believed to be the oldest existing house in Maine. Courtesy, Collections of Old York Historical Society

SIR FERDINANDO GORGES

Despite his odd, Spanish-sounding name, Ferdinando Gorges represented the flower of English aristocracy. He was a direct descendant of those Norman knights who had crossed the channel with William the Conqueror and ruled over the lowly Anglos and Saxons. He won his knighthood on the battlefield, fighting the Spanish in the Lowlands. Among his cousins were Sir Walter Raleigh and Sir Humphrey Gilbert. He imbibed their enthusiasm for conquering new worlds for England. He later became part of a privileged coterie clustered around King James I's oldest son, Prince Henry, which included geographers from Oxford and Cambridge, and helped plan an empire. Part feudal lord, part budding capitalist, always an imperialist, Sir Ferdinando received a large area north of the Piscataqua River, Maine's current boundary with New Hampshire, as his personal fiefdom. There he rented land to adventurous fortune-seekers, mostly from his home shires in the West Country.

Cod was long a staple of the Maine economy and diet. Some of the earliest European exploreres were fishermen here to take advantage of the huge stocks of fish swimming in Maine waters. Salted, dried cod was sent back to England and later was part of the trade industry that sent Maine ships around the world. Into the twentieth century, cod remained an important commodity. Racks of salted fish could be seen—and smelled—drying in the sun along the coast. Of course, cod was the main ingredient in the milky chowder that was a staple in Maine homes for generations. From A Popular History of the United States *by William Cullen Bryant and Sydney Howard Gay, volume II, 1878*

Gorges planned to build a capital city—a typical English market center complete with an Anglican cathedral—at a spot in the wilderness the local Indians had named Agamenticus. It was desirable because its forests had already been cleared by the natives for agriculture, they could grow corn there and it was on the ocean with a sheltered harbor. Most conveniently, a plague in 1613 had depopulated the hinterland. The rush of immigrants was not spectacular, but by the 1630s, this area was slowly filling with English families. Sir Ferdinando sent his nephew, Thomas Gorges, to govern feudal style and also to build him a grand manor house.

The city was renamed Gorgiana. Today it is York, the second town one drives through after entering Maine. The manor house is gone, but a few people say they know where its foundations lay along the York River. The old knight never did come to live in it. He had a ship built to carry him over and when she was launched, she didn't float but sank immediately. Then the English Civil War intervened. Gorges fought for his king against the Puritan forces of Oliver Cromwell and lost, was imprisoned, later freed and died at the age of eighty-one. Maine does not commemorate him, except through Fort Gorges in Portland Harbor. Without this pioneer Maine might have had a much different flavor.

OF PILGRIMS, PURITANS, AND WEST COUNTRYMEN

Allegedly, the unexplained sinking of Sir Ferdinando's flagship brought forth from the Puritans of England, when they heard of it, cries of joy that God had intervened to punish one of their fiercest foes. History does not record talk of an act of sabotage, yet a deliberate inside job of scuttling would not have been surprising. As in England, where the bitter contentions of different factions—partisans of King Charles I, Anglican Church of England and Royal rule versus Calvinist dissenters, Oliver Cromwell and Parliament's rule—broke out into murderous fighting. Those divisions were mirrored in North America, though less dire, since they did not lead to open civil warfare, but rather a good deal of fierce political enmity.

In the south, in the land to which today's Virginia has been reduced, the "Cavaliers"—adherents of the Stuart monarchs—were dominant. Up north in Massachusetts Bay, the "Roundheads," who loathed the king and his bishops, held sway. As for Maine, the people there became a quarrelling mixture.

European market goods were popular items when fur trading with Native Americans in Maine and eastern Canada. Originally, European traders would trade their own hat bands and brooches, but as trade grew, more types of silver jewelry were imported. Used to decorate clothing, ornate brooches with cutouts, like the one pictured below, were usually made in the late 1700s and early 1800s. Courtesy, Collections of Maine Historical Society

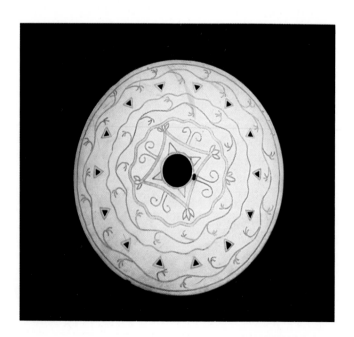

Early on, soon after 1620, those initial refugees from religious persecution in their own country, Pilgrims, as we know them, established ties to the north of them in Maine. The corn grown near Plymouth was traded for fish, which were delivered by the fleets that arrived annually to dry their cod on offshore Maine islands, like Damariscove. In return for their maize, the Pilgrims also traded for furs, particularly beaver, which the Indians in the colder climes would supply them. Soon, they had permanent trading posts in Maine. There were two small posts far down east on the coast at Machias and Castine. The main post was at the first falls of the Kennebec River, a place called Cushnoc, which is now Augusta, the state capital.

These were monopolies jealously guarded by the Pilgrims, who garnered funds to pay off their creditors in England. An example of this "jealously" was demonstrated in 1634 when an interloper in the pay of certain English lords was shot and killed aboard his ship—but not before he had gunned down one of the defenders. This was Maine's first double murder, so to speak, and a crime for which the well-known John Alden, present at the scene, was arrested in Boston and held until his bosom friend Myles Standish was summoned to prove his innocence.

The existence of courts in Boston at the time—and even the existence of Boston, the "city on the hill"—was due to the significant Puritan migration of the 1630s. The difference between "Puritans" and "Pilgrims" was slight: they were first cousins in religious belief, both opponents of the Anglican Church hierarchy. While the Pilgrims broke away, "separated," from the parent denomination, the Puritans nominally kept their membership, but with the goal of reforming the faith from within, "purifying" it. The Pilgrims, who went to Holland before America, numbered in the hundreds; the Puritans fled to Massachusetts by the thousands.

Originally, the latter intended to huddle in a single, special, godly community confined to the three hills, "Tremont," that comprised their settlement of Boston. Nevertheless, inevitably, the Puritans

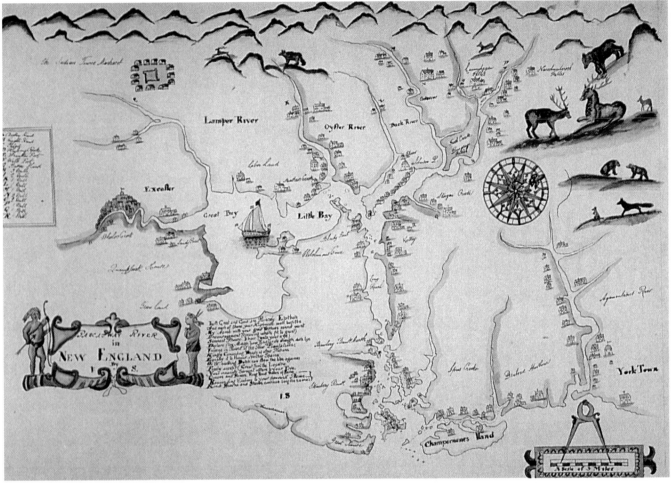

Map of the Piscataqua River shows developed communities in southern Maine in 1665. Homes and businesses lined the waterfront of rivers and the coast. Waterfront access was essential for travel, sawmills and gristmills, as well as to provide water for people, livestock and crops. Courtesy, Baxter Rare Maps Collection, Maine State Archives

spread, as a second generation of them sought land. The primary expansion was north and before long they reached New Hampshire and eventually crossed the Piscataqua River into Maine, where a conflict between their strict but democratically inclined mode of life collided with the rowdy, heavy-drinking, games-loving, maypole dancing folkways of the West Countrymen.

In 1652 Massachusetts Bay started its overt conquest of Maine, preempting lands technically belonging to Sir Ferdinando Gorges, taking Kittery, York and Wells, all that had been retained of the original "Province of Mayne," and continuing on through the "Province of Lygonia," named for Sir Ferdinando's mother's maiden name, Lygon, until they acquired the Portland area. A combination of persuasion, infiltration of Massachusetts's people, and shows of armed force had accomplished the takeover. Until 1820 Maine was to become a mere district of Massachusetts.

THE MELTING POT

If anyone fully exemplified the "Cavalier" aspect of Maine's heritage, it was Henry Josselyn. That is not to say that the "Squire of Scarborough" was fond of maypole dancing or addicted to the bottle. His demeanor was as grave as that of any Puritan magistrate, but he was feudally-minded, a firm believer in the king's "prerogative," a power ordained by God, which it was blasphemous to contest. The "leveling" tendencies of the Puritans who elected their church ministers were anathema to him. Their land distribution practices were equally abhorrent: no tenants, no humble peasants who paid their rent to the "squire" and showed unfailing respect to their "betters." Why, all a Puritan had to do was get himself elected as a church member and he automatically received a plot of land and it was his to own—as if he were an aristocrat. What a state of affairs!

The Massachusetts juggernaut rolled steadily, if slowly, northward from Kittery, York and Wells. By 1657 it was Scarborough's turn and the technique was always the same. A communication labeled "a loving letter and friendly" was sent ahead of time, requesting a meeting of the locals with Puritan "commissioners" who were always accompanied by an escort of soldiers. In Henry Josselyn's case, he and another like-minded local leader, Robert Jordan, were summoned to York. Neither responded.

The Puritans waited a year to pressure Scarborough. In England the Cromwell forces were in total command. King Charles I had been executed. The home form of government was a republican "Commonwealth," the same title that Massachusetts bears to this day. Jordan and other of Josselyn's neighbors submitted, but Henry Josselyn's signature was not on the document of surrender.

His loyalty to the Stuart Kings soon paid off. The beheaded king's oldest son was reinstated as Charles II in 1640 and Puritans were once more objects of the royal ire. Massachusetts became a target, its freewheeling government deemed too independent, and returned to the monarch's control. Henry Josselyn was created a justice of the peace, a powerful position. Maine was once again recognized as the property of the Gorges family.

There is a word picture of what Scarborough and its surroundings were like in 1663 in the writings of Henry Josselyn's brother John, who visited from England that year. The return to the king's "prerogative" was apparently not total. John Josselyn, Gent., as he styled himself, wrote, "Of the magistrates, some be Royalists, the rest perverse spirits" (i.e. Massachusettsans).

In a topsy-turvy turn of events, however, as soon as the forces sent by Charles II felt their job of coercion was done and had departed Boston by ship, the Puritans reasserted their authority. John Josselyn describes what happened next in Maine.

> ...the Massachusetts enter the province in a hostile manner with a troop of horse and foot and turned the judge and his assistants off the bench, imprisoned the major or commander of the militia, threatened the judge and others that were faithful to Mr. Gorges's interests...

The "judge," of course, was his brother Henry and the scene where the old gentleman was turned off the bench took place in York. Rival delegations met there and argued about who had governing jurisdiction. A rather comic opera ending to the affair had Josselyn's group taking over the seats in the First Parish Church that their opponents had vacated when the meeting broke for lunch. However, they were ousted, themselves, once the Puritans, with drummers and sword-waving military on horseback, returned.

England was far off. A tense calm reigned in the subdued Province of Maine, which ran not much farther north than Casco Bay. Beyond were a few scattered settlements, arbitrarily formed by Charles II's fiat into a "Duke's Province," belonging to his brother

James, Duke of York who later was crowned James II.

A dozen years elapsed, time for political tempers to cool and for settlers in Maine, with their differences of religious belief, geographic origin (the Puritans were mostly from the east of England, the Royalists from the west), even accent (the West Country people, much more Celtic in their roots, had brogues) to get used to each other, if not to begin one of America's first examples of a melting pot—albeit of different examples of English people. The impetus for this process of cooperating together was highly accelerated due to the outbreak in 1675 of serious fighting against the Indians.

KING PHILIP'S WAR

The fighting did not start in Maine. Friction between the native population and the English in and around "New Plymouth," as the Pilgrim colony was called, burst into open warfare in southern Massachussetts. The first settlers had been befriended by the great Wampanoag chief of Massasoit but his son Metacom was strongly opposed to the whites. Known derisively as "King Philip," he went to war after three of his warriors were arrested and hanged for the alleged murder of a pro-English Indian.

This soon led to generalized hostility between the indigenous tribes and the settlers and then spread to Maine. Its purported genesis was an incident that took place on the banks of the Saco River. A group of English sailors from a fishing vessel anchored nearby were lolling on one of the riverbanks, getting drunk. A canoe approached in which an Indian woman paddled with her baby. One of the men suggested that Indian infants didn't have to learn to swim; they knew how instinctively. To test their alcohol-inspired theory, the

Known as Metacom, the son of the Pilgrim's friend Massassoit, his opponents mockingly called him King Philip. Harper's Popular Cyclopaedia of United States History, volume 1 by Benjamin J. Lossing, 1893.

canoe was upset, and its occupants thrown into the water. The child who didn't dart off like a seal pup but sank and drowned, was the son of Squando, the Saco Indian chief. Not much time elapsed before houses were burning in Maine and scalped victims left lying in their embers.

Until that incident, relations in Maine between Indians and the English had been perfectly friendly. John Josselyn had written about these interesting people. He described them as "Tatarian-visaged" and "tall and hand timbered people." Their women were "comely" of face with bodies "as smooth as moleskin." These indigenous neighbors mingled among the English and shared the natural resources of the Scarborough environment, such as lobsters, which were so prolific that Josselyn saw an Indian boy spear thirty in less than two hours. One weighed twenty pounds. He expressed his amazement, too, that the Indians sold silver-bellied eels to the settlers for three pence the half dozen while in England, they would cost eight to twelve pence a piece.

The closeness of Scarborough to Saco, which lay just on the north side of the river of the same name, would indicate the Indians in question were Sacos, although Josselyn didn't identify their tribe. This English "Gent" admired the natives but viewed them with a certain haughty Anglo disdain, likening them to the Irish, who were seen then by the upper classes in England as little better than savages. So, attitudes were important in understanding the tragedy that soon enveloped these different ethnic communities in what had been, until 1675, a benign coexistence. Nor did it help matters that fugitive Indians from King Philip's defeated forces had fled to Maine and were inciting revenge against paleface intruders.

Heeding their words, Squando first attacked the settlement at Saco, but the townspeople, forewarned, crowded into a fortified garrison and defended themselves. Next, it was Scarborough's turn. Sections of the town at Blue Point and Black Point were raided separately. At the latter location, a Bostonian and Puritan, Joshua

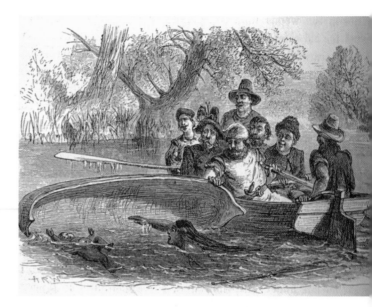

In 1675 English sailors overturned the canoe of the Wabanaki sachem, or chief, Squando, killing his infant son and causing tensions between the British and Indians to escalate. Squando, who had had a tenable relationship with the English, turned against the British and more fighting with the settlers ensued. From A Popular History of the United States by William Cullen Bryant and Sydney Howard Gay, volume II, 1878

Scottow, had bought land from Henry Josselyn and built a garrison. Those inside it repulsed Squando's initial attack, but subsequently faced a determined assault from another famous chief, Mogg, at a time when Scottow was away and Henry Josselyn himself assumed command.

"Grey Josselyn's eye is never sleeping," John Greenleaf Whittier wrote in his poem *Mogg Megone* about the incident. The old gentleman was described watching for Mogg. His eyes and ears, according to the poet, were "keener than those of the wolf and the fox." This particular battle was inconclusive, but in yet another fire-fight at Black Point, an English sniper killed Mogg.

The death of King Philip had occurred earlier in a Rhode Island swamp in August 1676. However, neither the news of the Indian rebel leader's demise nor the loss of doughty warriors like Mogg lessened the deadly hostilities up north. Two more years of bloodshed ensued until both sides finally, wearily, sought peace. Casualties were high in proportions to the populations—3,000 Indians and 500 Whites dead. In exchange for releasing his

The gaol (or jail) in York housed prisoners from 1719 to 1860. Records indicate that most of the prisoners were debtors, though drunkenness, infidelity, slander and even gossip could be considered crimes. The Old Gaol is now a historic landmark open to visitors and is regarded as one of the oldest public British-built buildings in the United States. Courtesy, Collections of Old York Historical Society

prisoners Squando extracted an annual rent of corn from the settlers, the amount equal to a peck for each English family in Maine.

Hardened by their experiences and woods-smart now, the English inhabitants in the north country had experienced their first transformation. Cavalier or Puritan, they had been comrades-in-arms. Indian arrows had been shot at both Joshua Scottow and Henry Josselyn. The people in Maine were on their way to becoming Mainers.

CUSTOMS OF THE TIMES

In writings about this period, mention is made of Henry Josselyn's wife Margaret. Her history points to several aspects of the subordinate role of women during these early colonial days in Maine. It was said that in marrying her first husband, Thomas Cammock, she had run away from her ancestral home. So the two of them had fled to America and amassed 1,500 acres of land in Scarborough, which she inherited when Cammock died unexpectedly. Suddenly, she was an independently wealthy, propertied widow. But after Henry

Josselyn wooed and won her, English law required that Margaret had to surrender her property rights to him, which she willingly did. On the other hand, if a man married a widow who had inherited debts, he could avoid them by staging a "shift marriage," symbolically taking a wife who had come to him "naked," or as happened in these ceremonies, wearing nothing but a shift, which was a flimsy undergarment.

Maine women could be very feisty and Joanne Andrews of Kittery was a notorious case. She was hauled before the town court again and again for her foul speech and cheating ways, like packing heavy stones into the butter she was selling by the pound. At one time she was sentenced to receive twenty lashes, but reprieved when she was discovered to be pregnant. Another well-known female miscreant was Ruth Bonython, daughter of the famous Saco troublemaker John Bonython, who was forced to stand at a town meeting in a white sheet to atone for her lasciviousness.

Puritan rules, whipping posts, stocks and dunking stools had come to Maine, but never did entirely subdue the more high-spirited original West Country immigrants. A certain leeway was also given to the Maine court system, although not in regards to the requirements for church attendance; it was against the law to belong to any church but the Congregational one.

Tall tales are another Maine tradition. The story of Michael Mitton, out rowing in Casco Bay, who had a scaly "merman" grasp the gunnels of his boat and with an axe cut off the creature's hands in a gush of purple blood, is told as if it were true. John Josselyn wrote of a sleeping farmer out of whose open mouth a big bumblebee flew and how his son could not awaken him until the bee flew back in.

Home remedies, many derived from this era, are still remembered in Maine, if not necessarily used— the juice of green pine cones for wrinkles; grinding deer horns or moose hooves into laxatives; hot fox fat for ear aches and tying fish skins around a child's feet to cure a cold. Medicinal plants by the score would be in a frontier woman's medicine chest, no doubt derived from her Indian neighbors, along with such necessities as pitchpine, hazelnuts, cod bones, loon beaks and even wolf dung.

NEW THREATS ADDED

Hostile Indians were a bad enough problem for the Maine colonists. On top of that, English politics then took a nasty turn. Charles II was fairly easy-going for a Stuart. The "merry monarch," a womanizer and a partier, never seemed to take anything too seriously, including religion. His family was crypto-Catholic in Protestant England, but "Charlie" never tried to push their Papist faith. Not so for his brother James, when the Duke of York became king upon his older sibling's death.

While alive, Charles had expressed open anger because of a trick Massachusetts played on him. Refusing to recognize the Bay Colony's claims to Maine, he had returned the disputed land back to the Gorges' heirs. So what did the sagacious Puritan fathers do on the sly? They approached Sir Ferdinando's grandson, who needed money, and without a word to the king, bought the entire grant. "We are not pleased," Charles II declared, or words to that effect, using the royal "we." But he declined to divest the purchasers of their legal title.

James II was made of sterner stuff. An autocrat whose not-so-secret goal was to return England to Roman Catholicism, he was also a major landowner in Maine. His "Duke's Province," known as Cornwall, but most commonly by its Indian name of Sagadahoc, encompassed the area that ran from north of Portland to an imaginary boundary around Pemaquid—a line that separated the last English settlement from territory the French designated as theirs and in cases occupied.

At the mouth of the mighty Penobscot River, a French stronghold was in the making. Castine, as it is still called today, after its originator the Baron de St. Castin, a Gascon adventurer and ex-soldier who left his regiment, went quasi-native and married Molly Mathilde, the beauteous daughter of

DU HAVRE DE PAINTAGOUET.

les chiffres marquent les brasse d'eau, qui restent en basse mer.

Echelle de Mille Toises Pour Vingt lignes.

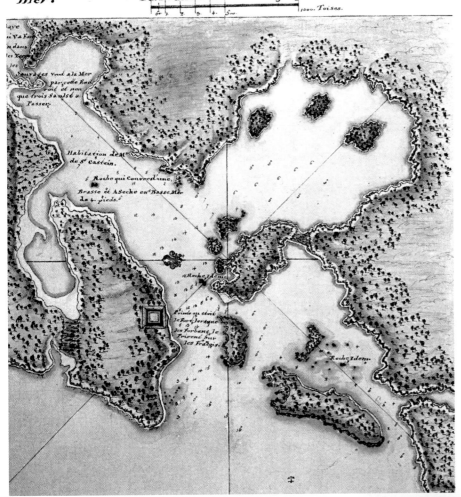

"The Harbor of Paintagouet"—more often spelled "Pentagoet"—a French map of the original Gallic stronghold at the mouth of the Penobscot River that today is Castine, Maine. Castine changed hands various times during the fight for control of downeast Maine and once was even briefly under the rule of the Netherlands when held by Dutch pirates. Attributed to French cartographer, Pasquine, 1688. Bibliotheque Nationale, Paris. Courtesy, Alaric Faulkner

Madockawando was born in Maine around 1630. A Penobscot Indian sachem during the Frontier, or French and Indian, Wars, Madockawando agreed to the 1676 accord that ended King Philip's War with the British. He lived at the French Fort at Pentagoet, and his daughter, Molly Mathilde, married the Frenchman, St. Castin. Bronze statue by Maine artist, Jud Hartmann. Courtesy, Jud Hartmann Gallery.

Madockawando, the powerful chief of the Penobscots.

In Boston, those French encroachments south became noticeable—and annoying. Until the 1680s, the prevailing wisdom in Massachusetts had been that the huge Penobscot Bay watershed would be out-of-bounds to the "New France" regime in Canada. Earlier in the century, in 1613, an attempt to land French colonists and Jesuit missionaries in the Mount Desert region had been thwarted by an English naval sortie out of Jamestown, with one of the priests killed in battle at St. Sauveur, identified as the current Maine town of Lamoine. For more than half a century, the French hadn't gone into what was essentially still a no man's land. Now, they had made several moves down the coast. One to Machias, once a Pilgrim fur trading post, but abandoned, and one

25

even closer to James II's Sagadahoc domain, wresting the strategic site that became Castine from a group of Dutch pirates. Worse than anything else, the French had become exceedingly friendly with the Indians.

James II's appointee to contend with the French and Indian threat was Sir Edmund Andros, an aristocrat from Guernsey, one of the Channel Islands that are practically in France, just off the Normandy coast. He was not only a French-hater, but had no love for Puritans either. Given extraordinary powers by his monarch, Andros dictatorially ruled the Dominion of New England— a cobbled-together amalgam of ex-provinces stretching from Manhattan, recently conquered from the Dutch—to the outer reaches of Maine.

In this arrangement, Massachusetts promptly lost all of its freedoms. Its charter from James I, on which it had based its jurisdiction over Maine, was arbitrarily revoked. No Puritan's liberty or property was safe any longer. To add to his unpopularity, Andros had brought with him to Boston where he made his headquarters, a group of carpet bagging fortune-seekers personified by one Edward Randolph, who led his employer's efforts to despoil the inhabitants of the land so many of them had arduously cleared from the wilderness, convinced they owned it. Assisting Randolph was a theory Andros had devised that all previous titles in Massachusetts and Maine were null and void. His reasoning was that the towns had given them out and the concept of a "town" did not exist in English law. With that excuse at hand, Randolph set out to seize vast acres of Massachusetts and Maine land for himself, Andros and their cronies.

Perhaps the greater threat to survival, troubles with France and the Indians, was Andros' doing, too, the Puritans insisted. True, the overbearing "Dominion" had entered King Philip's War and helped bring it to a close by sailing a fleet of war ships north to overwhelm the already badly mauled Indian forces involved. But that wasn't enough for Andros. The French had to be scourged out of the places they had invaded. He landed troops at Castine, with himself at their head. The French Baron was off hunting with a group of Penobscot braves and, before sailing home to Boston, Andros ordered all of his possessions to be ransacked and the buildings torched. When they returned from the forest, the belated ire of St. Castin and his father-in-law Madockawando was to cost the English dearly.

The midcoast town of Castine is named for Baron de St. Castin (1652–1707). He first came to the New World at age twelve or thirteen as an ensign on a regimental ship, but returned to France after peace was signed with England. He returned in 1670 and lived at Fort Pentagoet. In many ways, the French had a better relationship with the native people here, and some of the French explorers, including St. Castin, lived among the Indians. St. Castin met his wife, Molly Mathilde, daughter of Madockawando, at Pentagoet. Courtesy, Maine Historical Society

On the domestic front, among the bitter enemies of Sir Edmund Andros, were first and foremost a father and son, Increase Mather and Cotton Mather. Both men were ministers in Boston's establishment Congregational Church and also well connected to influential Protestant lords in England.

Presently, a step ahead of being arrested for sedition by Governor Andros, Increase Mather escaped from Massachusetts and sailed to the mother country. From there, protected by his friends in high places, he plotted against the Stuart regime. At the same time, son Cotton, no admirer of Indians, railed against Andros' attempts to negotiate with them and his failure to crush those "Satanic Devils" who had teamed up with the Romish French.

Events in England finally decided the struggle. James II had overplayed his tyrannical hand, alienated too many important people, and frightened the mass of the populace with his own now undisguised allegiance to the Pope. In a bloodless political *coup d'etat* known as the "Glorious Revolution," he was overthrown and replaced by his Protestant sister Mary and her Dutch husband, William of Orange.

New England followed suit. When delirious mobs heard the news of James' downfall they surged through the streets of Boston, subdued Andros' guards, and imprisoned him, Randolph and other lesser henchmen, interestingly enough. The date was April 19, 1689, eighty-six years to the day before the gunfire at Concord and Lexington. Rebelliousness was hardly a foreign trait among these budding Yankees.

Overseas, as soon as William and Mary were safely installed, Increase Mather worked hard to reinstate the Massachusetts Charter and the Puritans' lost liberties. Unfortunately, he was only partly successful.

The Dominion of New England was dismantled without a problem. Massachusetts received another charter wherein they were guaranteed their rights to Maine, with the Pilgrims' New Plymouth incorporated in their "Commonwealth." Still, the main sticking point was the structure of government allowed them by the crown. Prior to James II and Andros, the Puritans had elected their governors. Now, they were to be appointed by the king, following the advice of his Privy Council.

Admittedly, once more there would be a body of elected legislators, as Andros had abolished the "House." However, added to it was a counterbalancing sort of Senate, the "Council," chosen by the governor from nominees of the lower body over whom he had veto power. A messy, semi-democracy including strong "Crown" input, was the best that Increase Mather could attain.

The selection of governor, therefore, was crucial. Here the Puritan divine had his way. Sir William Phips was his man. Not your usual aristocratic knight, Phips was Maine-born, in the frontier town of Woolwich. He was the son of a shipwright, one of twenty-two children, self-made, rough-hewn, one the common people of Massachusetts Bay could accept as a local boy made good. He had won his fame, fortune and knighthood by salvaging a sunken Spanish treasure in the Bahamas and splitting the fabulous $300,000 proceeds with Queen Elizabeth. Settling down in Boston and becoming a parishioner of Cotton Mather's, Billy Phips was now respectable enough to hold high office.

His placement in the "chair" at the Province House marked an essentially new era for his native district of Maine. Its "beginnings" had been as lowly and precarious and storm-tossed as those of Phips. But here was Maine settling down, too, officially placed for the first time, snug in Massachusetts' embrace, seemingly forever.

Just as Sir William Phips was to have a hard time governing, Maine would undergo one of its most severe trials in the period ahead. For the next 100 years, seemingly perpetual warfare turned all of the state's magnificent scenery, forest and farmland, lakes, rivers and ocean into a wide-ranging battleground.

2

INTERNATIONAL WARS ON MAINE SOIL (1689-1783)

Fort Halifax is the oldest surviving wooden fort in the United States. Built by the Kennebec Proprietors in 1754, the fort was located in what is now the town of Winslow in the region once inhabited by Penobscot and Kennebec Indians. Intended to guard against attacks by Indians and French soldiers in the frontier wars, the blockhouse was never forced to defend itself and fell into disuse a decade later. Courtesy, Maine Historical Society

AN AGE OF EMPIRE

Despite the Treaty of Tordesillas and the blessings of the Pope, Spain and Portugal never did succeed in dividing up the world between themselves. They did amass large territories, particularly in South and Central America, and to a certain extent in Asia and the Pacific. Nevertheless, certain rivals began to surpass them in extent of conquest—none more so than France and England, who soon saw themselves as each other's biggest enemies in contention for world empire.

Louis XIV ruled France. His nickname the "Sun King" signified the splendor of his reign and his imperialistic reach. His armies were everywhere, attempting to dominate Europe, fighting for control of India and in North America they allied themselves with the local Indians to oust the English.

These were not necessarily all religious conflicts. The Catholic French had previously fought the Catholic Spanish, Austrians and Portuguese. The Protestant English clashed with the Protestant Dutch. England had a Dutch king, chosen precisely because he and his wife were Protestants. The greatest menace to their combined two realms came from Louis XIV, who was trying to occupy Holland and reinstate James II on the English throne.

In New England the first real struggle that included the French was referred to as King William's War. For the most part, only French officers were involved—assigned by King Louis' governor of Canada, the pugnacious Count de Frontenac—to fighting units made up purely of Indians. Occasionally, a French colonist like Castin, or even a war-like priest joined the raiding parties.

The governor in Massachusetts, Sir William Phips, was equally as offense minded as Frontenac. He commenced his first major military action by launching a full-scale attack upon no less of a fortress than the city of Quebec. The utter failure of that attempt was the impetus for his eventual political downfall. In 1690 he retreated from Canada. Two years later the English, again

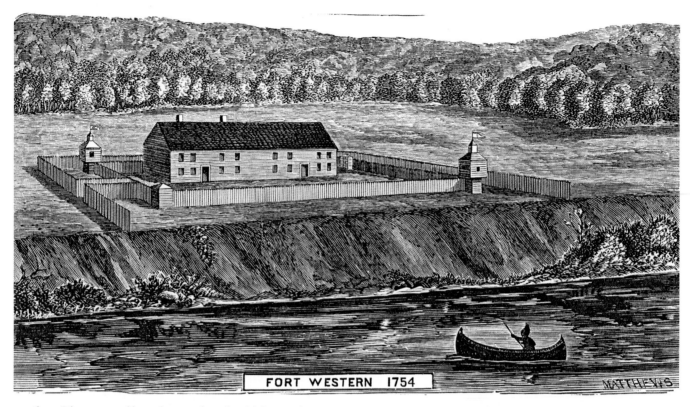

FORT WESTERN 1754

Fort Western was built in 1754 by the Kennebec Proprietors. Located at a desirable point for navigation on the Kennebec River, the fort was a useful preparation point for Benedict Arnold when the soldiers under his command embarked upon an attack on Quebec in 1775. Courtesy, Maine Historical Society

under Phips, suffered another bad blow when Captain Pascho Chubb surrendered Fort William Henry, their intimidating redoubt at Pemaquid, without a shot having been fired. Castin and Madockowando had led the French and Indian force of 200 men.

The same year, Madockawando and other French operatives devastated the frontier town of York, killing forty people and carrying more than 100 women and children off as captives. Civilian refugees from this southernmost tier of Maine fled by droves into Massachusetts. Boston, itself, felt alarmed.

A French victory may have been in the offing, except that all of the important decisions were still being made in Paris and London. Higher priorities existed than the fate of those "howling wildernesses" in Maine and Canada. A peace treaty signed at Ryswick in Holland in 1697 put an end to King William's War—inconclusively—constituting nothing but a fleeting truce. The raiding, the burning, the killing and the kidnapping, would continue. Both sides committed numerous atrocities.

Until the French in eastern Canada were ultimately beaten, four more wars wracked Maine. They were colloquially called Queen Anne's War, 1703–1713; King George's War, 1744–1748; the French and Indian War, 1756–1763 and squeezed in between, a strictly localized set of hostilities generally expressed as Dummer's War, 1722–1724. Dummer's War was named for William Dummer, the Massachusetts' lieutenant governor who presided over a peace treaty signed at Casco Bay. In Europe the same major conflicts had different names, advertising their dynastic politics, like the War of the Austrian Succession, which was also referred to as of the War of the Spanish Succession.

Whatever their historical monikers, the pattern was always similar. Maine would empty out as soon as enough damage occurred, or certainly the frontier edge would be evacuated. That is, until the lawmakers in Boston, fearing their own buffer against invasion from the north might vanish, decreed that the inhabitants of various designated border towns could not leave under legal penalty of having their property confiscated. "We are a poor scattering people, necessitated to watch, ward, scout, build garrisons and fortifications...and at every alarm driven from our employment," wrote the officials of Kittery in pleading for help from the General Court in Boston—as the Massachusetts Legislature was, and still is called.

Over time, the farmers of Maine became soldiers. Their militia outfits were not much to look at on the drill field, yet learning the art of fighting with the skill of warring Indians was far more of a necessity than being able to march straight. They learned how to shoot from behind trees and rock walls, how to scout and how to stage a surprise attack.

Norridgewock, on the Kennebec River, was a major Indian encampment that a ranger battalion from York totally destroyed in such covert fashion in 1724. Some historians view, and still

debate, this famous event as a major calamity for the tribes, the first genuinely grievous loss that put them on the defensive.

As a result, the Kennebecs ceased to exist. Some of the survivors fled north into Quebec province; others west, to mingle with the Penobscots and Passamaquoddies in Maine. Dead, too, at Norridgewock was the French Jesuit priest, Father Sebastian Rasle, a controversial figure, cut down by musket fire at the cross he had erected for his flock in the village center. Perceptions of Father Rasle were split by nationality. If one was French, he was a martyred saint. The English felt he was a deservedly slain war monger.

One fact was certain—the leaders of the attack had a score to settle. They were from York, the town devastated during the 1692 Candlemas eve "massacre." Captain Jeremiah Moulton, then a feisty four year-old, had seen his parents slain right in front of him before evading their killers. He regretted the way in which Father Rasle died. Moulton had wanted to take the Catholic cleric alive and hold him for a war crimes trial, but others of the militia unit argued that it was retribution for the slaying of a Puritan minister in York. The shocking revelation that they had scalped the priest was never excused; far from it, the gory pelt was displayed during a victory parade in Boston.

French Jesuit missionary, Sebastien Rasle served the Wabanaki Indians living at Norridgewock. He actively advocated on their behalf, detailing their complaints and conditions in frequent letters to the British. The British, in turn, saw Rasle as an instigator of Indian unrest. He was killed in an attack on Norridgewock in August of 1724 as a part of the conflict known as Dummer's War. Courtesy, Maine Historical Society

Another considerable loss for the Indians in that same overall campaign occurred at Lovewell's Pond near Fryeburg in Maine's western mountains. The fight was not a victory for either side. The equally high casualties, however, favored the English. They had large growing numbers that would eventually overwhelm their Indian and French foes.

THE CAPTIVES

French and Indian attacks on English settlements had several objectives. For the French, the prime goal was to extend their influence southward and chase out the implanted English populations they considered interlopers. The Indians, too, wanted to see the Yenghis gone, but they also had an additional motive. They sought prisoners, women and particularly young girls, whom they could ransom back to their families for good prices or sell to the French, who would raise the young females *a la francaise* to increase the numbers of their scant population.

After the 1692 "massacre," more than 100 captives were hustled out of York and were forced to walk to Canada, an action symptomatic of what happened to people across Maine during these wars. The only stop Madockawando's men allowed their victims was a brief pause in Cape Neddick, where they sent word to York of the prices they wanted for redeeming their human booty.

On the march, no lingering was allowed since there were usually English militia in pursuit. Tales are told of crying, sickly babies tomahawked so their mothers could keep up. The widow of Pastor Dummer, the English minister slain in York, although elderly, insisted on accompanying her young son. Shortly after he died en route, she succumbed as well, which the French said was of unhappiness.

Three young girls, the Sayward sisters of York and their cousin Esther Wheelwright of Wells, illustrated in their experiences how the French made converts of impressionable youngsters. All were delivered into the hands of Quebec province nuns who raised them. Mary Sayward, age eleven when captured, built a career in the church as Sister Marie des Anges, rising to the rank of mother superior and running several convents. Her younger sibling, also named Esther, chose a non-religious life for herself, and married a French Canadian merchant, bearing him many children. As the widow Madame de Lestage, she voyaged in her later years to York, seeking out her aging English mother, Mary Plaisted, who, herself had been ransomed right after the 1692 raid. Indeed, the image of a mother and daughter meeting after all those years, barely able to understand each other, was reported to be a touching one.

The gravestone of the Honorable John Wheelwright of Wells, 1745. Photograph by Mason Philip Smith. Courtesy, Maine Historical Society

The encounter between Esther Wheelwright, mother superior of the Ursuline Convent in Quebec City and her brother, Major Nathaniel Wheelwright, has the same heart-tugging quality. The English militia officer had journeyed to the French capital during a time of truce in order to tell his sister of their father's death back home in Wells. With him, he had brought a copy of John Wheelwright's will, which he read to her. Never forgotten, Esther had been left $100 in English currency, various heirlooms and a portrait of their mother. The father's last testament poignantly expressed the vain hope that his offspring, even after thirty years away and professing another religion, might still "return to this country and settle here."

Few of the York captives who had spent any time in Canada did go back. A twelve year-old boy, Charles Trafton, proved an exception. Rechristened by the French as Louis Marie Trafton, he stayed in Canada long enough to serve in Count de Frontenac's retinue but at last returned to York. Another who repatriated himself after considerable exposure to both French and Indian culture was the famed interpreter, John Gyles. Seized at age eleven while out haying with his family near Pemaquid, he spent six years with the Maliseet Indians before being sold to a Frenchman. In time, he was redeemed, after becoming fluent in two of the Wabanaki languages. He made himself indispensable to any parley the English authorities wished to have with the natives during these turbulent decades.

NEARING THE END

Until the next round of warfare in the early 1740s, English immigration into the District of Maine increased exponentially. The Puritans multiplied from a population base already huge, compared to any competing ethnicity. Proprietors, big and small, won title to the "Eastern Lands" from the Massachusetts General Court, which sold to wealthy individuals or to town governments, who then sold to landseekers who were willing to move

Samuel Waldo (1695–1759) obtained the rights to the Muscongus Patent, a large tract of land that encompassed the area that would become Knox and Waldo Counties. Waldo, like other land speculators, planned to sell plots of land to settlers looking to make a living on the Maine frontier. The land later came under the ownership of General Henry Knox, the Revolutionary War hero who had married Waldo's granddaughter Lucy Flucker. Courtesy, Maine Historical Society

and establish new communities in the wilderness. Potential settlers were sought. The Muscongus proprietors, essentially a real estate company controlled by Samuel Waldo, a Boston entrepreneur, hired an agent in Germany. The pious Protestants, whom he had shipped to America and who were fleeing the Catholic Rhineland, founded the Maine town of Waldoboro. Scottish-Irish Presbyterians who came directly from Northern Ireland populated mid-coast Maine towns named for Whig ministers in England. Walpole and Newcastle are two of the surnames that have survived. The Massachusetts contingents, spreading north, west and east, honored the municipalities they had left; thus Maine has New Gloucester to this day and used to have New Marblehead, now Windham. New England Yankees, out of Rhode Island and Connecticut, showed up too, to push back the "northern frontier."

The District of Maine had a critical mass of manpower when war was declared overseas again in 1744. England and France, it appeared, could not long stand to coexist without a showdown. Other countries entered the fray—Austria, Spain, Holland, Prussia—and massive battles of infantry, cavalry and artillery exploded on the continent of Europe, then flared into further hostilities in India and North America.

In the case of England (or more correctly, Great Britain, since the country now had amalgamated with Scotland, Wales and Ireland), opening gunfire provided nothing but military disaster. Therefore, the morale of the Brits was possibly at its lowest ebb when news of a small triumph of Anglo arms in Canada was seized upon by the Whigs in power and magnified far beyond its size. A force of New England colonial troops had captured Louisbourg, the impressive French fortress in Nova Scotia, with help from a detachment of Royal Marines, a Royal Navy fleet and colonial ships. The commander of this expedition was William Pepperell of Kittery Point, a Maine businessman and politician, not a professional soldier. Overnight, the powers-

that-be in London turned him into a British national hero.

SIR WILLIAM PEPPERRELL, BART.

The "BART." William Pepperrell was allowed to put after his name stood for *baronet*—the lowest rung of the British system of nobility, which rises up through Count and Marquis to Duke and Prince. The "Sir," in this case, did not stand for knighthood, but automatically accompanied his title of baronet. He was technically the first "American" ever ennobled by the crown.

Which is to say, he was American-born, but still an Englishman in his allegiance. Yet by the eighteenth century, a clear sense of differentiation had

German immigrants began settling in Maine in 1739 and the final group arrived in 1753. They settled on land owned by General Samuel Waldo (1695–1759) in a section of Waldoboro called Broad Bay. This German Protestant Church was built before 1773, but was dismantled and moved to its present site in 1795. Courtesy, Maine Historic Preservation

begun to develop in the thirteen colonies along the Atlantic coast. America, to Sir William, was his "country," while England, from which his father had emigrated, was "home."

Colonel William Pepperrell, the senior of the family, was a West Countryman. He had left Devonshire as a common seaman and settled at Kittery Point, where he'd founded a merchant empire, trading with Europe and the West Indies. His second son, William, joined the business alongside him and eventually entered politics, rising to become the head of the powerful "Governor's Council" in Boston. The Pepperrells had also gone into land speculation. By the time of the attack on Louisbourg, William Pepperrell, the younger, was purported to be the richest man in the colonies. It was said that he could leave his house in Kittery Point and ride his horse north to Scarborough, thirty-five miles away, and never leave his own land. Such wealth was one of the reasons he was picked for the command. He could afford to pay some of the expenses from his own pocket—and he did.

Private aid aside, the governments of Massachusetts and other colonial provinces had made significant financial sacrifices, not to mention the "American" lives lost, in conquering a massive fortress defended by regular army French military units. They were immensely proud of their effort for "king and country." What extraordinary disappointment they were to feel, particularly throughout Massachusetts and the District of Maine, which had supplied one-third of the troops, when, for reasons of state, the British government handed Louisbourg back to the French.

Diplomats contrived that bitterly resented deal known as the Treaty of Aix-la-Chapelle in 1748, swapping Louisbourg for Madras, a French-captured fortress in India. It prompted the grumbling remark printed in a Boston newspaper, that maybe New England itself, someday would be traded to the French. The menace from Canada had hardly disappeared. The new Sir William Pepperrell, after a triumphant visit to England during which he

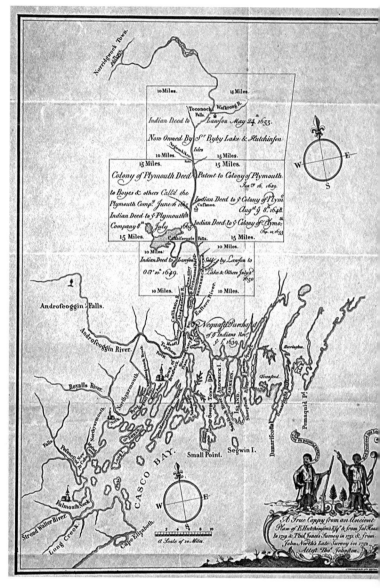

The Plymouth Company owned land and established a fur trading post at Cushnoc on Kennebec River in 1630. In 1752 the Plymouth Company lands were acquired by the Kennebec Proprietors who sold off plots to settlers looking to establish farms. Courtesy, Maine Historical Society

In an effort to gain dominion over the region, Sir William Pepperrell led British troops in an attack on the French at Louisbourg on Cape Breton Island. Pepperrell successfully took the fort and was named the first baronet in America. Courtesy, Maine Historical Society

received his rewards directly from King William and Queen Mary, returned to Maine and continued his role in business and politics. Among his emoluments, he was given the right to raise a regiment where he could make money by selling officers' commissions and supplying the enlisted men. The Yankee soldiers he organized were ready when the next—and last—round of fighting the French commenced in 1756.

But by then, Sir William, suffering from a rheumatoid condition contracted at Louisbourg, was in no condition to go to war again. Visiting him in Kittery were the two British generals, Jeffrey Amherst and James Wolfe, most credited with ending the French reign in Canada. They were on their way north to recapture Louisbourg and finally conquer Quebec City.

Their successes led to the 1763 Treaty of Paris, and now there was no thought of compromise. Its terms signaled the total domination of Great Britain in North America. Unfortunately, Sir William Pepperrell, BART. did not live to hear the triumphant chimes of the church bells of his southernmost Maine community.

AN IMPORTANT MAINE MILESTONE

One event of this final phase of the French and Indian War, although it did not involve any actual shooting, had a major—if unforeseen—influence on the future of Maine. Thomas Pownall was the governor of Massachusetts in 1759.

Decidedly young for the position to which he was named at age thirty-five, Pownall owed his appointment to the influence of his older brother in London, John Pownall, the indispensable secretary of the Board of Trade, the subcommittee of the King's Privy Council that handled all affairs dealing with the English colonies. On May 23, 1759 Governor Pownall, at the head of an expedition he had organized, buried a lead plate under a large white birch tree on the east side of the Penobscot River in what is today the town of Brewer, Maine. The inscription on the plaque read: "May 23, 1759, Province of Massachusetts Bay. Dominions of Great Britain. Possession confirmed by T. Pownall, Governor." A flagpole was erected and the Union Jack, the British flag, run up for Pownall's contingent to salute.

This casual ceremony was to establish the English claim to all of present-day northern Maine. It was a claim that for four more years still had competition from the French; after that, from Nova Scotia and, through the years of the American Revolution, from Great Britain itself, on behalf of Canada.

Whether there was an air of quiet tension to underscore the portent of Pownall's act has never been recorded. But moments later, something bizarre happened. Accompanying the governor from Boston had been that immensely rich landholder Samuel Waldo, earlier commissioned a general for the Louisbourg campaign. He was showing his fellow officers and the governor that they had reached the northernmost edge of his own vast property in Maine. "Here are my bounds," he declared, only to clutch his chest suddenly and collapse to the forest floor, the victim of a fatal heart attack. His body was brought back to the fort Pownall had built at the mouth of the Penobscot River, where funeral services were held. He was finally laid to rest in Boston once the gubernatorial party returned to the Massachusetts capital.

Two major effects of Pownall's expedition on Maine's subsequent history were the strategic barrier Fort Pownall, later called Fort Point, presented to further incursions southward by the Indians and the opening up of the Waldo lands to settlement. While the French and Indian War continued, its final conclusion was already seen as inevitable. The French would leave. The Indians would be defenseless. The British had grown too strong.

ON TO THE REVOLUTION

Paradoxically, Great Britain's strength in North America also concealed a weakness. For the Americans began to think: "With the French gone and the Indians weakened, we no longer need the British military to protect us." Also, the colonial capture of the mighty fortress of Louisbourg had taught them, "We can do it by ourselves and don't need to be afraid of any army." Consequently, as soon as serious quarrels arose with the home country and troops were sent by the king's government to overawe them, the colonists suspected they need have no hesitation in combating the "lobster-backs," those red-coated English regulars they reviled.

This Yankee attitude of defiance, increasing ever more fiercely since 1763, spread northward with the huge wave of emigration into Maine that followed the Treaty of Paris. Quebec still had not fallen in 1762, when the Massachusetts General Court, already selling land in southern and mid-coast Maine, carved out more than a dozen new townships farther downeast in Washington and Hancock Counties and put them on the block. A year later, the abandoned coastal settlement of Machias was reoccupied by a group from Henry Josselyn's old community of Black Point in Scarborough. The Waldo lands, in and around the Penobscot River, likewise received a stream of settlers before the break with Great Britain. This influx of "Americans" went directly into Canada, to the part of Nova Scotia that became New Brunswick. In June 1775, two months after the "lobsterbacks" had retreated from Concord and Lexington, the first fighting in Maine broke out at Machias.

Caught up in the eighteenth century border disputes between the French and the British, thousands of Acadians were rounded up and forced from their homes unless they swore allegiance to the British crown. Known as Le Grande Derangement, *this forced evacuation scattered Acadians throughout colonies along the eastern seaboard of North America. Some eventually made their way back home and formed communities along the border between Maine and Canada, but many went into Louisiana and were the ancestors of the Cajuns. From A Popular History of the United States by William Cullen Bryant and Sydney Howard Gay, volume III*

THE REVOLUTION DOWNEAST

The Machias incident was a naval battle, if such it can be deemed—not a clash of many-cannoned dreadnaughts, but a determined effort by local farmers who were wielding muskets and even pitchforks to overpower the crew of the cutter *Margaretta,* a small Royal Navy vessel. The ship's captain, an arrogant young officer named Moor, had threatened to bombard the town if the inhabitants refused to cut down a liberty pole they had erected. Instead of submitting, the settlers, led by a veteran of the Louisbourg expedition, Benjamin Foster and young Jeremiah O'Brien sailed out in a commandeered sloop and boarded the cutter. Captain Moor was fatally wounded in the resulting clash. The nine sailors who surrendered were transferred to a prison outside of Boston, while the *Margaretta,* America's earliest prize of war, was refitted as a U.S. privateer under O'Brien and captured several merchant vessels trying to provision British forces.

Maine's natural resources were an important part of the colonial economy. The rich lumber stores were made into boards, barrels and even partially fabricated homes before being shipped worldwide. The sawmill shown here under construction in Machias is a very early view by F. W. Des Barres in 1777. Courtesy, Library of Congress

ROLE OF THE MAINE INDIANS

Despite the victory of the American patriots at Machias, the situation in this remote region of Maine bordering Canada could at best be termed "dicey." It soon became evident that the Indian tribes of the Passamaquoddies, the Maliseets (then called the St. Johns), and the Micmacs directly downeast, as well as the Penobscots, held the balance of power. Their loyalty, whether to the crown or the American colonists, would be crucial in determining the future of northern Maine.

Previous warfare had essentially reduced the original Maine tribes to these four groups. Their decision was to have a critical bearing on their own destiny, as well, with their final choice, generally in support of the American cause, resulting in the toleration of their continued presence in the United States.

As early as June 1775 the Penobscots, led by their blond, blue-eyed chief Joseph Orono, had met with the Massachusetts Provincial Congress, then in exile from Boston at Watertown. They had their territorial claims recognized in return for their allegiance or, at least, neutrality.

A year later the extra-legal Massachusetts government was still meeting at Watertown in preparation for moving back to Boston, which the British had recently evacuated. Meeting with the Yankee lawmakers were representatives of the other three "eastern tribes." From these discussions emerged the Treaty of Watertown, a document still frequently used by the Maine Indians to insist that George Washington promised them their land rights.

The American commander-in-chief, however, was not present at Watertown, except as a personage much revered by the Indians. Ambrose St. Aubin, the Maliseet leader, declared, "We shall have nothing to do with the old England and all that we shall worship or obey will be Jesus Christ and General Washington." The upshot was that the tribes agreed to furnish "600 strong men" for

Sopiel Selmore (1806–1903) was the grandson of Passamaquoddies who fought in the American Revolution. As such, he joined the patriotic organization, Sons of the American Revolution. In his own right, Selmore was the Wampum Keeper of the Passamaquoddy people. He collected and preserved the stories of the tribe, and served as the messenger to spread news and information to his people. Courtesy, Maine Historical Society

Right
Though they lived primarily a mobile life, moving between good hunting, fishing and gathering spots throughout the year, the Passamaquoddy people were adjusted to a more settled, agricultural lifestyle after a 1795 treaty with Massachusetts. The Passamaquoddy gave up the rights to their lands in eastern Maine for 23,000 acres along the St. Croix River, which included the village of Sipayik shown here. From The Abenakis and their History *by Rev. Eugene Vetromile, 1866*

Washington's army, whom they planned to march to New York to join their hero.

During the course of this July 1776 conference in Watertown, the United *Provinces* of America became the United *States* of America, when the Declaration of Independence was issued on the fourth of July. Much as the Indians admired George Washington, they did not fight directly under him. Fight, they did, though, in the north country. They were commanded by a man they also came to respect greatly, Colonel John Allan who, although the Scotch-born son of a career British Army officer, was forced to flee his Nova Scotia home with a price on his head because of his patriot sympathies.

INVASIONS OF CANADA

In all, three American attempts were made to "liberate" eastern Canada from the British. Two were launched out of Machias, where John Allan, appointed superintendent of the Eastern Indians by the Continental Congress, had established headquarters and provided a refuge for exiles like himself, who were driven out of the Maritime provinces. The initial attempt to rouse the considerable ex-Massachusetts population in Nova Scotia was not the work of Allan but of a displaced ex-Massachusettsan named Colonel Jonathan Eddy.

With population diminished by war and disease, and Europeans encroaching further into tribal lands, many of the Wabanaki people made agreements with colonial forces in Massachusetts in exchange for badly needed supplies. They signed the Treaty of Alliance and Friendship in 1771 in which the Wabanaki were to provide 600 men to aid the colonial army during the Revolution. But the Micmac, because they lived close to British towns along the border with Canada, were unsure of where to place their loyalties. When France entered the war on the side of the Americans in 1778, many Micmac people decided to support the colonies with their old friends, the French, and in 1777 Micmac raiding parties began targeting British loyalists along the Miramichi River in New Brunswick. Shown above is a family at a Micmac encampment. Courtesy, Canadian Archives

Spurred on by the Reverend James Lyon, a fiery Presbyterian minister, who had gone into exile with him from Nova Scotia, Eddy assembled a strike force of 200 men, which included twenty Micmac and Maliseet Indians. As it turned out, it was an absurdly small invasion ensemble. His attack on Fort Cumberland, garrisoned by English regulars, was easily repulsed.

Later, the same fate awaited a regiment-sized attack led by Colonel John Allan. His orders had been to capture Fort Cumberland and, once that was done, the Nova Scotian capital of Halifax. Obliged to retreat back to Machias after failing in the first objective, Allan and his men were essentially rescued by his Indian allies who guided them in canoes through a maze of water routes to safety.

In 1775 Benedict Arnold led an expedition up the Kennebec and Chaudiere Rivers in an attack on British forces at Quebec. The ill-trained and provisioned American troops trekked through the Maine wilderness only to suffer humiliating defeat in Quebec, losing half of the 1000 troops to death or capture. Courtesy, Library of Congress

Indian guides likewise played a key role in the third attempted Yankee invasion of Canada that passed through Maine territory. Known as "Arnold's March," it was commanded by Benedict Arnold in the days before he became a traitor to the United States. The object of this large-scale campaign was to capture Quebec City and the expedition followed a route up the Kennebec River and overland via dense forests and swamps to the former capital of New France. Their hopes were that French Canadians, oppressed under the British, would rise up and greet the Americans as "liberators." Yet just as in Nova Scotia, the inhabitants never budged. Arnold arrived in Quebec with only 700 soldiers, far too inadequate a siege army for subduing that walled fortress. Another American retreat took place, back into Maine, again with help from local Indians. Yet worse disaster for the patriot cause, on a different major Maine river still lay ahead.

AS BAD AS PEARL HARBOR

The fighting downeast was a tug of war. The British, stung by the American incursions into Canada, counter-attacked. Their initial target was Colonel John Allan's headquarters of Machias. An amphibious battle group of their warships, loaded with Royal Marines, initially moved up the Machias River. However, they were met with a storm of bullets and cannon balls from Allan's men. Long celebrated by posterity in the American victory that followed was the prodigious musket shot by Chief Francis Joseph Neptune of the Passamaquoddies who downed a British officer from an unbelievable range. His fellow tribesmen attributed the miraculous shot to his "magic" as a powerful shaman. The Indians' blood-curling war whoops added another psychological effect also credited with inducing the British to withdraw.

Only temporarily, as it turned out. In the next invasion from Nova Scotia, Machias was bypassed and Castine wrested from the Americans and soon developed into a base from which the Brits threat-

The Penobscot Expedition of 1779 is regarded as one of the worst naval disasters in American military history. An American fleet was sent to Penobscot Bay to expel British troops who had taken possession of Castine, but a string of miscommunication coupled with poorly provisioned troops resulted in catastrophe. When the British trapped the American ships in the river, colonial troops fled their vessels and scrambled up the steep river banks. The men scattered, making their way back to Boston through the Maine wilderness. England held Castine for the remainder of the war. Courtesy, United States Marine Corps

ened not only all of Maine, but also Massachusetts.

Boston assembled a large fleet, carrying a strong cohort of infantry and artillery that embarked in June 1779 to recapture the Maine port. This rescue armada reached the mouth of the Penobscot and invaded Castine, but Commodore Dudley Saltonstall, the Connecticut naval officer in charge, seemed loathe to risk any of his ships in a vigorous counter-attack. There was only a short window of opportunity. A superior British fleet appeared, trapping Saltonstall and his nineteen armed vessels in the river, whereupon they fled upstream. All were ultimately sunk or scuttled and their wrecks to this day still lie on the bottom of the Penobscot.

Of the 1,000 army men aboard, most escaped to fight another day and many were helped to safety by friendly Penobscot Indians. Most of the 344 cannon were lost. None other than Paul Revere was in charge of that artillery. Revere was court-martialed but acquitted. Not so for Commodore Saltonstall, who was drummed out of the service for cowardice.

ELSEWHERE IN REVOLUTIONARY MAINE

Most of the military activity in Maine during the Revolution occurred in the northern and eastern parts of the "District." Particularly around Machias and Eastport and certainly in present-day Aroostook County, the status of these lands was not settled until long after the war. In western Maine the only act of hostility was "Tomhegan's Raid," a pinprick, but still remembered in the Bethel area. In 1781 pro-British Androscoggin Indian warriors who had taken refuge in Canada followed their leader to attack Bethel, then known as Sudbury, Canada. Surprise was complete. Three settlers were killed and three others, including two militia officers, were carried off as prisoners of war. But it was strictly a one-time affair.

Unremembered and unrecorded for the most part were the numerous acts of privateering off the Maine coast. Both sides preyed on fishing and merchant shipping. Settlers inland especially around Penobscot Bay never felt safe from British naval sorties and the danger was especially acute on the offshore islands. Commando operations like the one at Thomaston where British marines captured General Peleg Wadsworth, grandfather of poet Henry Wadsworth Longfellow, were a constant threat. This British derring-do, all the same, had a happy ending from the Yankee standpoint, when Wadsworth and a fellow inmate pulled off a hair-raising escape from their prison in Castine and safely returned behind the American lines.

Under British control, Castine was being groomed as a possible haven for Tories—American Loyalists—who in large numbers were, themselves, escaping from the thirteen colonies. A plan was floated to detach the northern Maine region from Massachusetts and make it into a separate province slated to be named "New Ireland." However,

General Peleg Wadsworth (1748-1826) was taken captive during the Penobscot Expedition in 1781. Making a daring escape by cutting a hole in the ceiling of his cell, Wadsworth lived to build a successful business in Portland and become the paternal grandfather of poet Henry Wadsworth Longfellow. Courtesy, Maine Historical Society

the premier Massachusetts Tory of them all, Thomas Hutchinson, the Commonwealth's ex-governor, then living in England, shot down the proposal through his contacts in London. Sure that Massachusetts would be returned to King George's hands and he once more would rule the area, Hutchinson refused to have his native constituency dismembered.

The farthest south in Maine where there was gunfire, with the exception of offshore naval action, was Portland, known at the time as Falmouth. Early in the war, in October 1775, a brutal bombardment unleashed by Captain Henry Mowatt of the Royal Navy practically leveled Maine's largest city-to-be to the ground. For almost twelve hours, Mowatt's sixty-four guns pounded the flourishing port. Miraculously, no one was killed, although the cannonade demolished almost all of the municipality's buildings, including its public library, town hall and Anglican church. Historians dispute whether this was an act of war or of personal revenge. Months prior to this atrocity, Mowatt, while ashore in the city, had been briefly imprisoned by a Sons of Liberty militia unit. Released on parole, with only his word of honor to keep him out of future fighting; he not only violated his pledge but also reduced an entire community to ashes.

Sally Sayward Barrell Keating Wood (1759–1855) of York, Maine is credited as America's first female novelist. She published her earliest novel, Ferdinand and Elmira *in 1804 after being widowed. Known as Madame Wood, she published several novels, one of which,* Tales of the Night, *was published in Portland in 1827. Courtesy, Maine Historical Society*

MADAME WOOD

Mowatt and the Tories left bitter feelings among Maine people that lasted for years. But there was another side to the Loyalist story—a human dimension. In an act requiring no little courage, a remarkable Maine woman dared to plead their case when doing so was still politically incorrect. She had been born Sally Sayward Barrell in the town of York, but known as Madame Wood—the pen name under which she achieved fame as America's first female novelist.

Among her ancestors were the same Sayward sisters who had been carried off to Canada and raised as French Catholics. Her Tory sympathies derived from more immediate kin such as her grandfather Jonathan Sayward and her father, Nathaniel Barrell. The former had remained steadfastly loyal to the king; the latter merely suspected of harboring pro-British tendencies. Neither, though, suffered as severely as Tories frequently did. Jonathan Sayward, the richest and most distinguished man in York before the Revolution, was put under house arrest. He was not driven into exile but deprived of all offices he'd held, such as judge and representative to the Massachusetts legislature. His son-in-law was also kept under close surveillance since he belonged to a religious sect, the Sandemanians, who would not condemn King George.

War, the Parent of Domestic Calamity—A Tale of the Revolution was Madame Wood's attempt to restore her relatives' honor and reputation. A love story between a Tory and a patriot, its literary merit was never strong enough to raise it to the status of a classic. Nor were her other books—like *Julia and the Illuminated Baron, Dorval or the Speculator* and *Amelia*—that memorable. But her distinction of being the first of her gender to have fiction published in the U.S. has kept her name alive, at least in Maine.

As Madame Wood, the wife of General Abiel Wood, a former militia commander and noted ship owner, she scored another "first" in her public insistence on the worth of "American" literature, as opposed to a slavish copying of English models, a fashionable trend then. "Why must the amusements of our leisure hours cross the Atlantic?" she asked. "Why should we not aim at independence?" She even delved into nonfiction with the work *Reminiscences*, about the history of York. Madame Wood also included a vignette on her mother superior ancestor's visit back to Maine.

THE PEACE TREATY

Victory by force of arms alone, was not enough to win the thirteen colonies their freedom. Between Cornwallis's surrender at Yorktown on October 19, 1781 and the signing of the Treaty of Paris, creating the United States, there was a hiatus of sixteen months. Part of the wrangling that went on among the negotiators and the British involved the future of downeast Maine. Who would own the land comprised of Maine's Washington, Hancock, and Aroostook counties? If Benjamin Franklin, the original chief diplomat on the scene in Paris, had been allowed to set conditions, all of those many thousands of acres would have ended up in Canada. The Pennsylvanian was perfectly ready to acquiesce in the British claim for them, which was based to a large extent on their occupation of Castine.

It was the arrival of John Adams as another member of the U.S. team that saved the day for Maine. As a Massachusetts lawyer, he had practiced

This watercolor genealogy shows the Samuel and Lydia Libby family of Scarborough. From the number of farm buildings shown, the Libbys would appear to have been a successful and prosperous farm family. The traditional death symbols shown here, a tombstone, an urn and a weeping willow, are thought to be in tribute to the Libby's unnamed child who died at birth. Painted by Portland artist James Osborne in 1830. Courtesy, Maine Historical Society

in Maine courts. He was familiar with the history of the District of Maine and had access to the legal documents that had set forth its bounds. Forewarned and forearmed, he had brought these research materials with him in his trunk to Paris. His adamant opposition to the British demands saved a considerable region of northern and eastern Maine for the United States. Adams' only concession to the British was to leave the final determination of borders to a commission, which both parties would set in motion following the signing of the treaty.

No doubt, the expectation was of an imminent decision. Most certainly, John Adams never dreamed that a final settlement would remain half a century away and nearly cause another war between Great Britain and its former American colonies.

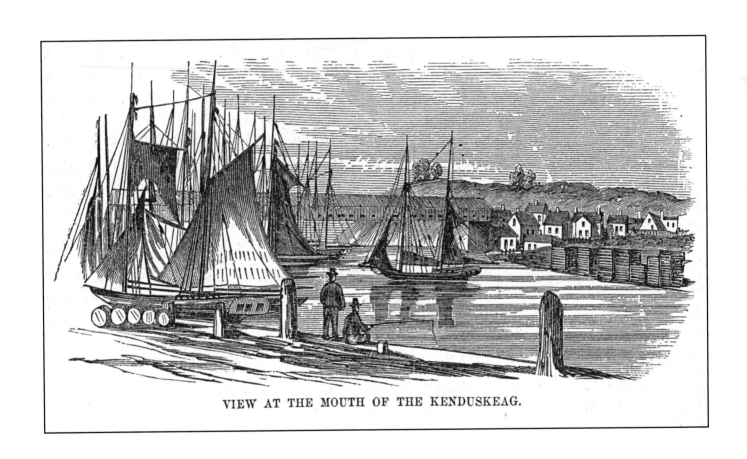

VIEW AT THE MOUTH OF THE KENDUSKEAG.

3

MAINE BECOMES
A STATE
(1783-1832)

Bangor was known as "The Lumber Capital of the World" because of the amount of wood that was shipped through the city. It grew rapidly during the early nineteenth century expansion period, providing lumber for new homes, ships and for heating fuel. Like many parts of Maine, Bangor's population exploded after the Revolution, going from just over 2,000 in 1825 to nearly 8,000 in 1834, when the city was incorporated. From Harper's Popular Cyclopaedia of United States History, *volume I, by Benjamin Lossing, 1893*

ROOTS OF RESTLESSNESS

The British threat had been lifted from Maine proper, at least temporarily. In the War of 1812 the redcoats were back, capturing Castine again, defeating the Americans at Hampden, burning Bangor and not evacuating their troops from Eastport until a year after the Treaty of Ghent ended hostilities. Consequently, they remained a lurking presence in Canada, in disputes with both Maine and the United States over precise locations for the still-undefined borders.

Until 1820 Maine was not really a free agent. In hindsight, it may seem inevitable that the "District" sever its ties with Boston. Yet that was hardly the case. Decades prior to 1652, when Massachusetts seized control, the seeds of separation were probably present and ready to sprout. In the long run, it meant nothing that most new settlers after 1652 originated from Massachusetts. Boston was a far-off capital and many Maine communities never sent representatives to its legislature, although they were entitled to do so. A sense of identity grew, seemingly, out of the geography. Partisan politics, as will be seen, also were heavily involved.

The War of 1812 was a major catalyst. When William King, the commander of the Maine militia, urgently requested reinforcements from the governor of Massachusetts to help stem the British invasion, he was turned down cold. Half a century later in Washington, D.C., proof of how that rejection rankled Mainers was shown during the unveiling at the U.S. Capitol building of a statue of William King. On that occasion, Maine's James G. Blaine, a historian as well as a nationally known politician, scolded Massachusetts in his speech for its past sins, especially its desertion of Maine in the 1812 contest. Blaine's diatribe was so biting that Massachusetts lawmakers came rushing to rebut him. The year Blaine ran for president in 1884, his opponents in Massachusetts made a point of reminding their fellow Bay Staters of his unfriendly remarks.

THE LONG PROCESS

For Maine to break away from Massachusetts, it took seven referendum votes over thirty-five years and then frantic efforts in Washington to reach a compromise with the southern slave states. The earliest indication of organized separatist sentiment was evidenced in Portland in September 1785, barely two years after U.S. independence. Then, the public notice of a meeting was called by distinguished local citizens, including General Peleg Wadsworth, the Revolutionary War hero, and Stephen Longfellow, his son-in-law and father of the poet, Henry. At this gathering, these original supporters of statehood were Federalists, members of the party of Washington and Hamilton, who

The 1807 Non-Intercourse Act (or embargo) under Thomas Jefferson was disastrous for Maine's coastal communities. Goods could not get into or out of U.S. ports meaning that Maine goods were not sold, Maine ships couldn't sail and the need for Maine-built ships diminished. Economic hardship forced some to turn to smuggling goods to British ships waiting offshore or across the border into Canada. From Harper's Popular Cyclopaedia of United States History, *volume II, by Benjamin Lossing, 1893*

Congressman Stephen Longfellow (1776–1849) was a Portland lawyer, trustee of Bowdoin College and supporter of Maine's separation from Massachusetts. He was also the father of the poet Henry Wadsworth Longfellow. Portrait by Charles Bird King, 1824. Courtesy, Maine Historical Society

favored a strong constitution and central government. The question was put to Maine voters in May 1792 and handily defeated. Five more years passed before another vote and this time statehood won, but by 373 votes. However, Massachusetts refused to recognize that such a slim margin represented the will of the people of the District.

WILLIAM KING

The man who changed all this, rightly called the "Father of the State of Maine," was born in Scarborough of a formerly wealthy but impoverished family. One of his half-brothers, Rufus King, set an example of success in being elected a U.S. senator from New York, and William, no less ambitious, left home as a young boy to seek his for-

William King, a merchant from Bath, was one of the leaders of the movement to separate Maine from Massachusetts and form a separate state. King and many others felt that "Mainers" could better represent their own interests rather than relying upon decisions made in far off Boston. King became Maine's first governor in 1820. Courtesy, Maine Historical Society

tune. He found it nearby in the shipbuilding town of Bath, where he prospered as a merchant and owner of numerous sailing vessels.

A Federalist to begin with, he changed his political allegiance following an intra-party spat and assumed the leadership of the rival Democrat-Republicans, who were a definite minority among the Massachusetts electorate of that era. In the District of Maine, utilizing King's vigor, influence and political acuity, these followers of Thomas Jefferson soon turned into a burgeoning majority.

After three tries, King was elected to represent Bath in the General Court in Boston. There, at the epicenter of Federalism, he continued his agitation for taking Maine out of the Bay State.

It proved hard going. In 1807 President Jefferson caused his party untold harm along the eastern seaboard by clamping an embargo on all U.S. coastal ports. The economic disaster that ensued did not spare Maine. Bath shipbuilding was crippled. Unemployment rose to 60 percent. Democrat-Republican King had to lie low but not for long.

Matching Jefferson's ill-advised policy, which had been aimed at keeping American ships from being seized by European belligerents, was a blunder by the Federalists of New England. Opposed to the War of 1812, they disgraced themselves by holding a convention in Hartford and discussing actual secession from the Union. Their opponents cried treason, made the label stick, and capitalized on the Federalists' unpopularity when their minions in Massachusetts did not come to the rescue of Maine from an invading enemy.

This compass is built into a wooden box lined with hand-colored printed paper. The outside is red, with remnants of a chart on one side. It was the property of Jeremiah Clements, 1779–1866, of Westbrook, Maine. He served as a sergeant from September 8–20, 1814 at Portland in Captain J. Valentine's company; lieutentant colonel in J. Hobbs' Regiment and was a lumber surveyor and farmer by occupation. Courtesy, Maine Historical Society

As a result, postwar, there was a more favorable climate for William King's goal. The demographic of Maine had also undergone distinct change. For one thing, the Puritan's old religious monopoly through the Congregational church was dissipated by a significant influx of Baptists. In the early colonial period it had been against the law to be a Baptist in Maine, but by the start of the 1800s they were quickly turning into the majority denomination north of the Piscataqua.

In a smart political move, William King, although a Congregationalist, championed the newcomer sect. This allowed him, during his time in the Massachusetts legislature, to vigorously support public funding for a Baptist College that had opened in Waterville, Maine. The institution, the "Maine Literary and Theological Institute" (later known as Colby College), challenged the monopoly of Maine's higher education that Bowdoin College had enjoyed, backed by the Congregational church and the Federalist legislators of the General Court. Rejection by the Boston lawmakers of King's plea for financial aid to the Waterville school helped drive many Maine Baptists into the Jeffersonian camp.

Undoubtedly the greatest factor contributing to statehood's mounting strength was the squatter situation. Poor people were the clear preponderance of the settlers pouring into Maine following the end of the Revolution. Coincidentally, much of the wilderness land they cleared did not legally belong to them. Prior to their arrival, land speculators had purchased huge parcels of these "Eastern Lands." One was the "Bingham Purchase," covering no less than 2.5 million acres.

The story behind this massive accumulation of property begins with Samuel Waldo, that wheeler-dealer Boston land speculator who, before his abrupt death in 1759, had already assembled a small empire in Maine lands. His direct heirs, with a sole exception, were Tories and fled America, leaving only his granddaughter Lucy Flucker, the wife of Henry Knox, to claim the hundreds of thousands of Waldo acres downeast. After the Revolution, in which Knox was Washington's

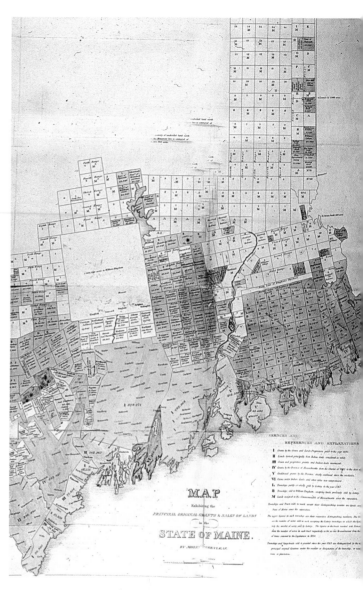

This 1829 map by Moses Greenleaf shows the land grant ownerships, and how lands were divided up for sale and new communities formed. Maine's population exploded after the American Revolution because much of the farmland in southern New England was overcrowded. Settlers flooded the Maine's backcounty region and the population went from about 30,000 in the 1770s to almost 100,000 in 1790. It would double again by 1800 and grew to almost 400,000 by 1830. Courtesy, Maine State Archives

right hand man, and his postwar service as U.S. secretary of war, the couple retired to Maine and bought several million acres more. Unable to sustain the investment, hard-pressed by creditors, they turned for help to a friend of Knox's from Philadelphia. William Bingham was a U.S. senator and reputedly the foremost landowner in the entire country.

Bingham bought the whole 2.5 million acres, while keeping Knox as a junior partner in the venture. Despite his war record and notoriety as a friend of George Washington, in Maine, where he built himself a mansion at Thomaston, Knox ended up as an archvillain to the "squatters" on his lands, when he sent surveyors to confirm his ownership and agents to collect rent.

General Henry Knox served in George Washington's cabinet as the first Secretary of War. A self-taught military expert, Knox had quickly risen through the ranks of the colonial army and was widely regarded as a hero of the Revolution. After the war, he and his family moved to Maine to manage the Waldo family lands they had inherited. They built a fashionable and extravagant mansion at Thomaston and brought a number of profitable industries to the area. The mansion fell into disrepair after Knox and his wife Lucy died. The citizens of Thomaston built a replica that stands as a monument to Knox and educates visitors about his life. Courtesy, Montpelier, the General Henry Knox Museum

THE WHITE INDIANS

Egged on by populist agitators like "the Reverend" Samuel Ely, the squatters fought back against the great proprietors. Knox was their number one enemy. Ely, who had been arrested for his role in Shays' Rebellion in western Massachusetts and deported from the Commonwealth, sarcastically labeled him "The Unmasked Nabob of Hancock County." Those surveyors the general had sent out were terrorized by bands of disguised rural frontiersmen wearing Native American war paint and headdresses—the so-called "White Indians." Their harassment tactics also involved out-and-out violence. In the "Malta War" of 1809, an incident near Augusta, one surveyor was shot and killed; elsewhere, others were wounded. The White Indian movement spread quickly throughout the backwoods areas of the District of Maine, involving so many people that they assumed the nature of a political force. William King set about winning their hearts and minds—and votes.

These Penobscot moccasins were made in 1834. Probably ceremonial, they're referred to as "mourning moccasins" and are most likely made of deer hide with a beaded fabric inserted across the top. Moosehide, a more rugged material, was generally used for work and travel, and was usually left unadorned. Courtesy, Maine Historical Society

THE FINAL STATEHOOD THRUST

King's appeal to the humble people down home was primarily through a piece of legislation he sponsored in the Massachusetts General Court. His "Betterment Bill" guaranteed that no settler could be evicted from a piece of land he and his family had improved, e.g., cleared of trees, lined with stone walls or erected a dwelling, unless the rightful proprietor paid him the value of these changes. The mere fact that King proposed the law made him a hero.

Another step King took, this time in the nation's capital, also advanced Maine's agenda. Through his half-brother, New York Senator Rufus King, he was able to repeal a federal "coasting law" that would have penalized Maine ship owners if Maine had separated from Massachusetts. Consequently, several former powerful statehood opponents on the coast changed their position.

A transformation was evident in Boston's

One of Maine's first two senators, John Chandler (1762–1841) also helped to draft the state constitution in 1820. Courtesy, Maine Historical Society

Maine's fate as a state hung in the balance in early 1820. John Holmes (1773–1843) codrafted the Missouri Compromise as a way to convince Congress that Maine could be admitted to the union without upsetting the balance of "slave" and "nonslave" states. Holmes then became one of the first two Senators elected to represent Maine in Congress in 1820. Courtesy, Maine Historical Society

attitude as well. The Federalists, seeing their political dominance threatened by the increasingly Democratic-Republican vote coming in from the District of Maine, decided it might be better to let the downeasters go their own way.

The seventh and ultimate vote in Maine was a lopsided 17,000 to 7,000. At last, Massachusetts conceded that Maine could leave. However, the suspense was far from over.

THE MISSOURI COMPROMISE

It is little known that the "Missouri Compromise" could just as easily have been the "Maine Compromise." Both future states were forever linked together in U.S. history by this temporarily successful conclusion to the first major crisis to wrack the nation because of slavery. Until Maine made its bid for admission, the balance between free and slave states had been almost equal. For Maine to enter the Union alone without slavery would have tipped the balance against those states with slavery. In Congress, the southern states firmly opposed Maine's bid.

Worse still, the agreement between Maine and Massachusetts had a time limit. Unless Congress accepted Maine before March 4, 1820 the deal was off. William King and his cohorts would have had to restart the statehood process all over again.

A hastily contrived extension bought some time. Into the breach stepped Henry Clay of Kentucky, the current speaker of the U.S. House—and a slave owner. His proposition was simple and seemingly fair—admit Maine as a free state and Missouri as a counterbalancing slave state.

A difficult problem for Maine supporters was to acquiesce in any gains for slavery. One of the loudest Congressional voices raised against the peculiar institution had been that of Senator Rufus King. Strongly anti-slavery himself, William King found himself torn. That in the end, he and others gave way in order to gain Maine its independence, drew heavy criticism back home. In spite of such flak, on March 15, 1820 Maine was incorporated as the twenty-third state.

MARTHA BALLARD

For a picture of ordinary life during this period of Maine's history, no better document is available than the resurrected diary of midwife Martha Ballard. Ballard kept a daily record of her life and work from 1785 to 1812 in the Kennebec Valley, where she lived in the river port community of Hallowell, adjacent to the future capital of Augusta.

In 1990 when Laurel Ulrich, a professor at the University of New Hampshire, published her scholarly revision of the Ballard papers entitled A Midwife's Diary, the book created a sensation. It won a Pulitzer Prize, spawned several television and radio programs and created a buzz among those seeking to portray a "lost subculture," i.e., female existence in the America of the late eighteenth and early nineteenth centuries. Like most Maine settlers of that epoch, Martha Ballard's saga began in Massachusetts in the town of Oxford near Worcester during the Revolution. Born Martha Moore in 1735, wed to Ephraim Ballard at age nineteen, the mother of eight children, three of whom died within days of each other during a diphtheria epidemic, she left for Maine with her surviving brood in 1777.

Ephraim had gone north first in April 1775, having secured land from the Kennebec Proprietors. He was a miller by trade and also a surveyor, a man with some education. Martha, too, could read and write, although her spelling needed improvement. What medical learning she had to acquire for her profession must have been gained informally. By 1785, when she commenced writing her diary, she already, according to Laurel Ulrich, knew how to make salves, syrups, pills and emulsions. She could dress wounds and burns; treat dysentery, whooping cough, and St. Vitus dance; lance abscesses; stop bleeding; relieve a toothache and, of course, deliver babies. Interestingly, her grand-niece, the granddaughter of her sister Dorothy Barton, a fellow emigrant to Maine, was Clara Barton, the founder of the American Red Cross.

Dolly Pollard of Augusta stitched this genealogical sampler in 1820 showing her connection to Maine midwife, Martha Ballard. Courtesy, Maine Historical Society

Martha's first "extracting" of a child occurred in 1778, less than a year after her arrival in Maine. Her diary records 813 more births at which she officiated. Ulrich estimates another 200 before she started writing. All in all, she brought at least 1,000 new Mainers into the world.

Needless to say, delivering babies and tending to the sick was only a part of her life. She has been described as "historian, mortician, pharmacist, farmer, wife and mother," giving birth to her ninth child in Maine.

Around Martha Ballard there also swirled the events of a turbulent time in Maine public life. Her husband Ephraim underwent several tribulations. Distrusted as an alleged Tory sympathizer throughout the years of the Revolution, he was at one time jailed for debt. Also, while acting as a surveyor for Henry Knox, set upon by the "White Indians," he was robbed at gunpoint of his documents, his compass smashed, and thoroughly cursed by the feathered squatters. That was in 1795. In 1809 this continued conflict about land ownership was brought directly into the extended Ballard family, but from another angle. Martha's nephew Elijah Barton, acting as a "White Indian," was tried for murder and implicated in the notorious fatal shooting of surveyor Paul Chadwick in the town of Malta (now Windsor). Martha, herself, paid little attention to newsworthy events like these. "In 1800 she was far more concerned with the death of Nabby Andros, a neighbor's daughter, than with the demise of General Washington," Laurel Ulrich writes.

Martha's entries were brusque, yet often quietly dramatic, telling an understated story of pioneer Kennebec life as in this 1787 sequence of events:

> Call'd from Mrs. Howard to Mr. McMaster's to see their son William who is very low. Tarried thru the night.
> At McMasters. Their son very sick. I sett up all night…"
> William McMaster expired at 3 O Clock this morn. Mrs. Pattin and I laid out the Child. Poor mother, how Distressing her Case, near the hour of Labour and three children more very sick…

After twenty-five years of keeping her diary, she made her final entry on May 7, 1812. The end was near for Martha. She had been working almost to the beginning of May, still birthing babies, although beset by fits of "ague." Her final patient was a Mrs. Heath, with whom she stayed for two whole days and ultimately delivered at 4:30 in the morning. Martha wrote on May 7:

> Clear most of the day & very Cold and windy. Daughter Ballard and a Number of her Children here. Mrs. Partridge and Smith allso. Revered Mr Tappin Came and Converst swetly and mad a prayer adapted to my Case.

Three and a half weeks from that day, Martha's funeral was held. Ephraim did not die until 1821, at the age of ninety-six, living to see Maine become a state.

Frances Western Apthorp Vaughan was a young bride when she moved to Hallowell with her husband in 1790. Both her husband and her father were members of the influential Kennebec Proprietors, Mrs. Vaughan undoubtedly had a cultural influence of her own in the new community. This portrait is one of a pair done of she and her husband, Charles Vaughan, circa 1820. Courtesy, Maine Historical Society

Charles Vaughan (1759–1839) was a member of the Kennebec Proprietors who obtained the Plymouth Patent, granting them thousands of acres of land between the Androscoggin and Kennebec Rivers. Vaughan settled in Hallowell in 1790. He organized the Kennebec Agricultural Society in 1787 and supervised the construction of a church and a boy's academy. But he also had a desire for profit that often guided him toward ill-advised schemes, including canals, bank stocks and even spruce beer meant to replace the more intoxicating beer made from hops. Courtesy, Maine Historical Society

Portland was the state's first capital when Maine became a state in 1820. The capital was moved to Augusta in 1833 when the State House was completed there. Watercolor by Anna Bucknam. Courtesy, Maine Historical Society and the Maine State Museum

Another famed descendant of the Ballards, in addition to Clara Barton, was Sanford Ballard Dole, the president of the Hawaiian Republic and the man most credited with making Hawaii a part of the United States. His mother was Emilie Ballard, a niece of Martha and Ephraim.

THE BRAND NEW STATE

Another condition of statehood imposed by Massachusetts on Maine also had a deadline, and this stipulation was met. Before their statehood bill

MAINE BECOMES A STATE (1783-1832)

could be submitted to Congress in 1820, the people of Maine had to hold a convention and produce a state constitution.

At the time, Maine had 236 incorporated towns and nearly all of them sent delegates to the First Parish Church in Portland, where the conclave was held. Notable Federalists, like Stephen Longfellow, were conspicuously absent.

The deliberations of the convention had to set a permanent governing foundation, answering basic questions such as: "What shall be the name of this new state?"

On that particular issue, the only competition for the final answer of "Maine" was "Columbus." The latter's sponsor, Daniel Cony of Augusta, argued that since battleships were named for states, and a USS *Columbus* already existed, why wait years for a USS *Maine* to be commissioned? It was tortured logic that was easily disposed of with the statement that the "State of Columbus" sounded like a country in South America. The question that still remained, however, was should Maine be a state or a Commonwealth?

Again, down-to-earth Maine reasoning won the day. It should be a state, naturally, a back country delegate argued. Why get fancy with Jonathan when plain old John would do?

The size of the legislature was vociferously debated at length. This fight pitted small towns against large towns. The original proposal of the rural communities would have had 700–800 members in the House. The prevailing compromise was 151, which editorial writers in big city newspapers in the state continue to complain is too large. The State Senate, again in keeping with a populist philosophy, based its number of thirty-one, since raised to thirty-five, not on wealth, as was the rule in Massachusetts, but on population.

No property qualifications for voters or candidates were allowed, unlike Federalist Massachusetts. There was freedom of religion—and from religion, No one had a "duty to worship," as would occur in the Bay State. There was even tolerance for Catholics. The education plank, according to William

Maine officially adopted a state seal upon statehood in 1820. The image comprises several traditional Maine symbols, including a pine tree, a moose—often looking like a deer—a husbandman to symbolize farmers and woodsmen and a sailor to represent the maritime trades. Land and sea are shown in the foreground and the north star can be seen at the top. Dirigo, written in the banner at the top means "I Lead" and is the Maine state motto. From Harper's Popular Cyclopaedia of United States History, *volume II, by Benjamin Lossing, 1893*

King, had been supplied by his friend Thomas Jefferson. Put to the people of Maine, the finished constitution was adopted overwhelmingly. Less than 800 out of 10,000 voters dissented.

Following Maine's official adoption into the United States, another election was held downeast for a governor. The results were completely lopsided, William King ran unopposed. Simultaneously, a legislature was elected and Portland was temporarily chosen as the site for its earliest sessions. It was an unwritten agreement that until a more central location could be decided, Portland would remain the capital.

In Governor King's address to the legislature three months after statehood, still more basics had to be covered—the creation of a State Supreme Court, the election of two U.S. senators, the design of a state seal, a state motto, and decisions on the state budget. With a *bona fide* state government in operation, its first law, "An Act to Incorporate the Augusta Union Society," apparently non-controversial, quickly was entered on the books. But Maine's freedom was not absolute.

Before granting separation, Massachusetts had insisted on keeping a significant amount of Maine property. Perhaps making the best of a bad bargain, Governor King openly praised the Commonwealth for only demanding an equal split of the unpopulated territory. This added up to millions of acres, the proceeds from which, when sold, went directly into the Boston coffers. The only condition the fledgling Pine Tree State could impose was that in the dividing up of these lands, those best suited for settlement would remain with Maine and those best for timber, alone, belonged to Massachusetts.

START OF THE LUMBER INDUSTRY

On the Maine state seal, under the motto *Dirigo*, meaning "I lead," in Latin, are pictured a farmer and a sailor, the North Star, a moose, and a pine tree. While most Mainers were farmers and many along the coast seamen, it was the pine tree that soon dominated the economy downeast. As soon

Lumber has been an important part of the Maine economy since the first Europeans arrived. Through ship's masts for the British navy, barrel staves, planks and boards for construction, shipbuilding and papermaking, lumber has been a cornerstone of Maine business for centuries. Now, the Maine woods are crucial to the tourist industry which draws thousands of visitors each year looking to rusticate in the Pine Tree State. From One Hundred Years' Progress in the United States, *1870*

This statue of Paul Bunyan on Main Street in Bangor was donated to the city in 1959 to celebrate its 125th anniversary. Said to be the largest statue of the mythic woodsman, the structure is built strong enough to withstand 110 mile per hour winds. Photo by Stephanie Philbrick

Plate VI (Grand falls of the St. John River) from the book Atlas of Plates Illustrating the Geology of the State of Maine Accompanying the First Report on the Geology of the State by Charles T. Jackson, engraving and lithography by Thomas Moore, 1837. Charles T. Jackson wrote, "At a time when the boundary line between the British provinces and the United States is proposed to be drawn, it is certainly a matter of no small importance that we should know accurately the nature and value of the district in dispute." Courtesy, Maine Historical Society

as those magnificent specimens of eastern white pine diminished in number, its evergreen relative, spruce took its place.

The loggers moved steadily north and Bangor on the Penobscot River gradually assumed a key role as the epicenter of the industry. Ten years after statehood, the "Queen City" was well on its way to enjoying the title "Lumber Capital of the World." Beyond the city, in places like Old Town, Orono and Veazie, mills by the dozens were erected to turn the giant logs into boards, laths, shingles

and other wood products. Miles from the ocean mouth of the river, Bangor was a major seaport, It was crowded with the sailing vessels that hauled Maine lumber away to destinations all over the world. Within the forests farther north, gangs of red-shirted lumberjacks created a legendary way of life—and a giant statue of Paul Bunyan in downtown Bangor stakes a claim that the mythic logger originated in the Penobscot watershed. No less colorful and facing no less danger in their work were the river drivers, who brought the logs out of

the woods and many miles down rushing rivers to the mills. Almost unconsciously, Maine was moving and looking evermore north.

AROOSTOOK

The vagaries of history might have made Aroostook County, now the largest of Maine's sixteen counties, even bigger than it is, or considerably smaller. Once Maine became a state in 1820 its people expected that its northernmost reach would be almost all the way to the St. Lawrence River, deep inside Quebec province, Canada. The special boundary commission, to which the Peace Treaty of 1783 had assigned the question of determining that border, still had not rendered a decision by 1820. The British kept arguing just as loudly why the correct line should give them half of Aroostook County. The two sides were more than a hundred miles apart.

This Camera Lucida view of Mucalesa Mountain from Mucalesa Pond is one of a series of images taken in Aroostook County in 1841. Hostilities over land and logging rights broke out in 1838 between Canadian and U. S. settlers. Captain Andrew Talcott led a crew to survey the region. The United States recognized the rich natural resources of the area and quickly moved to map and claim the region for the country. Courtesy, National Archives

Today the St. John River marks the boundary between the United States and Canada in this region. Then, it flowed through a vague, densely forested no-man's-land, encompassing Indian tribes, French refugees from Acadia (Nova Scotia), and occasional American pioneers, far out in advance of the wave of immigrants sweeping northward out of southern New England.

Three years before Maine became a state, these first Americans began to arrive in the upper Aroostook area. The most noted of them was John Baker. Building a saw mill on land he cleared in what presently is New Brunswick, he aggressively celebrated the Fourth of July, declared an American "Republic of Madawaska" and petitioned the Maine Legislature to absorb it.

Madawaska was a generic name for an undefined swath of territory on both sides of the St. John River. The French Acadians who had settled there in large numbers had originally been expelled by the British from their Nova Scotian homes, the story told by Maine-born Henry Wadsworth Longfellow in his immortal epic poem *Evangeline*. They resettled on the lower St. John, only to be uprooted once again after the American Revolution by displaced American Loyalists. Upriver, these French Catholics formed a unique community that, to this day, remains on both banks of the St. John, in Maine and New Brunswick. In the developing conflict between the Americans and the British Canadians in the 1820s, the French remained neutral.

John Baker's defiant "Republic" did not last. In 1827 he was arrested by a Canadian sheriff and unceremoniously hauled off to prison in Fredericton, New Brunswick. A vigorous protest followed from U.S. Secretary of State Henry Clay. Closer to the scene, Enoch Lincoln, Maine's governor, immediately dispatched state militia troops to the north woods where they created the town of Houlton—destined to serve as Aroostook's county seat. The road they cut through the forest is still called "the Military Road." Preparations were soon underway to extend it toward Canada as an invasion route, if Baker were not freed.

Happily, no war resulted. After the U.S. and Great Britain agreed to submit the dispute to a third party arbiter, King William of Holland, the American was released. Yet the problem remained unresolved. The Dutch monarch's decision, essentially splitting the geographic difference between the two rival claimants, was unanimously and indignantly rejected.

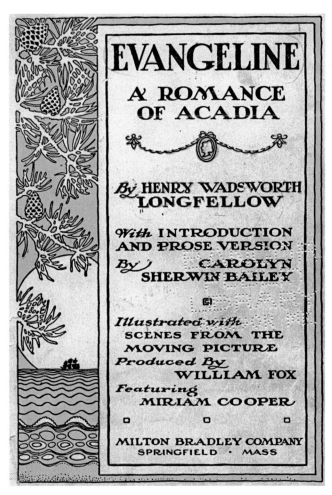

EVANGELINE

A ROMANCE OF ACADIA

By HENRY WADSWORTH LONGFELLOW

With INTRODUCTION AND PROSE VERSION By CAROLYN SHERWIN BAILEY

Illustrated with SCENES FROM THE MOVING PICTURE Produced By WILLIAM FOX Featuring MIRIAM COOPER

MILTON BRADLEY COMPANY
SPRINGFIELD · MASS

Henry Wadsworth's Longfellow's Evangeline *chronicles the deportation of more than 6,000 Acadians from Nova Scotia. The story follows two young lovers, Evangeline and Gabriel, as they are separated on the trip. It was and still is perhaps the nationally famous Maine poet's most popular work. From* Evangeline: A Romance of Acadia *by Henry Wadsworth Longfellow, a 1922 edition*

The border between Maine and Canada remained unsettled after the Revolution with Britain and the U.S. claiming overlapping portions of land. Settlers living in this secluded region were unsure of their nationality and not that interested since their remoteness meant that there was little government intervention in their lives. As lumber interests pushed into the area, competition over cutting rights escalated into conflict. The British and American governments were slow to react but eventually realized that valuable natural resources were at stake. Troops were sent to the area in 1838 and poised for a war that never came. When the bloodless Aroostook War, or Northeast Boundary Dispute, ended in 1839, the borders were finalized and Maine took the familiar shape we know today. Courtesy, Library of Congress

Next, Maine unilaterally declared through legislation that it would incorporate the town of Madawaska within its bounds, a gambit that didn't work either. Although a town meeting was held and a representative elected to the Maine legislature, the governor of New Brunswick, accompanied by soldiers, occupied the French settlement and chased Baker out of his Canadian home for good. There, the matter rested in an uneasy truce for another eight years.

BOWDOIN COLLEGE

The Massachusetts Puritans who took over Maine in the 1650s implanted a strong tradition of supporting education—essentially so that members of their congregations could read the Bible. On a higher education level, this religious impulse translated itself into institutions to train clergy, which were the roots of Harvard and Yale universities. Not until 1793 would a similar impulse apply to Maine.

That year the General Court in Boston elected to pass a bill establishing a college in the district.

Governor John Hancock "refused or neglected" to sign it, but the next governor, Sam Adams complied. On June 24, 1794 the General Court issued a charter for Bowdoin College, having furnished it with the name of an even earlier governor, James Bowdoin. A battle over the school's future location ended when the town of Brunswick offered an acceptable site, but then had to seek support from the authorities in Boston to evict a group of squatters from their property.

Only in 1802 did the college finally open its doors. Considered an orthodox congregational establishment, Bowdoin, like Harvard and Yale, soon went well beyond simply being a theological seminary. The mid 1820s produced a series of star-studded secular graduates who were to play major roles in American public life and letters.

Out of the class of 1823 came William Pitt Fessenden, the outstanding Portland lawyer who, as a U.S. Senator from Maine, chaired the Senate Finance Committee during the first part of the Civil War and reluctantly let Lincoln name him secretary of the treasury for the rest of the duration. Following Appamatox, Fessenden is credited with having saved President Andrew Johnson from impeachment by his one unexpected vote.

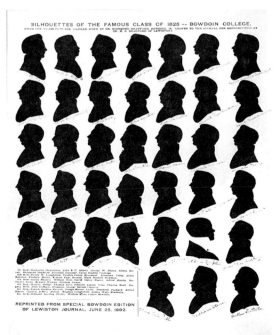

The class of 1824 contained the fourteenth president of the United States, Franklin Pierce. Pierce was a New Hampshire native, and, prior to entering the White House, a U.S. senator from that state and a general in the Mexican War. Also in the same year was Calvin Stowe, a minister and professor of religion not so much well known on his own account, but for having brought his wife, the former Harriet Beecher, with him when he returned to his alma mater to teach. Therefore, it was in Brunswick, Maine that Harriet Beecher Stowe wrote her immortal classic *Uncle Tom's Cabin.*

The most illustrious of all Bowdoin's classes is generally acknowledged to be that of 1825. Two American literary giants graduated that year, Nathaniel Hawthorne and Henry Wadsworth Longfellow. The two of them have been described as sitting two seats from each other in English class. Hawthorne, although forever associated with Salem, Massachusetts, had spent a good deal of his childhood from the age of ten on a farm bordering Sebago Lake in Maine, while Longfellow was born and brought up in Portland. At Bowdoin, Hawthorne's best friend was another classmate, Jonathan Cilley, who was tragically killed in a duel in Washington, D.C. while serving as a congressman from Maine. Also close to the author of *The House of the Seven Gables* was Franklin Pierce. Longfellow entered the class of 1825 along with his older brother Stephen, their politically-active father Stephen Sr. having been on the location search committee that sited the school. Henry was, as a history of Bowdoin attests, "given to writing melancholy verse in college." To no one's surprise, Henry Wadsworth Longfellow, in attendance at the class' fiftieth reunion in 1875, was declared the class poet.

The famous Bowdoin class of 1825 included writers, Nathaniel Hawthorne and Henry Wadsworth Longfellow, and Maine Representative Jonathan Cilley. Courtesy, Maine Historical Society

Jonathan Cilley, had he lived, would have completed a distinguished career in public service. Originally from New Hampshire, like Franklin Pierce, he, in contrast, stayed in Maine to study law and entered politics there. He ran successfully for the Maine House, where he acted as speaker before moving on to Washington, D.C. His fatal duel with a southern congressman was the last to take place in the nation's capital. So angered was his fellow congressman, and later governor, John Fairfield over Cilley's death, that he broke an unwritten rule not to condemn congressional dueling and pushed through legislation to abolish the deadly practice.

JONATHAN FISHER

Far from the refined educational atmosphere of Bowdoin and the town of Brunswick, at the same time that Longfellow and Hawthorne were matriculating, lived another Maine poet and writer. The Reverend Jonathan Fisher, to give him his full title, was more than a *litterateur*. This clergyman delivered 3,000 sermons in his lifetime. He was also a philosopher of sorts, a manufacturer of hats and, above all, an artist, best remembered for his paintings.

One of the breed of graduates the Harvard divinity faculty schooled, Fisher filled the Congregationalist pulpit in the frontier Maine town of Blue Hill, in which he had first settled in 1796. A jack of all intellectual trades, having studied languages, architecture, mathematics, in addition to theology, he resembled his less educated neighbors in the north woods community who had to be good at all practical things in this remote location.

Fisher's most famous painting is the allegorical *A Morning View of Blue Hill Village*, done in American primitive style. In one regard, it was a portrait of what was happening in many parts of early Maine. Here, the clearing of the forest wasn't only to send raw wood down the rivers to sawmills. The removal of the trees was permanent. Stone walls and agricultural fields and fences would follow.

Comfortable homes, a church and roadways are admirably depicted by Fisher in his work, along with a sailing vessel bringing commerce. Yet the foreground hints that the canvas is more than a simple landscape. The principal human figure is a man striking at a large snake—Reverend Fisher, perhaps, driving Satan from the "garden" that had been created in Maine out of a chaotic wilderness finally brought under control.

There is a horse in the scene that Fisher has included, too. Animal depictions were his specialty. Another memorable creation of his for which he has been praised was a book of drawings—*Scripture Animals: A Natural History of Living Creatures Named in the Bible*. It took him thirteen years to finish before he had the book printed in Portland after failing to find a Boston publisher. He sold most of the 1,000 copies himself.

One might, on the basis of this volume, call Jonathan Fisher an early if unconscious ecologist. The "Great Chain of Being" was the concept he pursued as a religious idea that he merged with science. Accompanying his illustrations was a poem expressing such a notion that he penned at the end of a section on whales.

> …all this world,
> This universe of being has its worth;
> Each link above to links beneath is bound,
> And each beneath by those above is held,
> And all existence is a mighty scale
> From to nothing downward and from man
> In grades ascending to the one supreme.

Not exactly Longfellow, but Jonathan Fisher was a Maine man of rare talent, nonetheless.

THE STATE CAPITAL FIGHT

By 1832, the year Jonathan Fisher began peddling his *Scripture Animals* portfolio, Maine had a new state capital. It had taken a dozen years to abandon the former stable in Portland where the legislature had initially been meeting. Despite the flies that still infested the site and promises to respect any decision on a more centralized location, the Portlanders had done everything they could to stall or defeat the move.

Almost immediately following statehood, the legislature had created a capital search committee to inspect several possibilities outside of Portland. Its first choice first fell on Martha Ballard's Hallowell, by then a thriving port, but that decision at once ran into trouble. What made it attractive to many—that it was thriving, wealthy and Federalist—made it unattractive to the majority Democrat-Republican lawmakers. The second search committee finally decided on a little politically correct village upriver from Hallowell—Augusta. Ultimately, the gift of Weston's Hill by a local Democrat-Republican judge clinched the deal. January 27, 1827 became a juridical earmarked date for the government's first meeting to be held in its future home.

Faced with this deadline, Portland and their southern Maine allies balked. A slim margin in the House turned down the gift of land from Judge Nathaniel Weston and, using that same small majority, the Cumberland and York County legislators delayed any additional votes until two years later. Even then, by a one vote margin, they once more put off settling the question.

But in 1827 Portland's resistance weakened. Permission to start work at Augusta was granted. To oversee the construction, William King, the ex-governor, accepted the job of building commissioner and in 1829 presided at the cornerstone laying. For the design of the structure, the supervising committee picked architect Charles Bulfinch, who had masterminded the Massachusetts State House, and his handsome, granite-faced edifice slowly arose on Weston's Hill.

Portland quibbled about cost overruns. Even having the machinery of state government firmly in place overlooking the Kennebec did not stop further attempts to take the capital back to Portland, the last of these efforts, incredibly, as late as 1907. Soon afterward, Augusta and central and north-ern Maine amended the state constitution to ensure that the capital would never be anywhere, but where it had been installed in 1832.

When Bulfinch's State House officially opened for business, President Andrew Jackson sent a personal emissary to speak for him at the ceremony. Major Augustus Davezac's remarks concerned themselves with the one remaining unsolved problem still troubling the new state—the unsettled fate of Maine's northern border. Undoubtedly to cheering roars of approval, the Jacksonian military man, implying help if needed from Washington, declared to his fired-up audience, "The frontiers of Maine will never recede before the footsteps of an invader...her youth in defense of their native land can never be conquered." Such war talk aside, it was a nagging reminder of how vulnerable Maine could be.

Jonathan Fisher (1768–1847) was ordained as a minister in 1793 and moved to Blue Hill in 1796. For over a decade he worked on his book, Scripture Animals, *researching the animals of the Bible, creating detailed woodcuts and writing the text. William Hyde of Portland published 1,000 copies for him in 1834, most of which Fisher ultimately bought to sell himself. Neither he nor Hyde made any money from the venture, but the book is a beautiful and lovingly made piece of art. Courtesy, Maine Historical Society*

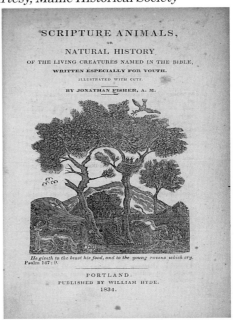

SCRIPTURE ANIMALS,
OR
NATURAL HISTORY
OF THE LIVING CREATURES NAMED IN THE BIBLE,
WRITTEN ESPECIALLY FOR YOUTH.
ILLUSTRATED WITH CUTS.
BY JONATHAN FISHER, A. M.

He giveth to the beast his food, and to the young ravens which cry.
Psalm 147:9.

PORTLAND:
PUBLISHED BY WILLIAM HYDE.
1834.

4

GROWTH
AND TURMOIL
(1832-1860)

Eighteen fifty-five was the peak year for shipbuilding in Maine, when the state led the nation in tonnage constructed. The end of the wooden ship era saw the end of such domination. Courtesy, Maine Historic Preservation Commission

THE WEBSTER-ASHBURTON TREATY

Once U.S. Secretary of State Daniel Webster and special British envoy Lord Ashburton finally settled the Aroostook boundary in 1842, it might have been thought that the Pine Tree State's future looked bright, indeed.

Immigration into Maine continued even during the tenuous decade following Major Davezac's boastful speech in 1832, when war with Great Britain at times appeared imminent. In addition, private entrepreneurs like the heirs of William Bingham, sought and found buyers for their northern lands. In fact, Lord Ashburton's marriage made him one of the Bingham heirs.

Lord Ashburton was born Alexander Baring, scion of the famed British banking family. Sent to the United States in his youth to acquire land for the company, he did so in Maine, taking a large share in the Bingham Purchase while marrying Bingham's oldest daughter, Anne—reputedly one of the most beautiful women in America at the time. The neighboring towns of Alexander and Baring in downeast Washington County are named for him.

Passamaquoddy Indian land in the county had already been acquired by a treaty signed in 1794 and furnished some of the area Maine and Massachusetts divided between them. Treaties with the Penobscots opened more land. With Aroostook County no longer prey to marching armies and sheriff's posses, a territory containing almost one-third of Maine's ultimate 33,000 square miles was added to the twenty-two year-old state.

Many Mainers groused it wasn't enough, that Webster had sold them out. British politicians made a similar charge against Lord Ashburton, that he'd given in too easily. In truth, since they were negotiating in Washington, D.C. in the summertime, Ashburton was anxious to escape the heat. With the help of a secret slush fund, Webster, assisted by Maine Congressman F.O.J. "Fog" Smith of Portland, quieted most critical tongues with gifts of cash, and the compromise was accepted.

At a time that saw Americans elsewhere pushing farther and farther west, in Maine other pioneers were extending the frontier way of life to the north. The lumber industry, though momentarily slowed by the economic "Panic of 1837," continued to expand. Aroostook, geologically much different from the rest of the state, proved to have significant deposits of fertile soil that were perfect for growing potatoes.

Just as Bangor, between the 1830s and the 1850s, dominated the lumber trade of the country, Maine potatoes, from five other counties in addition to Aroostook, quickly gained national fame.

BANGOR'S GOLDEN DAYS

Beautiful mansions, still found in Bangor today, are reminders of the "Lumber Barons" who made fortunes from the products from the Maine North Woods. Men like Rufus Dwinel and General Samuel Veazie, two of the most prominent who

River drivers used the cant dog to roll logs as they moved down river. In 1858 Joseph Peavey of Stillwater invented an improved version—the peavey—that added spikes at the bottom so that drivers could grab onto a log and maneuver it with more control. Courtesy, Bangor Public Library

grew up in small Maine towns, were immensely successful because of their skills and daring. A handsome bachelor, dashing and always controversial, Rufus Dwinel was a Rhett Butler-type who has figured both in Maine fact and fiction. General Veazie, who was a militia commander in the War of 1812, has left his surname on the town where he had most of his sawmills.

Other lesser known but also successful entrepreneurs were Amos Roberts and Hastings Strickland. Then, there was David Pingree who had left Maine for Salem, Massachusetts. There he earned a fortune in merchant shipping, was elected

The Penobscot County town of Veazie takes its name from General Samuel Veazie. A militia commander during the War of 1812, Veazie invested heavily in the lumber and sawmill industry. By the mid-nineteenth century, he owned fifty sawmills on the Penobscot, more than any other sawmill operator on the river. Courtesy, Bangor Public Library

mayor and made another fortune after amassing more than 1 million acres of Maine land.

One of the epic stories to come out of the Maine Woods in this era was the so-called "Telos War" between Dwinel and Pingree. This clash had its origin in a move by Maine lumbermen to keep logs cut in their state from being shipped north to Canada. The lumbermen changed the flow of a canal on the Allagash River from *south to north* into *north to south*, allowing logs to reach the Penobscot River and the sawmills around Bangor.

When Dwinel bought control of the canal, which acted like a sluiceway, his toll charges for the use of it were deemed outrageous by Pingree and he refused to pay them, but ran his logs through anyway. In response, Dwinel rounded up knife-wielding toughs from Bangor's many bars and insisted his fees be paid.

The barflies, recruited as Dwinel's musclemen in the woods, came out of a notorious section of the city known as "The Devil's Half-Acre" where the roughneck loggers came after months in the boondocks. Bent on spending their money, they mingled with the equally tough sailors from the boats that had sailed up the Penobscot. The place was like a Wild West town, packed with saloons, gambling establishments and houses of ill fame— the most memorable being Fan Jones' bordello, which had its chimneys painted pale blue and where bachelor businessman Rufus Dwinel was said to have spent much time. This "war in the woods," a bloodless stand-off, continued until the Maine legislature intervened. Pingree, the frugal Yankee, still has those 1 million acres to his name, controlled by his heirs.

The Bangor of these years was also a haven for foreign immigrants, the vast majority of whom were poor Irish Catholics, some of whom entered the liquor trade. Their presence had a twin effect on two major political issues—prohibition and ethnic religious intolerance—that soon roiled Maine's civil society. In the first instance, the legally imposed temperance movement originated in Maine, spread throughout the U.S. and various parts of the English-speaking world. In the second case, called Know Nothingism, some Mainers simply joined a number of their fellow Americans elsewhere in an ugly spate of essentially anti-Catholic immigrant-bashing.

THOREAU IN MAINE

Henry David Thoreau's connection with Maine dates to this era. His first visit was an exceedingly brief job hunt in Bangor in 1838. Not finding the teaching post he sought, he returned to Concord after a brief stop among the Penobscots on Indian Island. His subsequent trips, deep into the wilderness, were immortalized through his writings.

A number of present-day environmentalists credit Thoreau's statement, "in wildness is the preservation of the world," as the inspiration for all of America's wilderness-preserving activity. These words were the product of his 1846 expedition to climb Mount Katahdin. The Concord iconoclast had never seen raw nature until he encountered Katahdin. Walden Pond and its surrounding areas were tame compared to the primeval grandeur of Maine's highest peak.

Thoreau described the landscape as "Vast, Titanic, inhuman Nature." From the mountain's summit, once he'd climbed to the top, he stared in wonder and marveled at the "countless lakes" and "uninterrupted forest" he beheld. Others have reiterated his poetic reaction again and again in the more than a century and a half since it was written.

Nature was here something savage and awful, though beautiful. I looked with awe at the ground I trod on, to see what the Powers had made there, the form and fashion and material of their work. This was that Earth, of which we have heard, made out of Chaos and Old Night. Here was no man's garden, but the unhandseled globe. It was not lawn, nor pasture, nor mead, nor woodland, nor lea, nor arable nor waste land.

It was the fresh and natural surface of the Planet Earth, and it was made forever and ever—to be the dwelling of man, we say—so Nature made it, and man may use it if he can...

Did the wilderness movement really begin that moment at the foot of the Penobscot Indians' sacred mountain in the mind of a lyric, if cranky, philosopher from Massachusetts? Perhaps. Thoreau also, on his trips, witnessed Bangor in the throes of its lumbering craze...*how man was using nature*...and he watched General Veazie's saw blades, "sixteen in a gang, not to mention circular saws," and wrote that "the trees were literally drawn and quartered there."

On a later trip in 1853, he was back in the Maine wilderness and another idea had struck him that is still quoted to this day. United States' national parks may have come from Thoreau's thought,

again inspired by the wildness of Maine that this type of unspoiled habitat should be kept intact and untouched. Referring to the King of England's private hunting grounds, Thoreau called for "national preserves" that would hold "not the king's game merely, but to hold and preserve the king, himself, also, the lord of creation...."

Activist Lillian Stevens championed several causes during her life, including protection for neglected children, reforms affecting female prisoners and aid for Armenian immigrants to Maine. She is best known, however, for her work on temperance and prohibition. Stevens became the national president of the Women's Christian Temperance Union in 1898, and during her time there saw Georgia, Oklahoma, North Carolina, Tennessee and West Virginia pass prohibition laws, and the sale of alcoholic beverages banned on military bases. Courtesy, Maine Historic Preservation Commission

THE MAINE LAW

It is not generally remembered that the first law in America to ban the sale, production and possession of any and all alcoholic beverages was passed by the Maine legislature in 1851. From that moment on, the "Maine Law" was what people called Prohibition. The guiding spirit behind the movement was a young Portland fireman, born and raised a Quaker but always a feisty fighter, named Neal Dow. In time, he would become a Union Army general in the Civil War and before that, a highly controversial mayor of his native city. Dow never compromised. His position was that even a drop of alcohol was unacceptable and it mattered not whether the drink was wine, beer, rum or whiskey.

Such fanaticism made him many enemies. Trying to paint the abstemious Mayor Dow as a hypocrite, his opponents in 1855 brought a charge against him that he bought $1,000 worth of liquor for himself rather than the city, which could stock it for medicinal uses. A hostile mob gathered at the storehouse where the alcohol was being kept. When Dow sent armed police to contain the throng, troublemakers started throwing rocks. Dow then appeared at the head of a squad of rifle-toting militia and ordered them to fire. In the resulting volley, one man was killed and seven wounded.

The aftermath of the incident found the mayor put on trial for illegally selling liquor. Acquitted, he tried to retrieve his political career, only to suffer another setback when an associate of his, a Congregational minister serving as Maine's state treasurer, was caught lending public money to private individuals, including Dow.

The pioneer temperance law he aided in passing in 1851 was repealed a few years later, but not long afterwards it was reinstated. All of Maine, consequently, was technically "dry" from the mid-ninteenth century until 1933. During the Civil War, General Dow was captured by the Confederates, the highest ranking Union officer

TREE OF INTEMPERANCE

A law prohibiting the manufacture and sale of liquor was passed in Maine in 1851. As temperance gained political momentum, other states began to enact their own Maine Laws. Two key figures became important in spreading prohibition and temperance ideology to other states. Lillian M. Stevens, onetime president of the Women's Christian Temperance Union, and Neal Dow, the "Father of Prohibition," were both from Portland. This Tree of Intemperance links crime, vice, immorality and other less than desirable traits to the consumption of alcohol. Courtesy, Library of Congress

Anti-immigrant feelings ran high against Irish Catholics who moved into Maine during the 1840s and 1850s. Catholic churches were attacked, and this Bath church that local Catholics were using for services was burned on July 6, 1854. Painting by John Hilling. Courtesy, Maine Historical Society

to be held by the rebels. Eventually, he was exchanged for a relative of General Robert E. Lee.

An international figure, lecturing in England, Europe and throughout the U.S., Neal Dow was the most recognized prohibitionist of his time. His runs for president on the Prohibition Party ticket, though, were always unsuccessful.

THE KNOW NOTHINGS

Because many of the saloon keepers, bar owners, and liquor dealers in Maine and elsewhere were Irish Catholics, there was often more than a subtle link between anti-Catholic bigots and prohibitionists during the first half of the 19th century. The Protestant reaction, fanned by certain preachers, led to a political movement whose official title was the American party. Commonly, these were the "Know Nothings," since whenever you asked one of them what their party was about, he would answer, "I know nothing." Yet the violent actions of this secretive group spoke loudly.

Catholic institutions were physically attacked. In Bangor, the building used by local Catholics for

a church was burned to the ground. An established church building in Bath was torched. A priest trying to say mass in Ellsworth was tarred and feathered and ridden out of town on a rail. Such nasty hatred was all the more shocking in Maine since the Pine Tree State had been the first in the highly Protestant, Puritan tradition of New England to elect a Catholic to high public office. Edward Kavanagh who had been a congressman and then governor, stepped in from his position as president of the Senate to fill a sudden vacancy in the chief executive's spot.

As a political force, the Know Nothings, in Maine and in the U.S., were short-lived. Both state and nation soon had an overwhelmingly more serious issue to face—and this one, too, involved intolerance.

SLAVERY

In Maine there were varied reactions to the institution of slavery. Slavery had been legal once in Maine but officially was banned before the nineteenth century. Many Mainers were indifferent to its existence in the South or argued that it was a constitutional right for Southerners to own slaves, but the sentiment against the practice never ceased growing. This was evident in the severe criticism within Maine's congressional delegation in 1820 when they accepted Missouri as a slave state.

Further irritations that gained more anti-slavery adherents followed from Southern attitudes, plus perceived and real acts of aggression. "Free Soilers," acting as a separate political party, were formed in Maine and other parts of the North in a reaction to Southern attempts to extend slavery, particularly to the new territories absorbed from Mexico.

Additionally, a nasty fight developed between Maine and the state of Georgia. This event happened in 1837 when an escaped slave named Atticus slipped unnoticed onto a Maine ship which was docked in Savannah harbor. Surmising he had been on board when the schooner *Susan* left for home, Atticus' owners sailed to Thomaston, Maine where she landed. They secured a court order under the Fugitive Slave Law and reclaimed their "property" but not without an angry send-off from frustrated anti-slavery locals.

The incident might have ended there had not the slaveholders filed suit in Georgia against the ship's captain and mate for "slave-stealing." Thus began a decades-long quarrel between various governors of Maine and Georgia, the Southerners calling for the extradition of the two Maine men and the Northerners refusing on the grounds they had not known the slave was aboard until it was too late to turn back.

Georgia's legislature then contemplated drastic measures against Maine, including the closure of all of its ports to Maine ships and seizing Maine citizens as hostages. Cooler heads prevailed, at least temporarily, until a later Georgia governor, George R. Gilman, proclaimed in his legislative message that any Maine citizen found in Georgia would be presumed to have "intent to commit the crime of seducing Negro slaves from their owners…"

Maine's governor, John Fairfield, incredulously responded that this idea was so preposterous and unconstitutional, he couldn't believe the Georgia lawmakers would follow through. He was right. For his role in the dispute, Fairfield had a price to pay. At the Democratic party's national convention in 1844, after James Polk was nominated for the presidency, voting began for vice president. Fairfield led on the first ballot. However, on the second ballot the South turned against him and he lost to George Dallas of Pennsylvania.

It was not solely the Maine-Georgia fight that defeated him, although he acknowledged it had played a strong part. Equally important had been his vote against admitting Texas as a slave state. It should be noted that James Polk, the Tennessean who won the presidency that year, was a slave-owner and a dogged exponent of extending slavery.

John Fairfield (1797–1847) served as governor of Maine during some crucial, if little known, conflicts. He took office in 1839, during the Aroostook War and entered into an ongoing quarrel with Georgia over a runaway slave. This squabble cost Fairfield his bid to be James Polk's vice presidential running mate in 1844 since southern Democrats would no longer support him. From Maine: A History *by Louis C. Hatch, Volume II, 1919*

UNCLE TOM'S CABIN

The world's most famous book dealing with slavery is arguably *Uncle Tom's Cabin*, written in 1852. Though Harriet Beecher Stowe's novel is set in the Deep South, it was written in Maine. Harriet was brought to Brunswick by her husband Calvin Stowe when he came to teach at his alma mater, Bowdoin College. She was allegedly inspired one Sunday in the Bowdoin chapel by a vision she had of an aged slave being brutally beaten and then forgiving his murderers on his death bed. Having also been goaded by a relative that had been importuning her to write a book on slavery, she set to work.

The author had witnessed slavery first-hand when she lived in Cincinnati, just across the Ohio River from the slave state of Kentucky. It has been said that she even assisted in the escape of a fugitive slave.

She came from a devoutly religious Puritan family in Connecticut. Both her father, Lyman Beecher, and her brother, Henry Ward Beecher, were nationally famous Congregational ministers. Harriet was in Cincinnati because her father had been made the headmaster of the Lane Theological Seminary. After marrying Calvin Stowe, one of his teachers, in 1836, she moved to Maine.

The Compromise of 1850, which included a beefed up Fugitive Slave Act, also galvanized her into writing. Although not a professed Abolitionist as she thought their position too extreme, Stowe allowed *Uncle Tom's Cabin* to be first published serially in an Abolitionist newspaper, *The National Era*.

Overnight, the work became a sensational success. As a book, it was into its third edition within three weeks of publication. Worldwide sales eventually numbered 10 million copies. No wonder Abraham Lincoln, when he finally met Harriet Stowe, greeted her with, "So you're the little lady who started the big war."

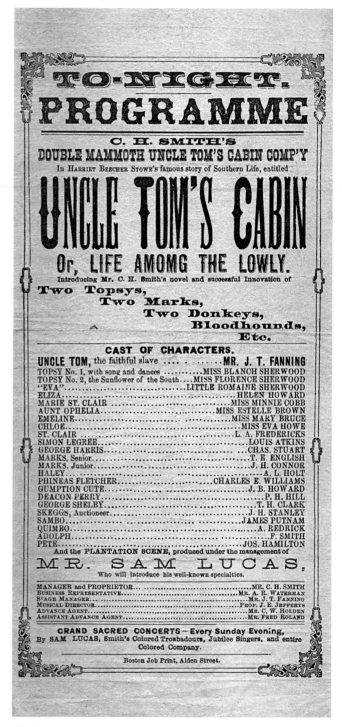

This program advertises a traveling theater company's performance of Maine resident Harriet Beecher Stowe's famous story. C. H. Smith's company did novelty renditions of the play throughout the 1880s and entertained audiences with trained bloodhounds and a double cast. Courtesy, Maine Historical Society

THE REPUBLICANS

Lincoln was the first president to be elected on the "Republican" party label. The name was not new in American politics. Jefferson's party, officially known as the Democrat-Republicans more often were referred to as simply Republicans. Their rivals, the Federalists, finding they needed to change their name, tried "National Republicans." That didn't catch on, so they became the Whigs. Then, due to the combined weight of three issues—slavery, Know Nothingism and temperance—a massive political change took place in the U.S. in the 1850s.

The year 1854 is usually noted as the beginning of today's Republican Party. That very same year, a meeting in the small western Maine town of Strong is generally credited with having started the GOP in the Pine Tree State. Various sources contributed to the amazingly swift growth of the new party in Maine. The Whigs had never been powerful in a state that had been founded by the party that now called itself Democrat. Consequently, a Whig contingent, with their organization disintegrating, formed a base for the opposing Republicans.

Possibly even more significant were disillusioned Democrats—including highly important and loyal members of the party—who could no longer support the Democrat's positions on slavery and prohibition. Their defections brought popular leaders into the new fold, providing instant credibility. For example, one such person was Hannibal Hamlin who went on as a Republican to become the vice president of the United States during Lincoln's first term.

Born in western Maine at Paris Hill, Hamlin, while still an infant, had a glorious future predicted for him by a locally famed Indian "medicine woman," Molly Ockett. As a Democrat representing Maine in the U.S. Senate and adjudged the most popular politician in the state, he seemed well on his way to fulfilling the prophecy, even before his dramatic switch of allegiance which took place

This iron collar and chain are said to have been filed from the neck of a negro field hand who came inside the federal lines from the Confederacy in 1862 at Pontchartrain, Louisiana. The collar was filed from the man's neck by Captain Charles C.G. Thornton, 12th Maine volunteers and presented by him to the Maine Historical Society. Courtesy, Maine Historical Society

openly on the Senate floor. Hamlin could no longer abide his party's support of the Southern position on slavery. Within months, he was running on the Republican ticket for governor of Maine. After being elected in a landslide, he almost immediately resigned and was reelected as a U.S. senator, this time by a Republican legislature, before going on to his vice presidential post.

Other major Democrats in Maine followed suit. Particularly noteworthy were two brothers, Anson P. Morrill and Lot M. Morrill. The latter left his position as state chairman of the Democratic Party to join the Republicans, primarily over the temperance issue. His sibling, who became governor, allegedly did so with the help of former Know Nothings, themselves forming an element of the Republican Party.

In addition, there were newcomers to Maine like James G. Blaine. A transplant from Pennsylvania, Blaine brought organizing skills, journalistic abilities and the enthusiasm of a young man in his twenties to the task of party building. Soon he was running the state party, which grew immensely in strength with the advent of the Civil War. From its initial victory in the gubernatorial election of 1856, Maine's Republican Party kept an iron grip on the state, with a few exceptions, for more than 100 years.

WHITHER MAINE'S ECONOMY

During the 1830s, 1840s and 1850s, Maine was one of the fastest growing and most populous places in the United States, proportionate to other parts of the nation. Then, Maine had six congressmen;

An anti-slavery, pro-temperance man, Lot M. Morrill (1813–1883) joined the newly formed Republican party because there was a movement in the legislature to undermine the Maine Law which prohibited the sale and manufacture of alcohol. Prior to the Civil War, Morrill was elected to three one-year terms as governor of Maine, then served in the U.S. Senate as the U. S. secretary of treasury. Courtesy, Maine Historical Society

Belgrade native, Anson Morrill (1803–1887) was Maine's first Republican governor, elected in 1855. He also served a term in Congress at the start of the Civil War. Courtesy, Maine Historical Society

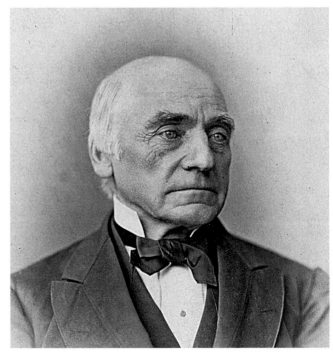

John A. Poor saw railroads as the key to Maine's future. Of his ambitious plans for them downeast, one reached fruition—The Grand Trunk from Montreal to Portland— and the other, the far more ambitious North American and European Railroad, never was completed. From Portland and Vicinity *by Edward H. Elwell, 1881*

today it has two. Portland, a booming port, was making a strong bid to outshine Boston. Plans were afoot to make Maine a keystone of American commerce with Europe, because of its closer position on the Atlantic coast. In shipbuilding and lumbering, it led the nation and its farms were flourishing. However, these ambitions were not realized. There are several reasons why they did not happen.

First, the state's railroad plans were flawed, beginning with a bang and ending more or less with a whimper. The key player in both instances was an entrepreneurial Mainer by the name of John A. Poor. A man of considerable daring, he engineered an astounding coup in 1842. Poor raced by horse and sled through a blinding snowstorm in subzero temperatures from Portland to Montreal, Quebec, in a race to gain an exclusive contract which was also sought by Boston railroaders. The contract was for nothing less than an American outlet on the Atlantic east coast for most of Canada's products that could be shipped by rail, and for return cargoes of Canadian imports from overseas that arrived by ship. The Grand Trunk Railroad thus promised whichever city won, Portland or Boston, the status of a major port and a glowing economic future.

Poor was successful. The Grand Trunk was built from Montreal to the potential Maine metropolis. Poor, always the dreamer, came up with a more grandiose scheme. His newest brainstorm bore the exotic title of the North American and European Railway. Linking railroad lines that already reached Bangor, it was to traverse the Maine woods to the New Brunswick border—passing through Vanceboro on the U.S. side, the town of McAdam in Canada, continuing on to Nova Scotia, Halifax and beyond. At the tip of Cape Breton Island, the railway would connect to steamships and carry freight and passengers to Ireland. Therefore, more than 100 miles would be shaved off any other competing route to Europe.

Poor devoted the rest of his life in an ultimately futile attempt to turn his vision into reality. After several decades, he got his tracks to Vanceboro,

This Grand Trunk Railway station in Portland was built in 1903, superceding an earlier structure built in 1855. It stood at the foot of India Street until it was torn down in 1966. Courtesy, Bethel Historical Society

and President Ulysses S. Grant traveled to Maine to cut the ribbon. However, the Canadians balked at completing the road and the whole project came to naught—except for an ancillary plan that became the valuable Bangor and Aroostook Railroad.

The success or failure of railroads had little impact on the lumber industry, the undisputed foundation of Maine's economy in the years before the Civil War. Its dependence on transportation was not tied to rails, but to rivers and ships. The weaknesses that began to reveal themselves in this epoch were those endemic to natural resources. The lumber industry began to run out of product.

The magnificent white pines were soon all cut; spruce, once scorned, became the tree of choice. Some Maine loggers, epitomized by the mythic Paul Bunyan, picked up and headed west to Michigan, Minnesota and Wisconsin. Thus, Bunyan and his blue ox, Babe, are associated with the Midwest, as well as Maine. Lumber remained important downeast, and later on, when paper began to be made from wood, it would prove to be much more important. However, this was not an economy to challenge the much larger manufacturing base that was developing in southern New England and the rest of the United States.

Lumbering left behind an ephemeral legend of a type of macho woodsman, heavily romanticized but based on real models. In 1851 John S. Springer wrote his classic *Forest Life and Forest Trees*, detailing the work of these loggers. The rhythm of their labor went from "the stump in the swamp to the ship's hold," in all its stages from toppling the trees, cutting roads, icing them in winter, moving huge logs by oxen-pulled sleds to the watersides of rivers, where they were finally floated in the most dangerous segment of the operation called the "drive." Springer described his own experiences, downing an immense "pumpkin pine," so-named for the orangey color of its interior wood, six feet in diameter and 145 feet high. When the giant crashed to the forest floor, it "seemed to shake a hundred acres." The stump was wide enough to stand a yoke of oxen on it. Five logs were sliced out of that huge mass, enough to load a six ox team three times.

This river driver wore spiked boots for sure footing as he rode the logs down river. Lumbermen are legendary in poetry and song for their hardiness. In one love song, a woman recalls her dead lover, a logger who only just buttoned up his coat at forty degrees below zero. *Courtesy, Bangor Public Library*

Some might say that Maine's soil is best for growing rocks. Old rock walls still snake their way through overgrown fields and housing developments, left over from the efforts of early settlers who cleared fields for farming. Even well-established farms find new rocks every year as the frost heaves move deeply buried rocks to the surface. *From Maine Agriculture, 1915.*

This watercolor sketch shows a surveyor by a campfire in the Maine woods. Surveyor James Bucknall Estcourt, (1802–1855) drew the pencil sketch while surveying the Maine-New Brunswick Border between 1843 and 1847. Estcourt, Quebec and Estcourt Station, Maine are named for him. Courtesy, Canadian Archives

Going downhill with such a load could be fatal if the sled tipped, and Springer once personally witnessed an accident when a driver was run over and practically cut in half. River driving caused even more casualties. Springer also wrote of the ultimate destination of the boards, slats, and staves produced from the lumber, whether in Boston "for building and cabinet purposes" or Cuba, the recipient of 40 million feet of Maine wood "for the one article of sugar boxes."

Another writer who apotheosized these rugged toilers in the forests downeast was John Greenleaf Whittier. In his poem "The Lumbermen," the Massachusetts bard snuck in a little Abolitionist propaganda as well, referring to the "Northland, wild and woolly," where:

Freedom, hand in hand with labor
Walketh strong and brave
On the forehead of his neighbor
No man writeth Slave!

Furthermore, Maine farming, except for potatoes, could not keep pace with the competition. Until the Civil War, agriculture, was the state's leading economic activity. Small farmers on rocky soil in a cold, cold climate, however, could not often sustain themselves. Opportunities that beckoned, like fertile lands opening in the west, drew many a Maine family. Meanwhile, the 1849 Gold Rush in California lured adventurous young Mainers who could pack up and leave, often sailing on ships out of Maine ports.

This period also saw the glory years of Maine shipbuilding. In 1855 Maine was the shipbuilding capital of the United States, with the weight of vessels constructed totaling 216,000 tons. The Gold Rush itself, which was draining the state of its male youth, also accounted for the undisputed superstars of this downeast fleet—the clipper ships—which were built for their speed in traversing the long route around Cape Horn to reach the west coast.

The total tonnage of the clippers was no more than 5,000, but the names of the fastest of them are still revered today by sailing buffs—the *Red Jacket*, the *Flying Dragon*, the *Nightingale*, the *Typhoon* and the *Snow Squall*. The latter raced *The Romance of the Sea*, built by famed Boston shipbuilder Donald McKay, from China, and beat her by two days. The *Nightingale*, built in Eliot, Maine, honored Jenny Lind, the great Swedish singer, whose likeness formed the ship's figurehead. Arguably, the fastest was the *Flying Dragon*, which made it from Maine to San Francisco in ninety-seven days. The *Typhoon* set a record on the Portsmouth, New Hampshire to Liverpool, England run. The *Red Jacket* was the largest and most handsome of

the Maine clippers and she was "wicked fast," too, as the locals would say. On her first trip, she surpassed the *Typhoon*'s record to Liverpool by nine hours. Another record, never equaled, was her run from the Cape of Good Hope off the coast of South Africa to Melbourne, Australia in nineteen days.

These tall ships, so entrancing to modern lovers of sail, had but a brief existence. Fast as they were, they could not compete with new technologies such as steam on merchant ships and ironclad armor on warships. Their beauty faded into nostalgia in books, paintings, films, museums, and replicas. Meanwhile, the nation lurched forward into a defining moment of its existence—the Civil War—and the many changes that conflict wrought.

Built in Cape Elizabeth at the Joseph Dyer yard in 1853, the clippership Portland *was owned by two Portland merchants, Joseph McLellan and Nathaniel Deering. Clipperships were fast vessels that sailed around the horn to ports in the Far East to transport American goods to China and bring fresh tea back to Britain and the U. S. Painting by Tudgay. Courtesy, Maine Historical Society*

5

MAINE IN BLUE
THE CIVIL WAR ERA
(1861-1865)

The Confederate ship Alabama *raided Union merchant vessels crossing the North Atlantic to Europe and captured goods valuing nearly $6 million. When the* Alabama *sailed to Cherbourg, France on June 11, 1864, she was confronted three days later by the Union vessel, USS* Kearsarge. *The* Alabama *sailed out to the* Kearsarge *and one of the great Naval battles of the Civil War ensued. Just a half hour later, the great raider ship of the North Atlantic was sinking and the crew was captured. This painting, by William E. Norton (1843–1916), shows the battle near its end. Courtesy,* Maine Historical Society

MAINE'S WAR EFFORT

The bloodiest four years of conflict in American history found Maine in the forefront of the forces who fought to preserve the Union and to put an end to slavery. Some 73,000 Mainers served in the U.S. Army or Navy, the highest percentage of any Northern state, and its ratio of fatal casualties was also the highest proportionately.

Its budding industries geared up fast. Approximately 5 percent of the powder used by Union troops was produced at powder mills on the Presumpscot River, just outside of Portland. The Navy benefited from the building of twenty-six warships at the nation's oldest public military shipyard located in Kittery, Maine, although it now bears the official title of the Portsmouth (New Hampshire) Naval Shipyard. One of these wooden ships, the *Kearsarge*, became especially renowned after she encountered the feared Confederate raider *Alabama* off the coast of France and sank her. Confederate privateers like the *Alabama* helped disrupt, if not destroy, Maine's pre-war trade in lumber, fish, and ice with other areas of the world. Since the *Alabama*, as well as several other Confederate cruisers, had been built in English yards at Liverpool, Americans who had suffered damages sued the British government—a litigation that lasted more than a decade and finally netted the U.S. plaintiffs $15.5 million. The indirect losses, such as the rise in insurance costs and higher prices for goods, were never reimbursed.

Part of those intangibles had to be the concern for Mainers that Great Britain, which early on recognized the South as a belligerent, might have joined the war on the Confederate side. Once more, Maine could have suffered an invasion from Canada. Consequently, coastal defenses had to be strengthened. An odd footnote was that the vice president of the United States, Maine's own Hannibal Hamlin, spent a good portion of the war years not at a desk in Washington, D.C., but at Fort McClary in Kittery, Maine, as a member of a coastal defense unit.

Maine's first wartime governor was Israel Washburn Jr., a member of an extraordinary family from the town of Livermore, whose sons typified the exodus west from the state's farms. In certain Midwest locations such as Illinois, Wisconsin and Minnesota, the Washburns became important political figures.

Israel, the eldest, staying home, was first a congressman who helped form the national Republican Party and then its downeast GOP branch, which was the dominant political force in Maine throughout the Civil War. He teamed with its rising young leader, James G. Blaine, to manage the Pine Tree State's military contribution to the Union. This was a huge mobilization that included thirty-two infantry regiments, three cavalry regiments, seven companies of coast guard and six companies to man coastal fortifications.

In addition to Hamlin being vice president, it also helped that Blaine had been a strong supporter of Abraham Lincoln's nomination in 1860 and that Governor Washburn's brother, the Illinois Congressman Elihu Washburne (he added the "e" to his surname after he went west) was one of

Nineteen year-old Wesley (or West) Cooper of Union enlisted in the army and was assigned to Company H, 4th Regiment Infantry. He was killed in the Battle of Bull Run on July 21, 1861. Courtesy, Maine Historical Society

It is estimated that 25 percent of the powder used by the Union Army during the Civil War came from the Oriental Powder Mill on either side of the Presumscot River in Gorham and Windham. The mills produced 2,500,000 pounds of black powder per year during the war, as well as making blasting powder for quarries and sport powder for hunting. Courtesy, Maine Historical Society

Above

Considered by many to be the first federal shipyard in the United States, the Portsmouth Naval Shipyard in Kittery is over 200 years old. Workers in the Piscataqua River region of Kittery, Maine and Portsmouth, New Hampshire had been building ships for generations by the time the shipyard was officially opened under Thomas Jefferson. During the Civil War, the USS Kearsarge, famous for destroying the Confederater raider, CSS Alabama, was built here in 1861. From Nooks and Corners of the New England Coast, 1878

Below

Companies from Houlton, Union, China, Presque Isle, Monmouth, Bangor, Portland, Fairfield, Biddeford and Bath were mustered in at Augusta in August 1861 as the 7th Maine Regiment. They saw action at Antietam, Gettysburg, the Battle of the Wilderness and several other key battles of the Civil War, and lost nearly 30 percent of the regiment's 1,165 soldiers to battle wounds or disease. Courtesy, Library of Congress

General O. O. Howard commanded troops at several key battles during the Civil War, including Bull Run and Gettysburg. Born in Maine in 1830, Howard championed the rights of African Americans and fought to secure land for freed slaves. From Maine: A History by Louis C. Hatch, Volume II, 1919

As much a moral crusader as a military one, General O. O. Howard was contemplating a career as a minister when the Civil War broke out. He was made head of the Freedmen's Bureau in 1866 and later founded Howard University in Washington, D. C. This jacket was a part of his uniform when he was a cadet at West Point, 1853–1854. Courtesy, Maine Historical Society

Lincoln's closest friends. Also, Ulysses S. Grant was one of Elihu's constituents and protégés.

In helping Maine's governor pick leaders for the Maine regiments, Blaine engineered the selection of a West Pointer from tiny Leeds, Maine, who came to have a distinguished military and post-Civil War career. This man was Oliver Otis Howard, the "Christian General," known to posterity because of Howard University, the Black college he helped to found after the war when he headed the federal Reconstruction effort.

THE WASHBURNS

Norlands was the name given to the third building which was erected atop a high ridge site in Livermore, Maine and settled by Israel Washburn Sr., a transplant from Raynham, Massachusetts. The first two dwellings, fairly crude structures, had burned down, but the final addition was an "Italianate mansion" built by the old gentleman's successful sons. For them, it was a summer vacation destination. For their father, described as a failed shopkeeper turned farmer, it was a more comfortable place to live out his life than either of the original homes in which his ten children had grown to adulthood.

The Washburn boys did well for themselves. There were seven of them in addition to three girls. Two of the males, Israel Jr. and Algernon Sidney, stayed in Maine, as well as all three females, Martha, Mary and Caroline, who married local men. The rest, like so many adventurous Maine youth in those times, had gone out into the wide world and mostly prospered.

Not that the stay-at-homes were any slouches. Israel Jr. was the wartime governor of Maine, a position to which he was elected after five terms in Congress representing the Bangor district. His two terms as chief executive, overseeing the state's war effort, left him exhausted. He declined a third term, opting instead to accept an appointment from President Lincoln as collector of the port of Portland, an important political and financial sinecure that he held for fourteen years.

Active in civic affairs in Portland, he was an officer of the city's board of trade, a trustee of its Maine General Hospital and extremely active with the Portland-headquartered Maine Historical Society. Nor did he neglect his native town, writing a history called *Notes of Livermore* and producing a historical piece on the Northeast Boundary controversy in which he deeply deplored the millions of acres Maine gave up to achieve a settlement. The other Maine-based brother, Algernon Sidney,

The seven Washburn brothers. Upper left, Sidney; upper right, Elihu. Center left, Cadwallader; center, Israel; center right, Charles. Lower left, William; lower right, Samuel.

The remarkable Washburn Brothers are a true rags-to-riches story. Raised in Livermore Falls, the brothers each struck out to find prosperity and all succeeded. A close-knit, loyal family, the sons returned home often and built "Norlands" for their parents. The home, farm, chapel schoolhouse and library still stand and are open to the public. Collections of Maine Historical Society

resided in Hallowell, was a banker, and quietly, it seems, bankrolled his brothers' careers.

Another Washburn who was successful in politics was Elihu, who had gone to Galena, Illinois after studying law at Harvard. The addition of an "e" to his last name was on the grounds that it approximated the ancestral spelling. He spent sixteen years in Congress, finishing his public service as secretary of state and U.S. minister to France during the Franco-Prussian War.

Cadwallader Washburn made his fortune in timber, minerals, and flour milling in Wisconsin. He was a congressman for ten years, a one-term governor and during the Civil War he formed a cavalry regiment and rose to the rank of major general. He was a founder of the Gold Medal Flour Company, today's General Mills.

William Drew, the youngest Washburn son who was also destined for politics, studied at Bowdoin. He clerked in the U.S. House of Representatives when three of his brothers were simultaneously members of that august body. He settled in Minnesota and ran Cadwallader's flour business. He made a fortune too, served in Congress and later was the only Washburn elected to the U.S. Senate. His other political siblings had tried for the upper body but failed. In the one term William had served, he was known as the "Flour of the Senate."

Brother Charles added California to the Washburn geography. He was a "Forty-Niner," not seeking gold, however, but anchoring himself in west coast journalism as an editor of the San Francisco *Times* and owner of the *Alta California*. A novelist also, he, like a number of literary Americans, turned diplomat. Lincoln appointed him U.S. Minister to Paraguay and he wrote a two volume history of that South American country after experiencing a series of hair-raising adventures during a revolution there.

Brother Samuel might have gone farther away physically than any of the other males had it not been for a Civil War wound. Instead of going to medical school, he ran away to sea at age eighteen. Later, as a captain in the U.S. Navy, he commanded

This statue of Joshua Chamberlain stands atop a miniature version of the battlefield at Little Round Top in Brewer's Freedom Park. Chamberlain saw at least twenty-four battles during his Civil War service, with Little Round Top and Gettysburg being the most famous. Photo by Stephanie Philbrick

an ironclad gunboat against the Confederates until lamed for life in battle. Whatever disposition he'd had for doctoring was put to use once he came home to Livermore and cared for his aging father and ailing brother Sidney.

Norlands at present is a 445-acre Living History Center, comprising the main house, farm buildings, school and library. All are available for educational programs built on recreating the past and relating the story of this extraordinary Maine family.

THE 20TH MAINE

One of the regimental commands offered by Governor Israel Washburn Jr. was to thirty-three year-old Bowdoin College professor Joshua L. Chamberlain. Characteristically, this modest, upright son of a noted family from Brewer, Maine, whose father had been a colonel in the War of 1812 and a state Indian agent, declined the highest rank on the grounds that he had no military experience. So the original head of the 20th Maine, the state's most famous regiment, was a West Pointer, Colonel Adalbert Ames, who had grown up in Rockland. After Bull Run, Ames was promoted to brigadier general and Chamberlain, now a full bird colonel and presumably feeling more comfortable, assumed the top post. Before its moment of lasting glory at Gettysburg, the 20th had seen hard fighting under Chamberlain's leadership.

As Civil War enthusiasts know, Gettysburg was the penultimate battle where General Robert E. Lee's invasion of the North was ultimately stymied, if not routed. The key climactic incident in which Lee might have succeeded had he flanked the Union positions took place at a hill called Little Round Top.

The 20th Maine was one of four regiments in the 5th Army Corps. Chamberlain, ordered to fill a gap on the extreme left wing of the federal army, led his men up the wooded slopes of Little Round Top and took possession of the site. When the Confederates, composed of a mixed brigade of

Joshua Chamberlain is undoubtedly the most glorified military leader from Maine. Born in Brewer in 1828, his career is chronicled in books, documentary film and movies. Chamberlain attended Bowdoin College before assuming leadership of the famed 20th Maine Regiment. Despite being wounded six times, Chamberlain went on to serve two terms as governor of Maine. Courtesy, Maine Historical Society

Alabamans and Texans, attacked, their first objective was the nearby Big Round Top, which they captured. From there, the 4th Alabama commenced its major assault on Chamberlain's position.

Despite his lack of formal military training, the ex-professor maneuvered his troops in a manner totally unexpected by the Southerners. The attackers were met by a fierce volley that stopped them cold. Yet, regrouping, on they came, shouting their blood-curdling rebel yell and soon engaged in hand-to-hand combat. Before long, the Mainers were out of ammunition, with a third of their numbers casualties.

Outnumbered, outgunned, this last Yankee bastion was saved by the daring and quick-thinking of its commander. Chamberlain called for the survivors of the 20th to fix bayonets and charge. Taken by surprise, the Alabamans recoiled. Then, they panicked, broke and ran when a company of Chamberlain's men got behind them and opened fire.

For his heroic exploits Joshua Chamberlain was awarded the Congressional Medal of Honor, but not until 1893—thirty years later. Belatedly, too, that high point of the Battle of Gettysburg has been recognized in modern times through several motion picture reenactments. Chamberlain, who became Bowdoin's president and then governor of Maine after the war, has had a number of books written about him and, most recently, a statue erected in Brunswick, where he lived most of his adult life.

MAINE TROOPS IN DIXIE

Virginia provided the baptism by fire for the young and untried volunteers from Maine. Bull Run, a Yankee defeat across the Potomac from Washington, D.C., saw four Maine regiments in action, three of them under the command of General O. O. Howard. The fourth was led by the legendary Colonel Hiram G. Berry of Rockland, a Congressional Medal of Honor winner later killed in action by a sniper's bullet.

Beaten once, the regrouped Mainers next joined in the Union's counterthrust attempting to capture Richmond. Under General George McClellan, who was to be Lincoln's Democratic opponent in the presidential election of 1864, they were somewhat more successful, capturing Yorktown and Williamsburg before the entire campaign fizzled out.

These veterans, eventually joined by new Maine regiments, also fought at Fredericksburg and Chancellorsville. Here, Hiram Berry was slain, causing his superior, "Fighting Joe" Hooker, the toughest of the tough, to weep like a baby over his body. Then, four more Maine regiments were at Antietam,

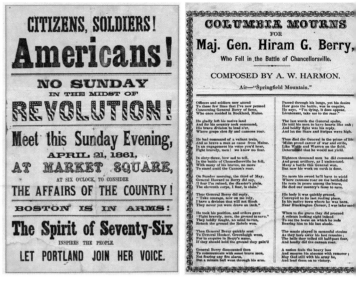

Above left
Mainers responded enthusiastically when the call to arms was issued during the Civil War sending thirty-two regiments of infantry, plus cavalry, artillery, sharpshooters and naval enlistees. Nearly 73,000 Mainers served and suffered over 18,000 deaths. With a population of just 628,279 in 1860, this was a significant percentage. Courtesy, Maine Historical Society

Above right
Born in Rockland in 1824, Hiram G. Berry served in the Maine Legislature and as Mayor of Rockland. When the Civil War broke out, he enlisted in the 4th Maine Regiment as a Colonel and showed unforeseen military skill at the first Battle of Bull Run. He was promoted to the rank of Brigadier General in 1862 and assigned to the 3rd Brigade, 1st Division, 3d Corps. He was killed at Chancellorsville a year later while leading a bayonet charge. Courtesy, Maine Historical Society

Maryland, fending off a Confederate northward surge in some of the war's bloodiest fighting.

It was not only in the northern part of the South that Maine men saw action. While some were with McClellan in the Virginia "Peninsula campaign," others were on the South Carolina and Georgia coasts, besieging Charleston and Savannah. Commanded by Lieutenant-Colonel Harris Plaisted, a War-Democrat destined to be a future governor of Maine, the 11th Maine captured Hilton Head Island, then Beaufort, South Carolina and Amelia Island, Florida.

Texas and Louisiana were other destinations for Maine soldiers. They marched into Corpus Christi and Brownsville and, on the Louisiana front, assisted in the capture of Port Hudson on the Mississippi. During this latter fighting Brigadier General Neal Dow was captured, while serving on the staff of General William Tecumseh Sherman. In the course of one of the assaults on Port Hudson that drew heavy fire, both generals were wounded. The Maine man received an almost spent rifle bullet in the arm and another wound in his left thigh. Out of action, he was recuperating in a nearby farm house when a rebel cavalry raiding party, tipped off by a local woman, seized him. Immediately, Dow was transferred to Libby Prison near Richmond, until the exchange that freed him.

The eventual surrender of Port Hudson put the Yankees in control of the Mississippi. On the other hand, their efforts to take over one of its tributaries—the Red River—were less successful. Helping the Union men retreat was a detachment of Maine loggers, cutting timber to dam the waterway so the federal gunboats would have depth enough to escape downstream.

Essentially, this was the end of the Maine regiments' campaigning in the Deep South. Many of the units went back to Virginia for some of the final critical battles, like Petersburg and the fall of Richmond.

As soon as Lee sought to surrender his Army of Virginia, the question arose regarding which Union Army group should receive his sword. The choice

One of the nine-month regiments, the 23rd Maine was mustered into service September 29, 1862. The unit saw no action but lost fifty-six soldiers to disease. In a letter to his cousin Deborah Rideout of New Gloucester in December of 1862, Mark Richardson reported that many of the men had contracted measles and typhoid fever preventing the regiment from moving out of camp. Courtesy, Library of Congress

was easy: the hero of Gettysburg, Joshua Chamberlain, now a general, of the 20th Maine. One more unexpected command came from this superlative officer. As the beaten Southern troops paraded through drawn-up lines of men in blue in utter, defeated silence, Chamberlain ordered his men to present arms. Such a sign of honor to a humiliated foe was said to have brought tears to the eyes of Confederate officers. "This was a magnanimity we did not expect," one of them explained. Chamberlain's graciousness was long-remembered and appreciated.

MAINE ATTACKED, BELIEVE IT OR NOT

Lee was halted at Gettysburg. Pickett's Charge, the last futile effort of the South in that epic battle has been called "the high water mark of the Confederacy"—they went that far and no farther in the North. So goes the broad scale of military history. Lost is the factoid that two small armed encounters took place in Maine, the northernmost Union territory—mere pinpricks, to be sure, yet the first hostile action in the Pine Tree State since the War of 1812.

Although Great Britain never entered the Civil War on behalf of the South, as once feared, one event did originate in Canada. Though little more than a bank robbery attempt, allegedly the purloined funds were meant to finance a Confederate invasion force of 5,000. The force was programmed to burst from New Brunswick and join up with the Copperheads, an underground army of Southern sympathizers in Maine to take over the state.

The presence of "Copperheads" downeast or at least those who were "soft" on the war was shown by the large vote a Peace Democrat, Bion Bradbury, had received in the gubernatorial election of 1862. That same year, the lumber baron Rufus Dwinel organized a mob to raid a Copperhead-sympathizing Bangor newspaper, destroying its presses and forcing its editor, Marcellus Emery, to flee for his life.

On May 3, 1863 the soldiers of the 6th Maine were the first to reach the top of Marye Heights at Fredericksburg and quickly planted their regimental flag to claim that part of the field in victory. One of the three forward

regiments to attack that day, the fighting was close range with point-blank battles over the stone wall. Nineteen enlisted men were killed and 100 wounded. Courtesy, National Archives

Preposterous as the idea of invading Maine might sound, a band of Confederates located in St. John, New Brunswick, resolutely set forth to undertake the first phase: the robbery of the only bank in Calais, Maine, the principal border town on the American side of the line in this northeastern region.

William Collins, a captain in the Confederate forces, was the ringleader and was in New Brunswick on the pretext of visiting members of his Irish immigrant family. A garrulous man, he spoke indiscreetly of his plans. He so alarmed his sister, Mary, that she communicated with another brother, John Collins, then a Methodist minister in York, Maine, and a Northern sympathizer.

The Yankee authorities were tipped off. On July 18, 1864 four men walked into the Calais bank and said they wanted to change their gold coins into paper money. As soon as one of them pulled out a small revolver, the signal was given and hidden federal agents emerged, guns bristling.

Along with his companions, Collins was sentenced as a common bank robber to three years in Thomaston State Prison Four months later, the Confederate leader pulled off a daring escape, reached New Brunswick and returned to the South before the end of the war.

The other attack on Maine a year earlier was much more serious in that one U.S. naval vessel was hijacked and destroyed. This assault exemplified the daring of Confederate privateering ship captains. Although naval lieutenant Charles W. Read, in the various Yankee ships he captured, never achieved the fame of the *Alabama*, his boldness on a dash from Brazil in the spring of 1863 was breathtaking. With the U.S. Navy in pursuit, Read captured fifteen vessels in less than two weeks before arriving in Maine waters. There, he and his crew continued their depredations by taking several fishing schooners. From two of the captured local fishermen, the rebels learned of a real prize in Portland Harbor—the U.S. revenue cutter *Caleb Cushing*.

To enter that sheltered space, Read had to navigate past three formidable granite forts. He did so

REBEL TERMS OF PEACE!

Citizens of Maine! The Copperhead Politicians of our State are crying out for "peace on any terms," and they tell you it is a very easy matter to "compromise with our misguided Southern brethren." To clearly understand the position of the enemy, read the following "CONDITIONS OF PEACE" on which the official organ of the rebel government, the *Richmond Enquirer*, of October 16, proposes to *settle and have "peace:"*

"Save on our own terms, we can accept no peace whatever, and we must fight until dooms-day rather than yield one iota of them; and our terms are:

"Recognition by the enemy of the Independence of the Confederate States.

"Withdrawal of Yankee forces from every foot of Confederate ground, including KENTUCKY and MISSOURI.

"Withdrawal of Yankee soldiers from MARYLAND, until that State shall decide, by a free vote, whether she shall remain in the old Union, or ask admission into the Confederacy. [This implies the surrender of Washington City and the District of Columbia to the Confederacy.]

"Consent on the part of the Federal Government to give up to the Confederacy its proportion of the Navy as it stood at the time of secession, or to pay for the same.

"Yielding up all pretensions on the part of the Federal Government to that portion of the old territories which lies west of the Confederate States.

"An equitable settlement, on the basis of our absolute independence and equal rights, of all accounts of the Public Debt and Public Lands, and the advantages accruing from foreign treaties.

"These provisions, we apprehend, comprise the minimum of what we must require before we lay down our arms. That is to say, THE NORTH MUST YIELD ALL—WE NOTHING. The whole pretension of that country to prevent by force the separation of the States must be abandoned, which will be an equivalent to an avowal that our enemies were wrong from the first; and, of course, as they waged a causeless and wicked war upon us, they ought, in strict justice, to be required, according to usage in such cases, to reimburse to us the whole of our expenses and losses in the course of that war."

These are the terms of peace, and the "Enquirer" says further:

"As surely as we completely ruin their armies—and without that is no peace or truce at all—SO SURELY SHALL WE MAKE THEM PAY OUR WAR DEBT, THOUGH WE WRING IT OUT OF THEIR HEARTS."

Voters of Maine! These are the terms of peace to which you are invited by the Copperhead politicians of our State—the destruction of the Union—the giving up of Maryland, Kentucky, and Missouri, which have all voted by immense majorities for the Union—the surrender of a large part of our Navy—the loss of more than one-half of our territory, the surrender of Washington City, *and the payment of the debt of the accursed rebellion of traitors,* by having it "WRUNG OUT OF OUR HEARTS!"

People of Maine! Will you give your assent to such a base surrender of our cause? If not, then rally only with those who "keep step to the music of the Union," who stand by our brave soldiers in the field, and are for "Liberty and Union, now and forever, one and inseparable."

Men of Maine! See to it that on the second Monday of September you pronounce for the Union.

SAMUEL CONY stands as the representative of those who will never surrender the Government.

JOSEPH HOWARD is the candidate of those who are willing to accept Peace on the terms dictated by Jefferson Davis.

PLEASE POST THIS UP.

Copperheads, also known as Peace Democrats and sometimes Sons of Liberty, were often seen as soft on the issue of slavery and sometimes suspected of disloyalty. The largest numbers were in the Midwest, and Copperheads were much less common in the abolition stronghold communities throughout New England. Many felt that the Republicans had provoked the South and started the war to impose their own views onto the rest of the Union. Furthermore, they felt that peace in the Union was in jeopardy and would be impossible to restore after a prolonged war. The broadside above, issued by die-hard supporters of the war, stated that the Copperheads were willing to accept the outrageous Southern terms, which amounted to: "The North must yield all. We nothing." Courtesy, Library of Congress

by switching his men to the *Archer*, one of the fishing schooners he'd commandeered. Two small boatloads of armed Southerners left the *Archer*, surprised the crew of the *Caleb Cushing* and sailed off with her. Pursuit was organized and in the vanguard was a large steamship, the *Chesapeake*. At one point, Lieutenant Read had thought of capturing that 460-ton vessel instead of the *Caleb Cushing*, only to learn that his engineer didn't know how to handle such large engines.

Those powerful machines were soon driving the *Chesapeake* into close proximity to the fleeing revenue cutter. Shots were exchanged. Out of ammunition, Read had to surrender. His prisoners were released and put into small boats. Then, after setting a fire aboard, Read and his fellow Confederates fled over the side and were taken onto the *Chesapeake* as prisoners of war. The scuttled *Caleb Cushing* soon exploded, and the excitement in Portland Harbor ended.

THE HOME FRONT

With the exception of the two aforementioned minor incidents, Maine was spared the more immediate ravages of war. But the conflict remained uppermost in people's minds with letters home from loved ones at the front, notification of casualties and sending off more contingents as the Union government in D.C. continued to call for more and more levies. The draft was instituted, and not popular. Each town had a quota to fill and the system, which included allowing wealthier folks to hire substitutes, lent itself to manipulation and scams. There were acts of defiance in Maine, like the "Kingfield Draft Riot." Unlike New York, where such outbreaks caused untold damage and many lives were lost, the protest in this small western Maine mountain town, when militia troops appeared with draft notices, ended in distinct Maine style. Once the armed volunteers reached the outskirts of Kingfield, they found the whole population had turned out to invite them to a picnic, where they

Opened in 1866, Togus Veterans Hospital was built to serve soldiers returning from the Civil War. Today, Togus encompasses over 500 acres of land, offers a nursing facility, a sixty-seven bed medical facility and several out-patient clinics around the state to serve Maine veterans. Located in Augusta just east of the state capital complex, Togus is the oldest facility in the federal government's Department of Veterans Affairs. Courtesy, Maine Historic Preservation Commission

were served by the prettiest hometown girls in their best dresses. Everyone had a good time; the draft notice was served and the crisis amicably averted.

Maine politics, always spirited, did not take a vacation during the war. The Republicans, supporters of Lincoln and hometown boy Hannibal Hamlin and ultra promoters of the war, had a slight edge. After Israel Washburn Jr. stepped down as governor in 1861, James G. Blaine, the GOP chief in the state, chose Abner Coburn, the richest man in Maine, to run next.

Not a politician, Coburn made a poor showing in the election of 1862. Albeit victorious, his popularity as a public figure was marginal. One outspoken enlisted man whose unit Coburn reviewed, witheringly wrote in his diary: "Governor Coburn is, without exception, the most wretched speechmaker that ever punished the cushion of the Governor's chair." Alarmed by a strong display of Peace Democrat strength, Blaine, the master politico, made some adjustments. Coburn was out for the next annual election. In his stead came an ex-Democrat, Samuel Cony, known for his patriotism and largesse. Out, too, was the designation, Republican Party; Blaine changed it to the Union Party.

Nationally, there were Republican worries. Until Gettysburg, Lincoln's reelection in 1864 was seen as in serious jeopardy. But the string of Union victories following the pivotal clash in Pennsylvania helped him defeat McClellan. That, and another move, similar to Blaine's maneuvering in Maine, also involved a change of image and personnel.

THE VICE PRESIDENTIAL DEAL

Maine's Hamlin was no longer Abraham Lincoln's running mate when the "Union Party" went to the polls against the Democrats in November 1864. His replacement was Andrew Johnson, a Southerner, a Democrat and a man the president had appointed as the war governor of his native Ten-

THE UNION MUST AND SHALL BE PRESERVED

FREE SPEECH, FREE HOMES, FREE TERRITORY.

PROTECTION TO AMERICAN INDUSTRY

FOR PRESIDENT
ABRAHAM LINCOLN
OF ILLINOIS.

FOR VICE PRESIDENT
HANNIBAL HAMLIN
OF MAINE

Abraham Lincoln and his vice president Hannibal Hamlin (1809–1891) only met after they were elected in 1860. A Maine native, Hamlin was somewhat reluctant to join Lincoln's ticket but felt strongly enough about the abolitionist cause to agree to run. Hamlin was dropped from the ticket during Lincoln's reelection campaign to make way for southerner Andrew Johnson. Courtesy, Library of Congress

nessee. Had Hamlin remained on the ticket and succeeded to the White House after Lincoln's assassination in April 1865, American history would have been entirely different.

Classed among the "Radical Republicans," i.e., those most adamant about doing away with slavery, the first vice president's most signal achievement was said to have been his leading role in persuading Lincoln to issue the Emancipation Proclamation. Postwar, had Hamlin been president, he would have encouraged the forces in the North pushing for Negro suffrage, building a biracial Republican Party in the South, and resisting the return to power of the same Southern men who had helped lead the rebellion.

The deal to thrust the Maine Republican aside for a more bipartisan team—never mind that Hamlin once had been a Democratic office holder, himself—almost didn't happen. At the Union party's June 1864 convention in Baltimore, the

Hannibal Hamlin was originally elected to the U. S. Senate as a Democrat. His stance against slavery distanced him from his party and the Republicans successfully convinced him to change parties in 1856. This bold move caught the attention of Washington politicians and in 1859 Hamlin was chosen as Abraham Lincoln's running mate in his first bid for president. This statue of Hannibal Hamlin (1809–1891), erected in 1927, still stands between Central and State Streets in Bangor. The statue was designed by Brewer native and noted sculptor, Charles Eugene Tefft (1874–1951). Courtesy, Bangor Public Library

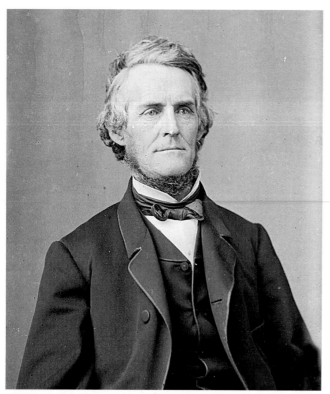

William Pitt Fessenden (1806–1869) grew up in New Gloucester and attended Bowdoin College. A staunch Whig and ardent abolitionist, Fessenden was elected to the United States Senate in 1854. He also served as Abraham Lincoln's secretary of treasury before returning to the Senate after the Civil War. He is often most remembered for casting the deciding vote against the impeachment of Andrew Johnson, leaving proponents— his own political party—one vote shy of the number needed to remove the president from office. Courtesy, Library of Congress

GOP's Pennsylvania boss, Simon Cameron, a Hamlin admirer, took the floor first and offered a motion for the joint renomination of Lincoln and Hamlin—and to do it by acclamation without a roll call vote. To his surprise, most likely since Cameron wasn't in on the deal to dump Hamlin cries of "No! No!" resounded.

Admittedly, the opposition wasn't against Lincoln and after Cameron's motion was shouted down, Honest Abe received an overwhelming vote of approval, 484–22. The separate contest for vice president was something else and involved three candidates: Hamlin, Andrew Johnson and a favorite son from New York Daniel S. Dickinson.

Historians ask if Lincoln secretly worked levers behind the scenes to change vice presidents. There are indications that he did, primarily because he wanted a Southerner. The floor managers for Andrew Johnson made no effort to quash rumors that the Tennessean was the president's favorite. Among the Republican leaders furtively scheming to oust Hamlin was Charles Sumner, the powerhouse U.S. senator from Massachusetts. Sumner had nothing against the Maine vice president, nor was he worried about his party's prospects. It was his hatred of another Maine politician that caused him to act.

He simply could not abide William Pitt Fessenden, one of his Senate colleagues from Maine. Consequently, his twisted reasoning formed a scenario under which Hamlin, deprived of the vice presidency, would go back to Maine, run against Fessenden and beat him. As illogical as this may seem, some writers insist that Sumner had never recovered, physically or mentally, from a brutal caning he'd suffered on the Senate floor from a Southern congressman before the war.

Poor Hamlin, unaware of the cabals against him, fully expected to be nominated again in Baltimore. In 1860 he hadn't sought the office, nor was he present this time to defend his cause since candidates simply didn't attend conventions. On the first ballot, the results were: Johnson, 200; Hamlin, 150; Dickinson, 108. Before the votes were announced and finalized, a groundswell for Johnson erupted as states switched their totals. Even Pennsylvania, which Cameron had kept solid for Hamlin, joined the stampede, prompting Thaddeus Stevens, its crusty old congressman and "Radical" leader, to growl, "Can't you find a candidate for vice president of the United States without going down to one of those damned Rebel provinces to pick one up?"

No one could foresee that within the year, Andrew Johnson, the poor boy from the mountains of East Tennessee, would be president of the United States. Proving himself much more sympathetic to the South than the "Radicals" ever dreamed, he was subjected to an impeachment trial and acquitted by a single Senate vote. Ironically, the deciding margin has always been attributed to William Pitt Fessenden, who was universally expected to vote for impeachment. Contrary to Charles Sumner's expectations, Hannibal Hamlin never ran against Fessenden.

WILLIAM PITT FESSENDEN

Born in New Hampshire, William Pitt Fessenden, a quintessential Yankee, spare and gaunt, moved to Portland, Maine as a young man and became its premier lawyer and a leading Whig politician. Later, as a Republican, elected to Congress and by the State Legislature to be a U.S. Senator, Fessenden found himself at the start of the Civil War in the all-important position of the chair of the Senate Finance Committee.

Thus, no person in Washington played a more critical role in financing the war effort of the loyal states. Expenditures of the government soared as high as $1 billion a year by the end of the war. Revenues, which were only $25 million in the year 1861, had to be increased proportionately with recourse to paper money, the famous "greenbacks," and borrowing through the sale of bonds. Pork barreling by individual legislators was a constant problem for Fessenden when his appropriation bills were treated like the proverbial "Christmas tree,"

on which self-seeking amendments were incessantly hung.

However, the old Yankee was the essence of toughness and probity. Toward the end of the war, when treasury Secretary Salmon P. Chase resigned unexpectedly, President Lincoln wanted Fessenden to take his place. The Maine senator, instead, urged the choice of a fellow Mainer, Hugh McCulloch, and went to plead his friend's case personally to Lincoln. Then the president informed him, "I have prepared an executive order naming you." Aghast, Fessenden cried that he couldn't accept. Lincoln cannily argued that Fessenden had to take over the treasury, otherwise there would be a financial crash and the war effort could be severely damaged.

They worked out a compromise. Lincoln agreed that as soon as Fessenden had the Union's finances as well under control as he had done with Congress', he could retire. That moment occurred in March 1865, shortly prior to Lee's surrender. Soon afterward, Fessenden was back in the U.S. Senate—right in the middle of the Reconstruction turmoil that ensued following the war's end, Lincoln's death and Andrew Johnson's ascendance to power.

IMMEDIATE POSTWAR

What to do with the South? Most pressing, what to do with the millions of former slaves suddenly released from bondage? Under slavery, at least, they had value as property and were cared for—well or badly—by their masters. The answer from the victorious Union in time became a governmental program summed up in a single highly charged word: Reconstruction.

This effort was the creation of the Radical Republican block in Congress, proceeding upon a period when these strong Union supporters stood by in frustrated anger as the same Southerners they had fought took control of their own states once again. Throughout the Southland, legislatures dominated by "Bourbons" or "Conservatives" passed laws in regard to the colored populations that more or less enslaved them anew. These laws were called "Black Codes."

In their furor, led by Congressman Thaddeus Stevens, the majority of Republicans defied the opposition of President Andrew Johnson and established a joint House-Senate "Reconstruction Committee," aimed at reversing the trend. The Senate chair of that body was Maine's own William Pitt Fessenden. One of its first acts, having overridden a veto to do so, was continuing the Freedmen's Bureau, earlier set up under Lincoln to care for ex-slaves. That operation, too, was headed by a Maine man, General Oliver Otis Howard.

The debate about Reconstruction has never ended. Throughout its existence, particularly in the South, it was reviled as a "boondoggle," an opportunity for "carpetbaggers" from the North and their sympathizers below the Mason-Dixon Line, "scalawags," to conduct corrupt governments with the help of Negro voters and to line their own pockets. The opposite mantra came from the victors, that protection was needed for blacks and Republicans in the Southern states against the violence of the Ku Klux Klan and other terrorist organizations and that former rebels should not be allowed back in power unless they observed the U.S. Constitution, including its newly enacted 13th, 14th, and 15th amendments.

Mainers other than Fessenden and General Howard were involved in the Reconstruction effort. One was a close friend of Howard's, Eliphalet Whittlesey, a professor at Bowdoin before the war, sent to North Carolina to help run the Freedmen's Bureau there. The culmination came when agents of President Johnson, forever seeking to discredit the bureau, seized upon an incident at a plantation where a Black man who had stolen clothing was shot and killed by a White overseer. Whittlesey partly owned the property with another Mainer.

Suddenly bureau officials, because they had been helping Blacks, were made to look like they were persecuting them. A group of them, including Whittlesey, were brought to trial. Although acquitted, Whittlesey nevertheless was forced to leave North Carolina but remained with the bureau as a staffer of General Howard's in D.C.

On a broader scale of Reconstruction, there were the trials suffered by the original commander of the 20th Maine, the West Pointer from Rockland, Adalbert Ames. At the end of the war, now a major-general, he was made the military governor of Mississippi. Despite the troops he controlled and the power he wielded, the harassment he received from the White Mississippians was no less dire than that endured by Whittlesey from the North Carolinians.

For one thing, Ames had married the daughter of probably the most hated Northern military man in the South. His father-in-law Benjamin Butler, the political ex-general from Massachusetts had earned the nickname of "Beast" during the war. Tough, mean, always controversial, the fiery Butler had stirred Louisiana's undying enmity by declaring that any New Orleans belle who openly insulted Yankee personnel would be treated as "a lady of the evening plying her trade."

Nor later, as a member of Congress, did he do anything to overcome his anti-Southern reputation. Most remembered and fought by friends of the South in Congress was his "Force Bill," aimed at the Ku Klux Klan (KKK). While debating the measure, he coined a phrase that was often used and misused in discussing the issue of North-South relations. "Waving the bloody shirt" assumed the meaning of any mention by Northern Republicans in political discourse of the Civil War and the Dixie Rebellion. In point of fact, Butler had waved a blood-stained shirt on the floor of the House— that of a carpetbagger county superintendent in Mississippi who was horsewhipped by the KKK.

Adalbert Ames, meanwhile, having brought Butler's daughter Blanche and their two children to live with him in Jackson, made further enemies by abolishing a color line in the selection of juries in Mississippi, taxing the rich more than the poor and by cutting state expenditures. Before long, the Republican-controlled legislature elected him to the U.S. Senate, along with a Black minister, Hiram Revels. They both voted for laws to enforce the 14th and 15th amendments to the U.S. Constitution, guaranteeing voting rights for Blacks, before Ames went back to Mississippi for another stint in the governor's chair. But when federal troops were removed entirely from the state, he knew his days were numbered.

Ames never returned to Maine. For a time after fleeing Mississippi, he joined his father who had emigrated to Minnesota and, like the Washburns, they were in the flour-milling business there. Then, he tried the Lowell area of Massachusetts, his father-in-law's home territory. He invested in textile mills, using his inventive mind to devise commercially successful gadgetry that made him millions and allowed him, in his old age, to go golfing with the likes of John D. Rockefeller and Henry Flagler, the Florida magnate. During the Spanish American War, Adalbert Ames put on a general's uniform again and fought at San Juan Hill and the siege of Santiago de Cuba.

Also involved in Reconstruction was that rising GOP star from Maine, James G. Blaine, who for much of the time was speaker of the U.S. House. Not exactly a Radical, he was nonetheless apt to "wave the bloody shirt" whenever it suited his or his party's purpose. The most famous instance was his effort in 1876, when he was minority leader, to keep the Civil War flame burning during a debate on an amnesty bill for Confederate leaders.

He offered an amendment to exempt Jefferson Davis from this final blanket pardon. His argument was essentially that he considered Davis a war criminal because as the South's president he had condoned the horrible atrocities perpetrated against Union prisoners in the infamous Andersonville prison. Stirring the embers once more won Blaine an immense Republican following nationwide, particularly among Union veterans. Betting professionals would soon wager that James Gillespie Blaine of Augusta, Maine, would someday be elected president of the United States.

Fairfield native, Selden Connor (1839–1917) was a lieutenant colonel in the 7th Maine Regiment and led the unit at Gettysburg. He was later commissioned colonel of the 19th Maine and was wounded at the Battle of the Wilderness. Connor served as governor of Maine from 1876 to 1879. Courtesy, Library of Congress

Lauf. No. 643.   New York, 16. Januar 1889.   13. Jahrgang.   No. 19.

What fools these Mortals be!

KEPPLER & SCHWARZMANN,

Herausgeber.

PUCK BUILDING, Ecke Houston & Mulberry St.   COPYRIGHT, 1889, BY KEPPLER & SCHWARZMANN.

ENTERED AT THE POST OFFICE AT NEW YORK, AND ADMITTED FOR TRANSMISSION THROUGH THE MAILS AT SECOND CLASS RATES.

PRESIDENT.

ER ist in Washington angelangt.
J. G. B.:   Hier bin ich!   Bringt Eure Administration her!

6

THE GILDED AGE
1876-1898

Rejected by his party in the two previous elections, James G. Blaine secured the Republican presidential nomination in 1884. It was a bitter and hard-fought campaign against Grover Cleveland, which came down to a very close vote in New York. Blaine lost, but the campaign created two of the most famous campaign taunts in U. S. history: "Ma, Ma where's my Pa?" aimed at Cleveland, and "Blaine, Blaine, the continental liar from the State of Maine" for Blaine. This cartoon, taken from Puck's *German language edition, shows Blaine five years later in 1889, after he'd been named secretary of state by President-elect Benjamin Harrison. To illustrate his influence in the Cabinet, he is quoted as saying in German: "Here I am (next to the president). Bring your administration here." Courtesy, Maine Historical Society*

BLAINE

On June 5, 1884, Augusta, Maine spontaneously held the most memorable celebration in the city's history. At about 4:30 p.m., the news reached an immense crowd gathered downtown on Water Street along the Kennebec River, that the state capital's favorite local son, James Gillespie Blaine, had been chosen as the national Republican party's nominee for president. Immediately, Postmaster Joseph Manley, Blaine's right hand man who had received the confirmation by telegraph, gave a signal and up went a huge banner, prepared in advance, that boasted, "JAMES G. BLAINE, OUR NEXT PRESIDENT."

Then, the processions began. The first one started that afternoon. In hilly Augusta, Blaine lived above the downtown, across the street from the State Capitol building. Led by a hastily assembled band, the joyous crowd headed for the "Blaine Mansion," where their hero had been lounging on his front lawn in a hammock slung between two apple trees. Alerted by one of his daughters that he had won the GOP's nod in far-off Chicago, he was ready with a short speech for the adoring throng of neighbors and fellow Kennebec County well-wishers who arrived to cheer him.

By nightfall, trains from all over Maine were bringing Republicans from every corner of the state. Proceeding under torchlight, five bands now led the happy revelers up from the railroad station to the Blaine home. A sudden rainstorm didn't dampen any of the enthusiasm and the crowd beseeched Blaine not to curtail his speech because they were getting drenched. "We been waitin' eight years for this shower," someone cried out of the dark.

It was true. Twice before, in 1876 and 1880, all political pundits had predicted that James G. Blaine would emerge from the Republican conventions as the party's standard bearer. Each time, internal politics had brought up a dark horse, instead—Rutherford B. Hayes in 1876 and James Garfield in 1880.

Now, Blaine at last seemed on his way to the White House. He had been Speaker of the House in the U.S. Congress, a U.S. senator, and secretary of state under his friend Garfield. However, after Garfield's assassination, he had resigned. Seemingly out of politics, he devoted the next few years to writing a mammoth best selling nonfiction book entitled *Twenty Years of Congress*.

In the days following the news of the nomination, Republicans from throughout the nation flocked to Augusta. The entire California delegation, having traveled to Chicago, kept on going east and visited Blaine *en masse* in the Pine Tree State. The convention's presiding officer, Senator John B. Henderson of Missouri, arrived to present the candidate his official certificate of nomination and hear him say he accepted it. So began one of the hardest fought, contentious and unpredictable elections in American history.

Blaine's opponent was Grover Cleveland, the Democratic governor of New York. Early on, the campaign got nasty. Republican operatives in Cleveland's hometown of Buffalo accused the then unmarried New York chief executive of having fathered an illegitimate child. "True," he admitted. From the GOP faithful there went up a derisive taunt of "Ma, Ma, where's my Pa?" Not to be outdone, the Democrats resurrected a similar personal tale about Blaine and his wife, whose first-born child, Stanwood, had died at the age of three. Using the couples' Pennsylvania wedding date and the birth date on Stanwood's grave, they charged that it had been a shotgun wedding. "Not so," the Blaines indignantly replied. They had been married much earlier in Kentucky, but because that state never sent them a marriage certificate they had gone through another ceremony some months later.

Yet the most damaging charges against Blaine, used both by Democrats and dissident Republicans who refused to support him, were also hangovers from his past. The notorious "Mulligan letters" episode was the key element, letters of Blaine's that had fallen into the hands of one James Mulligan, a

James G. Blaine (1830–1893) was at the center of Maine politics throughout the last half of the nineteenth century, and served as state legislator, a United States senator and as secretary of state for Presidents Garfield and Harrison. The Blaine House, the governor's mansion in Augusta, was donated to the state by Blaine's daughter, Harriet Blaine Beale. Courtesy, Maine Historic Preservation Commission

clerk in a Boston investment firm, which allegedly proved Blaine had lied to a Congressional committee probing his dealings in railroad stock. On the grounds that these letters were his private property, Blaine physically took the documents from Mulligan and read sections of them publicly in a sensational attempt to discredit his accusers. While partisans on his side cheered his daring, his enemies insisted for years that he hadn't told the whole truth. During the campaign, more of these letters surfaced. In the most damaging, Blaine, himself, had written a postscript, telling the recipient, "Burn this letter."

In 1884, to alliterative Republican chants of "Blaine, Blaine, James G. Blaine," the Democrats added the mocking refrain: "The Continental Liar from the State of Maine."

What proved to be the closest of elections came down to the vote in the state of New York. Even though it was Cleveland's home territory, Blaine was given a good chance to win it. Particularly important was the Irish Catholic vote, usually Democratic, but to which Blaine had made a strong appeal through his anti-British, pro-Irish home rule stance when he was secretary of state. Also, his mother was an Irish Catholic.

Conventional wisdom insists the final blow to Blaine's chances occurred when a Republican Prot-

estant minister in New York City made an offhand remark, referring to the Democrats as the party of "Rum, Romanism, and Rebellion," and Blaine failed to rebuke him for an anti-Catholic slur.

Blaine lost New York by only 1,200 votes and with it, his chance to be president. The Democrats picked up the former mocking Republican cry of "Ma, Ma, where's my Pa?" and added "Gone to the White House, Ha, Ha, Ha!"

Four years later, Blaine undoubtedly could have had the Republican nomination had he wanted it. He didn't and the prize went to Benjamin Harrison, who beat Cleveland. Blaine resumed his old job as secretary of state, the position he said he most enjoyed. He held it until about a year before his death in 1893. Arguably, James G. Blaine was the most prominent politician ever to emerge from the State of Maine.

THE "STATE STEAL"

A Gatling gun—the forerunner of the machine gun—on the steps leading up to Maine's capitol building in Augusta is the enduring image left over from a famous downeast political crisis of the Gilded Age. Undoubtedly the worst such uproar in the state's history, it has been cynically dubbed with the double pun the "State Steal."

The contested election of 1880 caused pandemonium in Maine government. This political cartoon shows the many parties vying for control. Democrats had teamed with Fusionists and Greenback Party supporters to defeat the dominant Republicans, resulting in a very close election. The threat of violence loomed as angry mobs stormed the statehouse and the Republicans took control of the building. The state militia, commanded by Joshua Chamberlain, was sent in to quell the situation and the outcome was eventually decided by the State Supreme Court. Courtesy, William David Barry

The Republicans accused the Democrats of trying to "steal" an election from them. At the same time the "state seal" itself, the emblem of state authority, was temporarily stolen by the Democratic secretary of state to keep it from falling into Republican hands. This whirlwind of events lashed the state capital during the last months of 1879 and the first months of 1880.

So emotional did the electoral hassle become that the State Militia, the National Guard of the time, had to be called out to keep the warring political partisans from going to war since both sides had armed themselves. The commander of that militia was General Joshua L. Chamberlain, the hero of Gettysburg. Although he had been a Republican governor, he warned his GOP friends and former supporters he intended to be neutral in the fight. He and his men, and their Gatling gun, were only in Augusta to keep the peace.

A year earlier, the utter dominance of the Republican party in Maine—ever since the late

In 1880 the Republicans accused the Democrats of trying to "steal" an election from them. Neither side was willing to concede the close vote, resulting in two governors and two legislatures vying to control the state. Courtesy, Maine Historic Preservation

1850s—hit an unexpected roadblock. The opposition Democrats teamed up with a new third party, the Greenbackers, and formed a Fusion coalition that ran as allies. The Greenbackers, active nationally, too, mostly were farmers and people in debt who demanded to use "greenbacks," paper dollars, for paying off their obligations.

The Maine branch was led by a long-jawed old Yankee named Solon Chase from the farming town of Turner, and he campaigned around the state with a pair of oxen he called "them steers." He used these work animals to illustrate how their price had fallen, and the need for cheap money. Fusionist voting strength in 1878 caused the Republicans, for the first time in almost thirty years, to lose the House of Representatives in Augusta. They failed to reelect their governor, who needed an absolute majority under then existing state law.

Consequently, the election, by the terms of Maine's Constitution, was thrown into the legislature. In this case, the Fusion-dominated House, which had the right to nominate, sent only the names of a Democrat and a Greenbacker to the senators who had the final decision. The Republican majority grudgingly chose the lesser of two evils—Alonzo Garcelon, a fairly conservative democratic businessman.

Maine went to the polls every year in those days, and in 1879 Governor Garcelon also failed to win a majority for reelection. Once more, the legislature would have to decide. But who controlled the legislature? Maine also voted ahead of the country and the initial returns from the September election indicated the Republicans were back in power. That's where the steal, sometimes called the count-out, came in.

The Fusionists set about undoing the results of the election. Votes were thrown out for the flimsiest of reasons. When thirty-seven apparent Republican victories were voided, the GOP struck back. James G. Blaine rushed home from the U.S. Senate to take charge, acting in his capacity as the long-time chairman of the Maine Republican State Committee. He led a large crowd to the

Farmer-politician, Solon Chase (1822–1909), a native of Turner, was the founder of the Greenback Party in Maine. He drove a pair of oxen around the country while campaigning for the Greenback Party and is remembered for his slogan, "Them Steers." His homely, vernacular style was ridiculed by his opponents, but he reached rural voters in a way that other candidates could not. From Maine Agriculture, 1909

State House and demanded that the returns be made public. Garcelon and his Fusionist council refused.

By Christmas, there was more than just talk of violence. Two wagonloads of rifles and ammunition destined from a State Militia arsenal in Bangor for Governor Garcelon's forces was halted and sent back by a Republican mob. Fusionist snipers mounted the dome of the State Capitol Building. One of them allegedly was preparing to pick off Blaine, walking in his yard across the street, when a comrade stopped him. During this period, General Chamberlain was summoned.

Bar Harbor began as the small town of Eden. By the late nineteenth century, it had become a fashionable summer colony for the wealthy. Rockefellers and Pulitzers had homes there, and several lavish hotels, the first built in 1855, catered to short-term visitors who had traveled downeast to avoid the summer heat in New York, Philadelphia and Boston. Courtesy, Maine Historical Society

One night, the Republicans simply sneaked into the State House and took physical possession of the House and Senate chambers. An angry Fusionist mob blamed Chamberlain. His life was threatened. He told the hotheads to go ahead and shoot him. But a Union Army veteran in the crowd, waving his weapon, said he would shoot anyone who harmed the general.

Two governors were "elected," as were two legislatures. Blaine, meanwhile, had gotten an opinion from the State Supreme Court that the Republicans had legally organized the legislature. They elected their candidate, Daniel Davis, and Chamberlain accepted the result. Heavily armed Augusta police took over the militia's duties and turned back the Fusionists when they physically tried to enter the Capitol. The primitive machine gun on the granite steps of the building was the sign of an end to this would-be Civil War.

VACATIONLAND

Despite the Augusta flare-up, Maine in that era was eminently the bucolic setting most people still think of today—lovely lakes, vast forests, and above all, the seacoast, more than 3,000 miles if measured by every nook and cranny of its oft-indented rocky shoreline. Inevitably, prosperous city people, in the rapidly urbanizing U.S. of the Gilded Age, sought havens from its noise, grime and bustle. They escaped to the soothing sounds of the sea or the haunting cries of the loon on an inland pond.

Mainers had a term for these visitors from "away." They called them "rusticators." Aside from peace and beauty, they were also searching for ties to a simpler past, a "rustic" way of life and people who still lived like their mostly Anglo-Saxon ancestors and talked like them, too. Some famous resorts resulted from this quest.

Bar Harbor is most likely the best known. Yet for many years, that name simply pertained to a small section of the town of Eden, one of a number of villages on the good-sized island, which Samuel de Champlain had christened *L'Isle des Monts Desert*, or Mount Desert, because of the bare rock and treeless slopes that ran breathtakingly down to the water.

The discovery of Mount Desert by America's "establishment" has been linked to an expedition, of sorts, in 1855 organized by Charles Tracy, a prominent New York City attorney. Among other distinctions, Tracy was the lawyer for the richest man in America, J. Pierpont Morgan, who had married his daughter, Frances, giving rise to the notion that the social prominence Bar Harbor and its surroundings were to enjoy in the future could be traced directly to these twenty-seven adventurous people. Yet the inspiration for traveling to such a remote, beautiful point in Maine has been credited not only to Tracy, but to another member of the tour, the only young artist Frederick Edwin

A Bar Harbor grand resort-type hotel was the Mt. Kineo House on Moosehead Lake. Built in 1884, by 1914 the resort could accommodate 600 guests and offered private bathrooms, electricity and long-distance telephone in a remote area of the state—and all at three to four dollars per day. Courtesy, Maine Historic Preservation Commission

Church who did sketches of the trip and later won national acclaim for his paintings of the area. Accompanying Church was his good friend Theodore Winthrop, a clerk in Tracy's law firm but best known for the immense promise of his writing, both fiction and nonfiction—a promise cut short by a Confederate bullet at the beginning of the Civil War.

A year after the trek to Mount Desert, Church and Winthrop explored another type of Maine vacationland experience—hunting, fishing, and mountain climbing in the deep woods. Church, as deeply affected by Katahdin as Thoreau had been, painted Maine's highest peak while Winthrop wrote a charming book about their adventures that publicized the state's attractiveness to tourists.

Accommodations, then, were sparse. Guest houses were all that was available to the Tracy party. Hotels in Bar Harbor were slow in coming, but by 1875 Frances Tracy Morgan was able to bring her husband J.P. to the village and stay at the expanding Rodick House, which soon grew to hold 600 guests. In 1887 the parent town of Eden, reflecting its transformation into a summer resort, officially moved to change its name to Bar Harbor.

Big hotels were followed by huge summer homes, ironically called "cottages," which the wealthy and in some cases famed vacationers built. The families of the Astors, Vanderbilts, Rockefellers and Pulitzers became connected with the region. James G. Blaine erected his cottage "Stanwood," named for his wife's family and brought President Benjamin Harrison to stay with him.

Exclusive social clubs were created. They found ways to skirt Maine's prohibition laws. As the community grew, so too did concern about preserving its quality of life. Because of the untiring work over decades of a transplanted Bostonian, George Bucknam Dorr, Acadia National Park was born. Today, perhaps in contravention of Dorr's intent, it is the second most frequented park in the U.S.

But Maine would not just be kept as just a playground for the rich. The development of another version of Bar Harbor in the south of the state, York Harbor, illustrates the divergence. Next to this enclave, with its "cottages," exclusive clubs and swank hotels, is York Beach, home of trailer parks and an amusement park with a Coney Island-like atmosphere. The two sections coexist within the town of York, a stone's throw from each other.

These Wabanaki women are shown at home, making baskets for the tourist trade. Generally made of brown ash or of sweet grass, the baskets were traditionally practical items used to carry and store household goods. As tourists "discovered" Maine in the late nineteenth century, Maine Indians recognized the market for baskets, birch bark crafts and other traditional crafts. Today, Maine Indian baskets are highly prized pieces of art, with skilled makers often selling their work for hundreds of dollars. From Hatch, *volume I*

Rusticators from "away" came to Maine to hunt, fish and hike in the woods. The remote wilderness attracted "sports" from all over the east coast, who traveled to Maine by steamship and train. Local guides led visitors to fishing and hunting spots guaranteed to be successful, and Maine earned the title "Vacationland." Courtesy, Bethel Historical Society

All through Maine, communities' populations swell in the summer, whether by seaside or lakeside, along rivers or in the mountains. The autumn brings in hunters by the thousands and the winter caravans of snowmobilers. Tourism is now Maine's largest industry.

SARAH ORNE JEWETT

In both high-toned Bar Harbor and York Harbor, among the exclusive clubs, each community had one called the "Reading Room." A literary veneer was fashionable during the Gilded Age and in York Harbor, several well-known writers of the day were founders of the establishment, such as Finley Peter Dunne creator of the fictional "Mr. Dooley," the national mouthpiece of a syndicated political satire column he'd created for a Chicago newspaper and Thomas Nelson Page, a Southern novelist.

The area around York was a magnet for American literati of the time. Mark Twain, who helped coin the term "The Gilded Age" spent summers in York. William Dean Howells, not only a best-selling author but also a famed editor, lived next door in Kittery. Henry Wadsworth Longfellow and John Greenleaf Whittier frequented the town. The latter set one of his poems there. Nathaniel Hawthorne, too, had visited, and based one of his short stories on an incident from York's past. Also, following in the footsteps of Madame Wood, female writers appeared. Among them were the poet Celia Thaxter, and possibly the finest writer of fiction Maine has ever produced, Sarah Orne Jewett, who was a country doctor's daughter from neighboring South Berwick.

Her novelistic collection of short stories about a Maine seacoast village, *The Country of the Pointed Firs*, has been ranked, by none other than the author Willa Cather, with Hawthorne's *The Scarlet Letter* and Twain's *Huckleberry Finn* as one of the top three American literary classics. Nearly a hundred years after Jewett's death, it is still being read.

At age nineteen, in 1868, Jewett published her first story under a pseudonym, afraid to tell her

Girls at a Maine summer camp in the 1940s. Maine's summer camps have been popular for decades, but popularity peaked in the 1920s and again in the 1950s. By 1990 30,000 children per year attended Maine summer camps and contributed to a $100 million per year industry. There are still over 200 camps in Maine and children from all over the world spend their summers here. George French Collection, Courtesy, Maine State Archives

family, particularly her father, with whom she was very close. Often, she accompanied him on his house calls. When she did at last reveal she was the published "Alice Eliot," he simply told her, "Tell things just as they are."

The growth of tourism in her home area was apparently what spurred her to document the Maine people she knew. Those from "away" were apt to make fun of the country folk and that, as she said, "fired me with indignation." Sarah Orne Jewett saw it as a mission to depict their "simple grand lives."

Her first book, *Deephaven* in 1877, was a collection of her sketches and stories that had been published by the prestigious *Atlantic Monthly*. John Greenleaf Whittier said of it, "I know nothing better in our literature of the kind." More than twenty books followed. Bowdoin College, where her father had studied medicine and later taught, granted her an honorary Doctor of Letters degree, the first woman the school had ever so honored.

Her family home in South Berwick, lovingly restored by the local historical society, is today a museum and, ironically, an attraction for the tourists who inspired her to seek a literary career.

THE MILLS

Harriet Beecher Stowe wrote in 1872, "City people come to the country, not to sit in the best parlor and to see the nearest imitation of city life, but to lie on the haymow, to swing in the barn, to form intimacy with the pigs, chickens, and ducks." But other much different people were also coming to Maine in these years. In addition to those from "away," from not-so-far-off Canada, people also came from *far away*—in that few of them spoke English. They were French-Canadians who first came to work in the textile mills.

Most of them were concentrated in certain cities where rushing river water provided abundant energy to run the machines. Lewiston, on the Androscoggin, undoubtedly attracted the largest contingent of "Francos," while Biddeford, on the Saco; Sanford, on the Mousam; Waterville, on the

"There was something about the coast town of Dunnet which made it seem more attractive than other maritime villages of eastern Maine," begins Sarah Orne Jewett's classic story, The Country of the Pointed Firs. *Born in Berwick, Jewett (1849–1909) began writing in her teens and published her first story in* Atlantic Monthly *when she was just nineteen. She is seen as representative of New England regional literature and many of her works,* Deephaven *and* The Country Doctor *among them, are still read today. Courtesy, Maine Women Writers, University of New England*

Mill supervisors recruited worker of all ages. Adults worked a twelve hour day for ninety cents. Their young children worked, too, usually for nine hours straight. Historian Yves Frenette has written that, "between 1850 and 1880, over 70 percent of French Canadian children in Biddeford and Lewiston aged ten to fourteen worked in the mills." The numbers dropped in the first part of the twentieth century, but children continued to work, leaving quickly when a truant officer visited the mill. Courtesy, Androscoggin Historical Society

Kennebec; Rumford, on the Androscoggin and Old Town, on the Penobscot, grew up as other centers of French-speaking workers fleeing hard economic times in Quebec Province. Even rustic, small South Berwick had mills situated on its falls and a railroad running through the town, a situation that Sarah Orne Jewett lamented in one of her sketches.

Until the 1870s most of the workers in Maine's textile industry were of Yankee Anglo-Saxon origin. Many of these were young women off the farm, who lived decorously away from home in closely-chaperoned dormitories. The Bates Mill in Lewiston was the quintessential model.

Owned by Benjamin E. Bates of Boston, who had bought it from local businessmen including Governor Alonzo Garcelon, the sprawling plant owed its rapid growth to U.S. government contracts for making tent cloth during the Civil War. The fortune Bates compiled led him to endow another college for Maine, located in Lewiston; named for himself, Bates College was also like Colby, a Baptist institution.

The infusion of Roman Catholic French Canadians into Lewiston was said to have started as early as 1866. By the spring of 1870 more than 1,000 immigrants had arrived in the city from Quebec, and within five years, their number had tripled. They weren't expected to become permanent residents but merely make enough money to go back to their native province and buy farmland, since most of them were agriculturists driven off the land by the poverty situation at home.

Textile mills—cotton, wool, silk and spool thread—proliferated throughout Maine communities from the mid-nineteenth century. Factories could be found in Westbrook, Lisbon, Lewiston, Biddeford, Saco, Old Town and many other riverfront towns. Spools of cotton at the Lockwood Mills of Waterville are shown here. Courtesy, Maine Historical Society

On the whole, they stayed; and their population swelled. Today Lewiston is the second largest city in Maine, surpassing Bangor. At present, close to 25 percent of the Maine population can trace its ancestry to French roots, either of the *quebequois* who came to toil in the mills or the *acadiens* in the northern most parts of the state.

The conditions under which the Franco workers in Lewiston had to live were poor, indeed. The tenements on Lisbon and Lincoln Streets in the heart of town were described as an "evil which ought to be remedied," an average of twenty-four people to each house. Sanitation was almost non-existent, health problems multiplied, and the adults worked a twelve hour day for ninety cents. Their young children worked, too, usually for nine hours straight.

The French were preferred by the mill owners because, as one report put it, "they are industrious in the extreme, do not grumble about pay and docile, and have little to do with labor agitation." In an era when strikes were erupting nationwide and unions were starting to form, even in Maine, this was a clear advantage in the eyes of management.

For that reason, if nothing else, these Canadians suffered discrimination from Mainers who thought they were taking jobs from them. They were likened to the Chinese "coolies" in the west. Their deep devotion to the Catholic church also set them apart in Protestant Maine, where there were perhaps still lingering memories of the French and Indian wars. Oddly enough, their co-religionists, the Irish who had preceded them, were not welcoming. It can still be pointed out in Maine cities which Catholic churches are French and which are Irish.

Woolen mills grew up concurrently with the cotton mills, expanding exponentially—26 of them in 1860 and 107 in 1870. The end of the Civil War saw no slowdown of production. By 1873 the cotton mills in Lewiston alone employed 7,500 men and women. Biddeford had 2,600 mill workers and nearby Saco had another 1,000.

While large employments by Maine standards, they, on a smaller scale, mirrored the massive industrialization sweeping the nation during the

As early as 1866 Roman Catholic French Canadians immigrated to Lewiston. In the spring of 1870 more than 1,000 immigrants had arrived from Quebec. Their number tripled within five years. Similar influxes occurred in many of the textile mill towns. Ku Klux Klan cells organized in reaction to the swelling Catholic population and, in some cases, "twin city" communities developed around mill towns as yankee citizens fled to suburbs to avoid living near their new neighbors. Pictured above is a KKK parade in Maine during the 1920s when the "secret organization" briefly flourished. Courtesy, Maine Historical Society

Gilded Age. With it came all the problems that America witnessed then: great disparities between the few rich and the many poor and labor unrest. Horrible living, working and health conditions existed for huge numbers of citizens, bad enough in Maine, too, for the sardonic comment from one Maine city, "In 1880 a man from the Middle Ages would have felt at home amidst the dirt and smell of Brunswick."

Nor was the industrializing trend confined to textiles and urban parts of the state. When it was learned that paper could be made from wood, not just rags as in the past, Maine with its endless forests was soon a target for immense manufacturing operations.

PULP AND PAPER

Maine's pioneer in paper making was the S.D. Warren Company, started by a Massachusetts businessman and located on the Presumpscot River which runs into Casco Bay, slightly north of Portland. The site, Congin Falls, where Samuel Dennis Warren first set up his operation in 1854, is now the downtown section of the city of Westbrook. Newsprint, Manila brown wrapping paper and high quality writing paper was produced there, all derived from various grades of rags and jute. It has been alleged that linen wrappings from Egyptian mummies were found among the rags used in Maine.

In 1874 S.D. Warren changed to wood pulp for its raw material. Poplar logs from nearby forests had their contents reduced through a chemical process developed by an English scientist in the U.S. In the 1890s the company was called one of the "most extensive of their kind on the globe."

But another paper making giant would soon create competition. International Paper was established by another foreign-born, far-sighted transplant to America, the Canadian entrepreneur Hugh J.

The S. D. Warren mill was the first to blend wood pulp with rag to make paper. This innovation was key; by 1880 S.D. Warren was considered the largest paper company in the world. Courtesy, Maine Historic Preservation Commission

Chisholm, who had settled in Portland in 1872. He had arrived via the Grand Trunk Railroad from Montreal on which he, along with Thomas Alva Edison, had been newsboys in their childhoods, an experience from which he had fashioned a successful business of publishing railroad tourism guides and photo albums of beautiful New England scenery.

On a trip in the mid-winter of 1882, Chisholm was in the Rumford area of the upper Androscoggin River. He was admiring a set of falls he planned to photograph. Suddenly he had a vision. He saw all the "water power going to waste." He described what happened next in his mind, "I pictured to myself the industrial community which might grow up there."

Out of this capitalist inspiration, Chisholm, who had already created several small paper companies in other parts of Maine, formed the Rumford Falls Sulphite Company and the Rumford Falls Paper Company. Both businesses employed a new "sulphite" process to break down wood fibers. These combined operations were on line and turning out reams of newsprint by July 1893.

Maine's paper industry developed in the 1850s as a shortage of rags led innovators to try making paper with wood fibers. Further development led to using wood pulp. Maine paper mills quickly became some of the largest in the world. Large rolls of paper, probably newsprint, are seen here in the cutting room of the Rumford Falls Paper Mill. Courtesy, Bethel Historical Society

The Rumford Falls Sulphite Mill is shown here under construction in the early 1890s. Courtesy, Maine Historic Preservation Commission

That wasn't all Hugh Chisholm did. Five years later, his organizing skills brought together twenty paper mills in Maine, New Hampshire, Massachusetts, Virginia and New York. Out of these a newsprint conglomerate emerged, the International Paper Company (IP), which controlled 90 percent of the U.S. market. Still active in Maine, Chisholm's IP remains a major player in the world's paper industry today.

Chisholm's model of moving into the Maine wilderness and creating an industrial complex on the basis of water power was copied more ambitiously only a few years afterward. In some respects, Chisholm's success and his monopoly of newsprint manufacturing led to the appearance of a rival, the Great Northern Paper Company (GNP), destined to play a bigger role than International Paper in the economy and politics of Maine.

An ex-employee of Chisholm's, Garrett Schenck, a New Jerseyan of Dutch ancestry, really made this happen with the help of rich investors in New York City, including the owner of the *New York World*, Joseph Pulitzer, who wanted another outlet from which to buy newsprint for his daily paper.

Likewise, aiding the huge project of building the whole new community of Millinocket in the depths

By 1909 there were forty-five paper mills in Maine, employing 8,647 workers and the number increased to 10,696 employees by 1914. By the early twentieth century, workers had unionized with the Pulp, Sulphite and Papermill Workers Union having nine locals in Maine while the International Brotherhood of Papermakers had twelve. This parade is probably the 1902 Labor Day Parade in Rumford Falls. The Livermore Falls Advertiser *reported that the papermakers union had purchased 180 matching suits for its members to wear in the parade. In 1903 over 1,200 people marched in the Livermore Falls Labor Day parade, the first Labor Day celebration ever held in that town. Courtesy, Bethel Historical Society*

of the Maine woods was the extension of the Bangor and Aroostook Railroad northward. A branch line from its intersection with a major fork of the Penobscot River could connect it with the amazing water power availability around Millinocket Stream. The vision in the company's first prospectus spoke of 23,500 horsepower, enough to create "300 tons of paper per day."

Once financing was assured, the project spurred forward. Construction workers, many of them Italians recruited at the docks in Boston and Providence as soon as they arrived in this country, had a

paper manufacturing plant completed within less than a year. Alongside it, a town grew up, one section called "Little Italy," a landmark in twenty-first century Millinocket. The foreign mix there, as in Rumford, had gone beyond the previous influx of Irish and French Canadians. It was not simply the Italians, but Poles, Lithuanians, Latvians, Finns, Estonians, Hungarians, Czechs and Slovaks, the latter grouping usually designated under the generic term of "Polacks."

It was not long before Great Northern was flexing its economic and political muscle in the state. The critical juncture was a fight over water control that developed between GNP and the Penobscot Log Driving Company, which was dominated by the most famous log driver in Maine history, John Ross. Despite the fact that Ross' son was a state representative and he, himself, a power-house in Bangor circles, Great Northern ultimately triumphed in Augusta when its bill to take over all driving rights was presented to the legislature.

For one Maine chronicler of this era, the Reverend Alfred G. Hempstead, this triumph of Great

Located on the West Branch of the Penobscot River near Mount Katahdin, Millinocket was a mill town with homes, stores and schools built by the Great Northern Paper Company. Founded in 1898 as the Northern Development Company, the name was changed to Great Northern Paper in 1899. The mill was manufacturing over 350 tons of paper daily at the time this photo was taken. Courtesy, Maine Historical Society

Northern constituted the beginning of "the period of corporate control" in the Maine North Woods. Lumbering had given way to paper making and the forests, themselves, were now industrialized.

KATE FURBISH

In the summer of 1880, a forty-six year-old female amateur botanist from Brunswick, Maine named Catherine "Kate" Furbish undertook a plant collecting trip into the wilds of northernmost Maine. She was going to Aroostook County, whose flora had not been well explored. Finally reaching Fort

Fairfield, that original military post Governor John Fairfield had established close to the New Brunswick border during the Northeast Boundary dispute, she made it her headquarters for six weeks, investigating the flowers of the Aroostook River. Then, she went north to the town of Van Buren and for the first time saw the mighty St. John River, the boundary between the U.S. and Canada. Clambering over the steep river banks on the American side, she noticed a particular type of blossom that most people, even a botanist less trained than she was, might not have bothered to inspect. At an immediate glance, it appeared to be a type of snapdragon, the "common lousewort," or, to give it its official Latin species tag, *Pedicularis Canadensis*, quite prevalent in the eastern United States. A closer look, however, revealed differ-

Immigrant workers found work in Maine's manufacturing industries, often taking the hardest or most undesirable jobs at low wages. The Italian workers shown here around 1900, are working on the Somerset Railroad near Bingham. Courtesy, University of Maine, Special Collections

ences. Several examples of this three foot high plant were put in her vasculum, or collecting case, roots and all. Although Kate couldn't have suspected it, she and the plant were about to make history.

It turned out the experts at Harvard to whom she sent her specimens confirmed that the plant was new to science. Moreover, after flirting with naming it *Pedicularis Johanensis*, for the St. John River, the director of the Harvard herbarium was persuaded to honor Miss Furbish for her discovery. The plant entered the annals of botanical science as *Pedicularis furbishiae*—the Furbish lousewort— a rare organism, found nowhere in the world except along a 130 mile stretch of the St. John River.

The Gilded Age, with its fast-paced industrialization transforming America, even in the Thoreau-trod wilderness of Maine, could never in its wildest dreams imagine that a day would come when the existence of a wild snapdragon could stand in the way of plans for a multi-million dollar federal hydroelectric project. But this is what seemingly occurred in November 1976 to the proposal for an enormous stoppage on the St. John at a site known as Dickey-Lincoln School. By then, the range of Miss Furbish's flower had narrowed to the point of disappearance. It was thought extinct, until a few clusters of them were found on the river banks in the vicinity of Dickey-Lincoln. Environmentalists cried that the project, which they opposed for various reasons including the flooding of 88,000 acres of wild land, should be stopped because of an endangered species. Behind them were private power interests, opposed to Dickey-Lincoln because it would be for public power, in competition with them. The Furbish lousewort made headlines nationally.

In the long run, the political opposition proved too strong and the dam was defeated. The gentle, dedicated lady from Brunswick, who was also an extraordinarily talented botanical artist, had left her mark on the world in those three-foot high plants waving along the waters of the northern St. John.

W. A. Rogers.

7

INTO THE
TWENTIETH CENTURY
(1899-1929)

On March 25, 1898 the gallery was packed with spectators when the president's message about the destruction of the USS Maine was read before the Senate. The Maine was the first modern battleship and was commissioned in 1895. For no known reason the USS Maine exploded in Havana Harbor off Cuba in 1898 and the act—whether accidental or hostile— brought about the beginning of the Spanish-American War. Courtesy, Library of Congress

REMEMBER THE MAINE

Along the gilt upper edge of the Gilded Age, it is not always possible chronologically to discern when exactly this period merged into the twentieth century. Industrialization that began within the glittery post-Reconstruction era may not have fully developed until after the new century commenced, as was the case in Maine with the Great Northern Paper Company, which did not fully blossom until 1903.

If a rather arbitrary dividing line is to be drawn, however, it might well be the Spanish-American War. This one year event started and ended in 1898. It cannot be argued that America was quite the same afterward. Overnight the U.S. had turned into a world power. An "imperialist" power, some critics complained. America had expanded beyond its continental borders in a fashion—they also carped—that the founding fathers and creators of the Constitution never foresaw nor would have wanted to allow.

Maine, despite its relative smallness and isolation in the northeast corner of the nation, played a surprisingly important role in this drama of American expansion.

It wasn't just that the battleship blown up in Havana harbor on February 15, 1898—the indisputable triggering event—bore the title of the USS *Maine*. Daniel Cony, in 1819, was right in predicting that many years would pass before the Pine Tree State had a dreadnaught named for it, but he could never possibly imagine what the upshot would be once it did. To the universal American cry of "Remember the *Maine*," the country went into battle and won territory in the Atlantic and Pacific from the Spanish empire. Some still held, like Puerto Rico and Guam, some held temporarily and then released, like the Philippines, and some freed right at the time, like Cuba. Also in 1898 the U.S. annexed Hawaii. Amazingly, Maine had a number of direct connections to the making of that formerly independent kingdom into a future U.S. state. One Hawaiian historian in his book on

When the USS Maine exploded in Havana Harbor off Cuba in 1898, the ship was moored there to protect United States interests, if necessary, but the country was not at war. The tragedy caught the country by surprise, and immediately foul play was suspected. No substantial proof has ever been found that the ship was attacked, but the event precipitated the Spanish-American War as cries of "Remember the Maine" spurred the country into action. Recent evidence suggests that the explosion was started by a fire in a coal bunker, but still no cause for that fire has ever been identified. Courtesy, Library of Congress

A poster for Along the Kennebec: A New England Story Laughingly Told, a comical play by C. R. Reno, circa 1900, about the role four Mainers played in Hawaii becoming American. There were nine posters printed for the play which featured an explosion and family disgrace along with the laughter promised by the title. Courtesy, Library of Congress

the annexation even includes a two page nineteenth century drawing of the Kennebec River with insets of four Mainers from the area who played key roles in seeing that Hawaii became American. They were Luther Severance, first U.S. minister to the Kingdom of Hawaii; Daniel Dole, missionary and father of Sanford B. Dole, president of the Hawaiian Republic; James G. Blaine, U.S. secretary of state and his one-time business partner, John L. Stevens, appointed by Blaine as the last U.S. minister to the Royal government and the man most credited with having overthrown the Hawaiian monarchy.

The *Kennebec Journal*, which is still the local newspaper in Maine's capital, unites three of these figures. For health reasons, Luther Severance, the *Kennebec Journal*'s original owner and editor, left Maine in 1851 for Hawaii where he had gotten a presidential appointment to represent the U.S. When he returned to Augusta, he spent time at his old paper, which by then had been bought by Blaine and Stevens, and he imbued those two younger men with his fervent belief that the Sandwich Islands, as Hawaii was known, should come under the American flag. Years later, Blaine, as secretary of state, began implementing his policy of American expansion and, with regard to Hawaii, he assigned Stevens as his personal and official emissary to the court of Queen Lili'uokalani. By encouraging U.S. marines to land in Honolulu, Stevens gave tacit approval to a coup by American businessmen who deposed her.

The fourth figure, David Dole, a missionary, supplied the finishing touch. His son Sanford was chosen to head up the "Republic" imposed by these Americans, prior to annexation. The elder Dole also hailed from the Kennebec Valley, farther up the river at Skowhegan. Allegedly it was Luther Severance's editorials in the *Kennebec Journal* that inspired him to go to the Pacific and settle on the island of Kauai. His wife, too, was a Kennebec Valley native, from Hallowell, nee Ballard, and a niece of the now-famous midwife. The town of Koloa where they lived was, in fact, an enclave of Kennebec Valley folks and Sanford Ballard Dole, himself, although born in Hawaii and only a visitor to Maine, married a girl from Castine. To finish this set of Maine-Hawaii links, the American minister to the Hawaiian "Republic" at the time it finally entered the United States was Harold Sewall, another Mainer and one from the lower Kennebec River city of Bath.

"CZAR" REED

In 1902, upon the occasion of the 250th anniversary of the town of York, a glittering array of celebrities—some of national renown—were on the speakers' platform, including ex-governor Joshua Chamberlain, the hero of Gettysburg; James Phinney Baxter, former mayor of Portland and president of the Maine Historical Society; and William Dean Howells, best-selling novelist and noted editor. Two persons in particular were speakers the crowd most looked forward to hearing. One was Mark Twain, who spent some of his summers in the Maine resort. The other was Twain's close friend, the Honorable Thomas Brackett Reed, a Portland native whose ancestors had come from York, but whose political stature—he was six foot three, weighing 300 pounds—was as big as he was. He had been the most powerful speaker in the history of the U.S. House of Representatives, nicknamed "Czar" because of the iron hand with which he ruled over his fellow congressmen. His wit was as famous as his pal Mark Twain's and his quips are repeated to this day.

For example, a pompous congressman who declaimed to the chair, "Mr. Speaker, I would rather be right than president," and received the prompt reply from Reed: "The gentleman need not be disturbed. He will never be either." Reed is rejoinder to a particularly garrulous congressman is also remembered, "Russell, you do not understand the theory of a five minute debate. The object is to convey to the House either information or misinformation. You have consumed several periods of five minutes this afternoon without doing either." "A statesman is a politician who is dead," ranks among his other oft-quoted ad-libs. So is another jewel of unrehearsed put-downs. After leaving an opponent speechless, Reed declared, "Having embalmed that fly in the liquid amber of my remarks, I wish to proceed."

His own family members were not spared his witticisms, either. His daughter Kitty had a favorite pet cat and, once to her horror, she noticed the feline asleep on a chair that Reed, with his great mass, was unknowingly about to sit on. Dashing over, she pulled the chair away and "Mr. Speaker" went crashing to the floor. Instead of roaring with rage, he rose calmly, dusted himself off and admonished, "Kitty, remember that it is easier to get another cat than another father."

But Tom Reed's fame in his own time rested on an action of his, rather than any clever use of words. As Speaker, he put an end to a practice of obstruction in Congress by which the minority party would not allow a quorum simply by refusing to answer to their names when called. Both political parties did this and Reed had participated when the Republicans were not in control. On the receiving end of the procedure when he was in the Speaker's chair, he suddenly one day, without warning, ordered his clerk "Mark him present" after a Democrat's name had been read off and the man had sat silently. The Democrat jumped to his feet, protesting, "I object, Mr. Speaker. I object."

"Does the gentleman deny he is present?" Reed shot back.

Amid bedlam, the portly giant had the roll call continue, declared a quorum existed and proceeded to conduct House business. "Czar," "Tyrant" and "Dictator" were among the kindlier names hurled at him. But Reed prevailed.

To the Republicans, he was a hero—and a potential candidate for president. Theodore Roosevelt was one of his strongest backers; William McKinley, his prime rival. It was no contest. McKinley's manager was Mark Hanna, one of the ablest politicians in the country, and Reed would not do the political things he needed to do to win

Portland native Thomas Brackett Reed (1839–1902), served as the Speaker of the U.S. House of Representatives from 1889–1891, and penned Reed's Rules which are still used by the House today. Referred to as "Czar Reed" because he wielded so much power as Speaker, he used his "Rules" to limit the minority party's ability to block any majority action. Reed is quoted as saying, "The best system is to have one party govern and the other party watch." Courtesy, Library of Congress

the GOP nomination. The Maine man lost on the first ballot.

Then, too, when the issues of "imperialism" emerged after the election of 1896—the annexation of Hawaii, the Spanish-American War and its conquests—Reed found himself on the wrong side. Nor was he shy about making his anti-imperialist views known, announcing from a sick bed that he would have voted "No" on the annexation of Hawaii and, in 1898, following his reelection

Democrat Arthur Sewall (1835–1900) was William Jennings Bryant's running mate in the 1896 presidential campaign. A successful shipbuilder from Bath with a number of big business interests, sharing the ticket with the populist Bryant must have seemed like an odd pairing. Indeed, Sewall had not sought the nomination. Sewall was an anomaly in Maine—a successful Democrat in a very Republican state. Courtesy, Library of Congress

to Congress by a huge majority, resigning his seat in protest against the war. Despite his views, he certainly would have been elected Speaker again.

"Office as a 'ribbon to stick in your coat' is worth nobody's consideration," Reed declared in a farewell address to his constituents, and added, "Whatever may happen, I am sure the First Maine District will always be true to the principles of liberty, self-government and the rights of man."

A MAINE VICE PRESIDENTIAL CANDIDATE

Arthur Sewall of Bath was another of those figures of note in Maine who straddled the Gilded Age and the start of the twentieth century. His son Harold, mentioned earlier, had been working for the U.S. State Department and even before his involvement in the annexation of Hawaii, was the U.S. consul in Samoa when half of that archipelago in the South Pacific was made an American pro-

tectorate. The elder Sewall, known as "the Maritime Prince," ran a major shipbuilding operation in the Maine city traditionally most dedicated to that industry. The Sewall Company was famed for building "the only fleet of steel deepwater ships sent overboard from an American shipyard." It had stopped making wooden ships in 1892, once it had built the world's largest wooden vessel, the *Roanoke*, weighing 3,400 tons, which carried the biggest cargo ever of Hawaiian sugar to New York City—88,000 bags.

Active, too, in Maine politics, Arthur Sewall was an anomaly for that period of time in the Pine Tree State. He was a Democrat, albeit a successful businessman, a leader of the distinctly minority party on both a local and national level. Yet Maine, which was referred to as a "Black Republican State," from its diehard anti-slavery, pro-Black stance in the Civil War and utter GOP domination downeast, seemed the last place in which the Democrats would want to pick their vice presidential candidate.

In 1896, however, they did just that and the strangeness of their choice was compounded by the "radical" nature of the principal standard-bearer, William Jennings Bryan. He was described as a "populist denouncer of corporations" and his running mate as a "man who had grown rich by manipulation of corporative property." The newspaper editorialist offering this comparison opined, "The Democratic Party cannot appreciate what a funny thing they have done."

Celebrating their native son's sudden, unexpected notoriety for Sewall had never sought the nomination, the city of Bath threw a great party for him when Bryan arrived in Maine to campaign. The contrast between them was also one of age and appearance. Bryan, the "boy orator" of Nebraska, was only thirty-six years old, thin and dynamic; Sewall, heavy-set and seemingly stodgy—until he scared Bryan half to death, driving him back from a clam bake with breakneck style in his fast-paced horse and carriage, while smoking one of his habitual black cigars.

The three Bath newspapers, all Republican, had helped arrange the welcoming rally for Sewall and his guest. Then, reverting to type, they proceeded to lambaste him, one of them stating, "We regret to believe that our fellow townsman's election would be a disaster not on account of any personal characteristics of Sewall, but because of the thoroughly objectionable platform to which he stands committed."

Sewall was as wedded to free silver and an inflated money supply as was Bryan—an issue overwhelmed in the election by "McKinley and gold," which was the reigning Republican slogan.

Bryan ran twice more for president and lost twice more again. Arthur Sewall, now a footnote in history, closed his shipbuilding business in 1903.

ICE AND GRANITE

Two native industries, taking advantage of Maine's natural resources, as the paper companies from "away" had done, gave the Pine Tree State a short-lived fame in their respective fields.

At its peak, Maine's ice-producing business was the largest in the United States and 90 percent of the product was shipped out of state, a good deal of it in the summer to hot southern cities like Baltimore, Savannah and Alexandria, Virginia. While the supply came from various Maine rivers that froze up in the winter, the most sought-after in terms of quality and purity was cut from the Kennebec River.

Shipping went on year round. Packed in sawdust, gladly supplied by Maine's many lumber mills, the ice would last for months, providing refrigeration and cold drinks in an age before electricity and well after Thomas Alva Edison opened the nation's first power plant in New York City. Until 1900 the blocks, sometimes fifteen to twenty inches thick, were sent down river on schooners and following that, on barges pulled by motorized tugboats.

Early on, in the nineteenth century, it had been a cottage industry, starting with a Portland ice cream maker who served his concoction to the Marquis de Lafayette when the French Revolutionary War hero visited Maine in 1824. A Boston businessman, Frederick Tudor, tried to corner Maine's ice market in the 1850s and ice, at the time, was even being exported to Liverpool, England, for use in British hospitals during the Crimean War. Maine ice went to Cuba and the West Indies, too.

The 1890s were boom years: 3,000 men working on the Kennebec River, alone, employing 1,000 teams of horses. During that time, a Bath businessman, Charles W. Morse, set out to do on a national scale what Tudor had previously tried locally— corner the ice market. By 1895 his Consolidated Ice Company had a capital of $10 million as Morse took over distributing companies in New York City, Baltimore and Philadelphia. He also controlled the tug boats.

The "Ice King's" consolidation, it has been said, was responsible for the "downfall" of the ice trade in Maine. In 1909 Morse dispatched his last cake from the Kennebec. Here and there, ice cutting went on long afterward. In 1962 a South Portland company was reported still at it commercially.

Granite rose and fell in the same fashion. In the 1890s, Maine was second nationally in the production of this important stone for building material, topped only by Massachusetts. When it came to paving blocks for street work, Maine actually led the nation.

The Bodwell Granite Company was the foremost leader in the state and the prominence of its founder, Joseph R. Bodwell of Hallowell, had propelled him into the Governor's chair for a term in the 1880s. Like Charles Morse in ice, Bodwell was known as the "King" of his trade. In 1895 the Bodwell company entered into a long-term contract to supply the granite for the foundation and support columns of the massive Episcopalian cathedral, St. John the Divine, in Manhattan. The pillars, themselves, were reputed to be the largest ever carved from a single block. Other major contracts handled by the firm included the Brooklyn post office, the Library of Congress building in Washington, D.C. and the guard house of the Philadelphia city prison. As the twentieth century began, Maine took the lead in national granite production, with 152 quarries in operation and 3,500 men at work.

Labor problems, changes in building fashions and the economics of the industry led to granite's decline in Maine. Some stone is still cut today, mostly for cemetery memorials.

THE CENTRAL MAINE POWER COMPANY

That electricity, and resulting refrigeration, would eventually put an end to Maine's ice business might not have been foreseeable when, in 1882, Edison's invention began producing power in New York City. But seventeen years later, small power companies in Maine were popping up like mushrooms after a rain. In 1899 a young man from the small town of Oakland, Walter Wyman, bought the local electric generating concern for $4,500. Once he received a contract from the neighboring city of Waterville for street lighting and a hydro station, the Messalonskee Power Company was on its way to statewide domination of the industry. A measure of its success could be seen in 1910 through two events: a name change to the Central Maine Power Company (CMP) and the nickname bestowed upon it by a legislator, angry that it had already swallowed up companies in Clinton, Dexter, Skowhegan, Solon and Vassalboro. To State Senator Kellogg, Wyman's budding business had become an "octopus."

CMP's momentum, however, continued without pause, spreading from Kennebec County into Lincoln, Oxford, Somerset and Androscoggin counties—an outreach finally to culminate in its conquest of the state's two most populous counties—Cumberland and York.

Not only was Wyman's company dominant in Maine's power industry, he, himself, became a force in the state's majority Republican party.

Water power control was achieved through his hold over the GOP members of the legislature. It was a known fact that on occasion bills or amendments to bills would be submitted under his signature although he was never elected to any position.

Wyman's cleverness was also illustrated during the Depression in avoiding a ruinous collapse after he had brought his company under the financial umbrella of a vast Chicago-based holding company, led by Samuel Insull, who had been Thomas Edison's private secretary. Realizing that Insull's overextended empire was about to crash in the 1930s, Wyman adroitly maneuvered CMP out of danger, then went on, making himself more and more indispensable to the Maine economy, literally taking on the role, long before state government was involved, of enticing outside industries to Maine.

Generators at the CMP power station in Buxton. Maine's many rivers and streams offered a good source of electricity. In 1899 Walter Wyman and Harvey Eaton purchased a small hydroelectric power plant in Oakland. That operation became Central Maine Power in 1910. Courtesy, Maine Historic Preservation Commission

THE MAINE CENTRAL RAILROAD

If anything, the Maine railroads, in their early days, were as diffuse and numerous as the power companies. Their consolidation was inevitable. The "octopus," in this case was the Maine Central Railroad, first organized in 1862 after the merger of two roads: the Androscoggin and Kennebec and the Penobscot and Kennebec, giving it a run from Lewiston-Auburn to Bangor. In time, the Maine Central was to encompass fifty lines and count among its presidents two former governors, Anson P. Morrill and Abner Coburn.

Two of the major railroads it acquired were John A. Poor's European and North American Railway, originally planned to extend into Canada and connect with sea travel to Europe and Hugh Chisholm Portland and Rumford Falls Railway, which the creator of the International Paper Company had once visualized reaching Quebec City, although the completed line never went farther than the Rangeley Lakes.

The former railroad was the site of an actual German sabotage attempt in World War I before

This Maine Central Railroad locomotive, the "Arthur Sewall," was built at the Portland Company in 1877. The Maine Central Railroad was first organized in 1862 after the merger of two railroads. Courtesy, Maine Historical Society

the U.S. entered the conflict. A lieutenant in the Kaiser's army was sent to try to stop the Americans from allowing the transport of Canadian troops through Maine, in violation of neutrality. Dressed in full uniform so he wouldn't be treated as a spy and shot, the German officer placed a charge under the Vanceboro Bridge on the Maine side of the border shared with New Brunswick. The sheriff of Washington County, tipped off about this strange man running around in field grey and spiked helmet, arrested him before he could set the charge.

The Maine Central didn't just run trains. It owned hotels, too, large ones, like the Mount Kineo House on Moosehead Lake and the Samoset Hotel in Rockport, and advertised heavily for tourists it could bring to Maine. Steamships and ferry boats, performing the same function, were also owned by the Maine Central.

THE STANLEY STEAMER

The western Maine mountain town of Kingfield was founded by the state's first governor, William King, after he received an entire township from the heirs of William Bingham as a reward for withdrawing his attack on their claim to vast Maine properties. It was here that the Stanley brothers, Francis E. and Freelan O., were born, identical twins with a mechanical, Yankee ingenuity bent.

Having initially produced hand-made violins at an early age, as young adults they turned to photography and invented a procedure using dry plates that was a significant improvement over the previous wet plate technique. Soon, the two male siblings established the Stanley Dry Plate Company in Lewiston-Auburn, which they sold to Eastman Kodak in 1905. Their female sibling, the beauteous Chansonetta Stanley Emmons, was a pioneer woman photographer, nationally known for her portraits of rural women, starting with "Aunt Hannah and Aunt Abigail, Kingfield," her "first genre masterpiece." Throughout the 1920s and 1930s, she was at work, photographing coun-

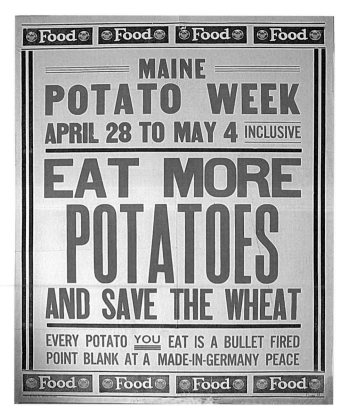

The Food Administration encouraged people to observe "Wheatless Mondays" and "Meatless Thursdays" during World War I. Potatoes were a filling alternative and Maine growers saw a market for their crops. This World War I poster encourages people to eat more potatoes and save wheat for the troops. Circa 1917. Courtesy, Maine Historical Society

Percival Procter Baxter (1876–1969), two-term governor, Maine legislator, Maine senator and noted animal lover, purchased Mt. Katahdin and gave it, along with 202,064 acres of land, to the state to create Baxter State Park. A lifelong public servant, Baxter wrote that the park, "shall forever be retained and used for state forest, public park and public recreational purposes ... shall forever be kept and remain in the natural wild state ... shall forever be kept and remain as a sanctuary for beasts and birds." Baxter's Falmouth home on MacWorth Island was also a gift to the state and is now Baxter School for the Deaf. Baxter is shown here in the shadow of Mount Katahdin in 1962. Courtesy, Baxter State Park

James Phinney Baxter (1831–1921) was a six-time mayor of Portland and a multi-millionaire thanks to a canning industry that he created. Mayor Baxter's legacy of philanthropy lives on today in a number of southern Maine landmarks that bear his name: Baxter Boulevard and Baxter Woods in Portland and the Baxter Library in Gorham. From: Maine: A History *by Louis C. Hatch, volume I, 1919*

fight in which he engaged with them. Who would own this source of electric generation? Would the people of Maine receive any financial benefit from the "white gold?" Epic battles erupted in that contest, pitting Baxter against the titans of downeast industry. For this reason, they made sure he didn't win the GOP nomination for U.S. Senate in 1926. They also fought furiously against all his efforts, both as a legislator and as governor, to have the state of Maine buy Mount Katahdin.

Percival Baxter was described as "a rich man's son who has antagonized every rich man in Maine."

His father, James Phinney Baxter, was six times mayor of Portland and a multi-millionaire because of his pioneer work in creating a canning industry that in the 1860s was considered "the largest food packing firm in the world."

An inspiration for his son's conservation interest most certainly was Mayor Baxter's long but successful battle to create park areas in Portland. Using his own money, he commissioned Frederick Law Olmsted, the designer of New York City's Central Park, to prepare a master plan for Portland. Its ultimate expression was the

"Boulevard," now called Baxter Boulevard, a greenway around the Back Cove section of the city.

As a youth, witness to this ferocious political struggle, Percival was also aware of the similar Maine conservation initiative by George Bucknam Dorr on Mount Desert Island to create the future Acadia National Park. While generally opposed to any federal funding for Maine, Percival Baxter did support Dorr in this instance.

It took "Percy" thirty years to put together the disparate pieces of his huge state park. Only after the death of Garret Schenck, the head of the Great Northern Paper Company and Baxter's inveterate enemy, would the pulp and paper giant sell its ownership of the mountaintop to him. Year after year, the aging bachelor ex-governor would bring a new purchase to Augusta for the legislators to accept. When he died at the age of ninety-three, his ashes were flown over the park and scattered upon the crest of Mount Katahdin.

Two decades after his death, one of the most beguiling mysteries about Percival Baxter was solved to an extent in a startling fashion. Why was it that this tall, handsome, charming man, eminently eligible, had never married? All sorts of rumors abounded. Then, a time capsule, planted during his governorship in the early 1920s at a war memorial in Kittery, was opened and a letter in it released publicly. It was a "confession" Percy had left about his "love life," how a prominent socialite in Portland had turned him down and how he, in turn, ready to propose to a beautiful Italian countess, decided she would never be happy living in Maine and so he let her return to Italy without having popped the question.

Cornelia "Fly Rod" Crosby (1854–1946) was a top Maine guide and one of the greatest promoters of Maine's natural habitat. From her hometown of Phillips, she wrote hunting and fishing stories for New York, Boston and Philadelphia newspapers, attracting vacationers to Maine's remote regions. Dressed in the daring hunting costume of a "short" skirt with a hem seven inches from the ground, Crosby also appealed as a role model to women who wanted to hunt and fish. Crosby is credited with naming Maine the "Nation's Playground," and with being the first publicity agent for the Maine Central Railroad. Courtesy, Phillips Historical Society

IMPORTANT MAINE WOMEN
OF THE ERA

CORNELIA T. CROSBY

An unexpected gift that Percival Baxter received from one of his admirers was an album of photographs of Maine fishing and hunting scenes. The note accompanying the package revealed they had been sent from the estate of the late Cornelia Thurza Crosby of Phillips, Maine, at her express wish, to the ex-state chief executive. "I want Governor Baxter to have this book to place wherever he thinks best," the woman had written, signing herself as "Fly Rod, Cornelia T. Crosby."

Fly Rod Crosby was famous in Maine. In a sense, she was the "Annie Oakley" of fly fishing. One notable record from the western Maine Rangeley Lakes region where she lived had her flycasting and catching fifty-two trout in forty-four minutes, the first female ever to do so. She was also the first, and for many years the only woman member of the Maine Sportsmen's Fish and Game Association.

Under the heading of "A Letter from Fly Rod," she began writing columns on hunting and fishing for her local newspaper, the *Phillips Phonograph*. Edwin R. Starbird, who had learned his trade studying with one of the Stanley twins, was a photographer for the same publication. A number of his pictures were in the album Fly Rod sent to Percival Baxter and also grace a recent biography of the noted angler, which is subtitled "The Woman who Marketed Maine."

Fly Rod's greatest skill appeared to be her knack for attracting attention to the Maine outdoors at Sportsmen's Shows and Expositions in major U.S. cities. One of the friends she made at these exhibitions was Annie Oakley, herself, the internationally reknowned rifle shooter. The *New York Times* wrote about Fly Rod, calling her "an athletic country girl from the State of Maine...as proud of her $1,000 collection of fishing tackle as most girls are of souvenir spoons and blue and white china."

The *Washington Times* and the *St. Paul, Minnesota Press* called Fly Rod the "Queen of Anglers."

For thirty years, Fly Rod Crosby wrote and boosted the Maine outdoors, all the while fishing and hunting, herself, and living until the age of ninety-one. One of her columns, written just as the twentieth century began, celebrated another "Fly Rod" in the making, a "sweet little nine year old daughter" of a New York couple who summered in the Rangeley area. The child's name was Augusta and Fly Rod dubbed her the "Queen of the Pond," because of her skill with her mother's fly rod and her knowledge of which flies to use. Fly Rod describes the girl reeling in a one pound salmon, quickly followed by several trout. Perhaps with her own childhood dreams in mind, Fly Rod ended the piece: "...little Augusta is going to keep on trying for a three pounder. Here is hoping she will get him and a dainty little fly rod for the August birthday which is always celebrated."

GAIL LAUGHLIN

One other reason, aside from fishing skill, that Fly Rod Crosby was easily accepted in the macho world of Maine sportsmen was her outspoken scorn for woman suffrage. The exact opposite was the case with Gail Laughlin. Born in the tiny Washington County town of Robbinston, she left the rural downeast for Portland and as soon as she earned enough money as a secretary, paid her way through Wellesley College, then went on to Cornell Law School, one of three females in a class of 123. By 1902 she was working for the National American Woman Suffrage Association. Her job took her out west to states like Wyoming, Colorado, Idaho and Utah, where suffrage had already been granted, but eventually homesick for Maine, she returned to Portland. By then, the suffrage battle had been won through the nineteenth Amendment, so Gail turned her energies to the idea of an Equal Rights Amendment to the U.S. Constitution, guaranteeing a whole range of equality circumstances for women in addition to voting.

Her activism led her to run for the Maine Legislature and she served three terms in the House and three terms in the Senate.

Elected as a Republican, she fought for a host of women's issues, like opposing a law to let girls marry at age thirteen and changing commitment of the insane rules to prevent husbands from falsely incarcerating their wives. An early environmentalist, she built a bird sanctuary in Mayor Baxter's Portland Back Cove parkland, fought the paper companies to try to establish a national forest in Washington County and worked for uniform lobster measures. Congress passed her Equal Rights Amendment in the 1970s. However, not enough states ratified it. Maine did, on its second try.

DORA PINKHAM

Gail Lauglin was not the first woman elected to the Maine Legislature. That honor belongs to another Republican, Mrs. Dora Pinkham of Fort Kent, the northernmost community in the state. Her election occurred only two years after the Woman Suffrage Amendment took effect in 1920. Standing up for her mostly French Acadian Catholic constituents, the Protestant Representative Pinkham made her maiden speech an attack against a proposed amendment to the state constitution banning all aid to parochial schools. She called the measure anti-Catholic and said it was "fanning the flames of fanaticism," a veiled reference to the Ku Klux Klan.

Her next target was Governor Percival Baxter, himself, the Klan's arch foe. Dora Pinkham's quarrel here was with his vetoes of her bills. Generous with his own personal fortune, Baxter was a veritable skinflint in the dispensing of state funds. Thus, down went Mrs. Pinkham's bill for a state of Maine building at the Eastern States Exposition in Springfield, Massachusetts, except she mustered enough votes to override Percy. Even fiercer fireworks erupted between Dora and Percy over a bill allowing Maine to receive federal funds to match a state appropriation for maternal and child

As early as the 1850s, national suffrage leaders were in Maine giving lectures and helping to organize the Maine suffrage campaign. A women's suffrage group was started in Portland in 1855. In 1873 the first Maine Women's Suffrage Association was formed in Augusta. Courtesy, Maine Historical Society

healthcare. The governor was adamantly against any federal funding for Maine. Defeat of the Pinkham bill, he declared, would return Maine "to the fundamental doctrine that the state is sovereign and will brook no interference in its internal affairs." Mrs. Pinkham's rejoinder: "That sounds almost like a declaration of Civil War. We once had a war to decide the same question of states rights."

FANNIE HARDY ECKSTORM

When Maine women received the vote in 1920, the first head of the town of Brewer's Women's Republican Committee was Mrs. Fannie Hardy

Eckstorm. Previously, she had been the superintendent of schools in her native community. But it was neither as a politician nor an educator that she achieved lasting fame in the Pine Tree State. Her literary talents, portrayed through the nonfiction books of history she wrote, have kept her works and her name alive.

She was born Fannie Pearson Hardy in Brewer, which lies just opposite Bangor on the Penobscot River. Right at the end of the Civil War, the town was then still in a very rural area on the edge of the great Maine North Woods. Her father, Manly Hardy, was a fur trapper and trader, with close ties to the Penobscot Indians. Fannie often traveled with him. From her firsthand experiences, she wrote with deep sensitivity and understanding of the lives of the lumbermen, the woodsmen and the river drivers who created a colorful subculture out of logging, hunting and fishing in those vast forested spaces.

Among these populations were Indians, too, and a group of them lived in Brewer. Their leader, the

Believed to be a photo of Mary Pelagie (1775–1867) or Molly Molasses, as she was known. A Penobscot Indian who grew up just as Maine's wilderness gave way to a booming natural resource economy, Molly had learned the traditional ways of life in her youth: moving seasonally to hunt, learning the old stories and the gift of m'teoulin (magic) that ran in her family. But by adulthood, she faced a different world. Huge stands of timber were disappearing from the forests where she had roamed as a child and Indians were forced into settled lives on reservations. Courtesy, Bangor Public Library

Fannie Hardy Eckstorm (1865–1946) was a noted Maine historian from Brewer. Her father had been a successful fur trader, working closely with the Penobscot Indians. Growing up around Maine Indians led to one of Eckstorm's life-long interests. She published Penobscot Man in 1904 and later wrote, Indian Legends of Mt. Katahdin. She studied Maine cultures and traditions that were giving way to modern life and her work has become part of the foundation of material for modern Maine history. Courtesy, Bangor Public Library

Penobscot Lieutenant Governor John Neptune, exiled from his home on nearby Indian Island because of internal tribal and personal problems, was a dear family friend. Many a night, Neptune and his common-law wife Molly Molasses sat by the Hardy's fireplace and young Fannie listened in wonder to the discussions.

Out of these and other girlhood episodes came Fannie's two most famous books, *Penobscot Man* and *Old John Neptune*. The former immortalized the West Branch of the Penobscot river drive led by John Ross, whose crews of "Bangor Tigers" were universally conceded to be the best such watermen in the nation. The latter detailed the life of a fascinating Indian figure, a crafty politician, trapper and hunter, but also a *m'teoulino*, in the Penobscot language, or shaman, about whom numerous myths were created.

Other Fannie Hardy Eckstorm writings included an extensive essay on Maine game laws and a published collection of Indian place names. There is a wonderful romantic tinge to her writing that has kept this now vanished Maine Woods life vivid, yet factual, and serves as an important resource for Maine historians of the period. One of them wrote "What would we ever do without Fannie?"

EDNA ST. VINCENT MILLAY

Beyond Maine, Fannie Hardy Eckstorm is hardly a household name. Edna St. Vincent Millay, on the other hand, has been considered one of America's major poets. She won the Pulitzer Prize in 1923, ostensibly for her collection of poems *The Ballad of the Harp Weaver*. Her first volume, *Renascence*, had appeared six years earlier in 1917, the same year she graduated from Vassar.

Born in Rockland, she was raised in Camden. Her unusual middle name honored St. Vincent de Paul, a cannonized French priest; to her family, she was always "Vincent." After college, Vincent spent time in Greenwich Village, living a bohemian life—today we would call it hippy—and she was also a member of the avante-garde theater

Pulitzer Prize winner Edna St. Vincent Millay (1892–1950) was born in Rockland and raised in Camden. She published her first volume of poetry, Renascence, *in 1917. Millay was a prolific writer, publishing poetry and plays and working under contract for* Vanity Fair. *In 1923 she became the first woman to win a Pulitzer Prize for poetry. Courtesy, Library of Congress*

group, the Provincetown Players on Cape Cod. One of her best known verses: "My candle burns at both ends/ It will not burn the night; But ah, my foes, and oh, my friends/ It gives a lovely light" reflects the wild, uninhibited style of her 1920s life.

Married in 1923, she and her husband returned to Maine a decade later and bought an island in Casco Bay. It became their summer home to which they returned every year. Although Edna St. Vincent Millay also wrote plays and even an opera libretto, she is best remembered for her lyric poetry, especially her sonnets.

LILLIAN NORDICA

Farmington is a small college town in western Maine and the birthplace of an opera singer who was a world class soprano in her day. Nordica was her stage surname. In Farmington she was plain Lillian Norton, daughter of a musical family, which moved to Boston when she was fourteen. Her early training came at the New England Conservatory of Music and the name change after she had studied in Milan, Italy. "Lily of the North" then made her Italian debut in Mozart's *Don Giovanni*.

Her singing took her all over Europe and to the Metropolitan Opera in New York City, where she was a leading member until 1907. She became especially adept at Wagnerian roles and performed at Richard Wagner's own Bayreuth Festival.

An ardent suffragist, Lillian sang the "Star Spangled Banner" to a 1911 women's rights rally in San Francisco that attracted thousands of participants. Grand diva that she was, with all the trappings of a star like her diamond tiara and private railroad car, she never forgot her plain New England roots. Her last appearance on stage was in 1913 at Melbourne, Australia after which she died in Java, Indonesia of pneumonia contracted on shipboard during her return voyage home.

Farmington has preserved her birthplace as a museum, with displays of her costumes, furnishings, musical scores and mementos.

Lillian Norton (1857–1914) was an American soprano who performed under the name, Madame Nordica. Born in Farmington and billed as the Yankee Diva, she was famous for her Wagnerian roles and for a Coca-Cola advertising campaign that used her likeness. Her life, in many ways, was as tragic as her opera. She married rather unhappily three times and she died unexpectedly at the relatively young age of fifty-six. Courtesy, Library of Congress

8

THE THIRTIES
AND THE FORTIES
(1930-1949)

Maine Governor Carl Milliken is shown here signing an act for women's suffrage into law on August 6, 1920. Efforts for women's voting rights started in the nineteenth century in Maine, but were sidetracked by support of Abolition and Temperance, two campaigns in which Maine women had great influence. Maine's state suffrage law was signed in March of 1919 just before voters ratified the national suffrage act, the Nineteenth Amendment, in November 1919. In an ironic twist, however, suffrage opponents called the Maine law up for referendum. In September 1920 Maine voters—men and women—voted on the meaningless question of whether or not women would have the right to vote in the state. The decision was an 88,080 to 30,642 yes vote. Courtesy, Maine Historical Society

PROHIBITION ENDS

Two decades of great challenges, imposed by the outside world, descended upon Maine at the close of the Roaring Twenties. For the most part, Maine had remained an isolated enclave in the Northeast, away from the shake-up of thinking and living that rocked the nation following the end of World War I. At the advent of the Depression, then World War II and with the global effect of these two international crises, Maine could not continue to escape untouched.

The stock market crash of 1929, the resulting collapse of the American economy and the election of Franklin Delano Roosevelt in 1932 were the preliminary tremors of an earthquake downeast, felt only to a small extent. When FDR had the Prohibition Amendment to the Constitution repealed in order to stimulate more business activity through a revival of the liquor industry, that was a direct blow Maine could experience. Since 1856 the sale and consumption of alcoholic beverages had been banned in the Pine Tree State.

This is not to say that Maine was ever as "dry" as it legally proclaimed itself to be. During the Roaring Twenties, the state's proximity to "wet" Canada made the Maine coastline and large unguarded border an ideal entry point for bootleggers. Aroostook County was a beehive of smuggling activity. Gangs formed in the northernmost French Acadian St. John Valley and shootouts did occur, although none of the crime and violence was anywhere near the scale of Al Capone's Chicago. "Joe Walnut," (the alias of Albenie J. Violette of Van Buren,) seemed to be the "Capone" of the region, rumrunning on both sides of the border and having a network of operations that extended south to the West Indies and north to St. Pierre and Miquelon, islands off the Canadian coast that to this day belong to France.

Maine had become a key transit point for illicit booze after President Calvin Coolidge in 1924 extended U.S. jurisdiction twelve miles out to sea, chasing a "Rum Row" of liquor supply ships

"Prohibition is a howling success" reads this post card. Maine, despite being the birthplace of temperance legislation, had a difficult time policing the consumption of alcohol. With its long international border and coastline, Maine was a notorious inlet for foreign liquor. Smugglers came in from Canada or even smuggled rum up from the West Indies—an industry unto itself that supported importers, merchants and even shipbuilders who built the small, fast boats called rumrunners. Courtesy, Maine Historical Society

Smugglers and bootleggers brought liquor into Maine from Canada all throughout Prohibition, and other entrepreneurial types made their own. Kitchen bars, like this one here run by Marie Cyr in Biddeford around 1930, could be as simple as obtaining some liquor and opening your home for a night of drinking. The "proprietor" would make money from the sale of drinks and food, and someone would probably bring a guitar, fiddle or accordion, making it a real party. It's unlikely that much advertisement was needed. Underground liquor sellers never had trouble selling their wares. Courtesy, Maine Historical Society

away from ports like Boston and New York City and dispatching U.S. Navy destroyers to make sure they didn't return. The complicity of Aroostook officials in the contraband trade was revealed that same year with the arrests in Houlton of Aroostook County Sheriff Edmund W. Grant and County Attorney Herschel Shaw. Nevertheless, the smuggling went on, keeping the Maine State Police and special liquor enforcements officers busier than they had ever been until Repeal.

THE QUODDY DAM

Franklin Delano Roosevelt was almost a Maine summer resident. Unless he reached his family's home on Campobello Island in New Brunswick entirely by water, he had to drive through Maine and across the bridge at Lubec to reach the compound where he had been vacationing since he was a child. He knew the area, the geography and the local people. He was even friendly with some members of the Passamaquoddy Indian tribe at nearby Eastport and particularly the artist Tomah Joseph, who built him a canoe and sold the future president a number of his unique carvings on birch bark.

In 1920 young FDR was a candidate for vice president on the Democratic ticket and during a brief campaign visit downeast, spoke of a visionary project to bring prosperity to that generally poverty-stricken region. It was the vision of the engineer Dexter P. Cooper, who also had a summer home on Campobello and knew the Roosevelts. Cooper had worked on the massive Wilson Dam at Muscle Shoals on the Tennessee River and his concept for Passamaquoddy Bay was even more grandiose. He wanted to tap the energy of the immense tides, which are the highest in the world. For more than a decade, he battled opposition to the project, making slow progress. Then, his summer neighbor became president of the United States, and Cooper went to Washington to see him. The idea fit well with FDR's plans to help the country out of the Depression through government invest-

The Quoddy Dam project was a New Deal program designed to create jobs in Washington County and to harness the tides of Passamaquoddy Bay. Five dams were planned to create electricity from Bay of Fundy tides and work was welcome in the region. Congress appropriated $10 million for the start of the project, though it was never completed. Young men at the National Youth Administration camp at Quoddy are shown here, circa 1933. This program was part of a job training and placement program called The Quoddy Regional Work Experience Project. Hundreds of young men gained practical experience while finishing their education in a quasi-military environment. Courtesy, William David Barry

ment. The Public Works Administration granted a $43 million loan. The Maine state government had changed, too, because of the Depression and now had a Democratic governor, Louis Brann, who was an enthusiastic Quoddy supporter. A State Authority was proposed for the venture and federal work was begun on "Quoddy Village," a housing site for those who were to build the dam project. This advance construction, alone, employed 5,000 workers.

However, the homes were never occupied as intended and the dam never built. The opposition proved too strong. The House Appropriations Committee in D.C. was persuaded to halt all further financing. FDR then seemingly walked away, saying he couldn't take the money out of his work-relief funds. The U.S. Senate followed the House in denying Quoddy money. Dexter Cooper died and, with him, the project until a brief attempt to revive Quoddy was attempted when John F. Kennedy became president. The power of the enormous tides remains unharnessed.

Morning exercises in 1941 at the National Youth Administration Camp at the Quoddy Tides Project. This program was also part of The Quoddy Regional Work Experience Project. Photo by Barbara Wright for the Office of War Information. Courtesy, Library of Congress.

men who visualized development of pride in accomplishment. They got it. The CCC turned boys into men. . . . They paid back then and later the nation's investment in youth."

LABOR UNIONS

Until the validation of the Wagner Act by the U.S. Supreme Court in 1937, American workers had no protected right to organize. Often, the Sherman Anti-Trust Act was used against them, on the grounds that union activity was as much a restraint of trade as the monopolistic practices of trusts. The pre-1937 situation often led to labor violence, even in bucolic Maine.

There had actually been unions in Maine prior to the 1890s. The most unlikely of them was "The Lobster Fishermen's National Protective Association," headquartered on Vinalhaven Island and containing in 1907 more than 1,000 of those cussed, ultra-individualist, macho harvesters of the sea. The American Federation of Labor (AFL), after a shaky start in 1891, reinstated itself in 1904, trying to penetrate the textile mills and factories that had become prevalent in some Maine cities. Shoe factories, called "shoe shops," also began to play a prominent role in Maine's economy as the twentieth century advanced.

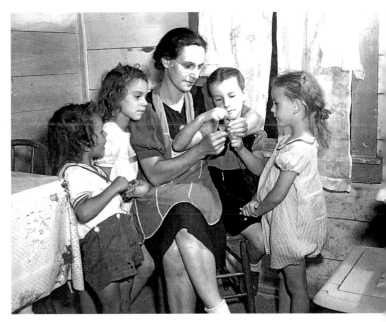

Young girls in the Edward Daigle family of Fort Kent learning to knit in 1942. This photo is part of a series on the United States as it mobilized for war taken by photographer John Collier for the Office of War Information, which had absorbed the earlier Farm Security Administration. Courtesy, Library of Congress

The Lewiston-Auburn area was one of the largest shoe manufacturing centers in the country after the Civil War, sparking a statewide industry that lasted into the late twentieth century. Even before that, the shoe industry was the largest in Maine. One historian found 3,500 people listed as shoemakers in the 1850 census, not counting people who did piece-work in their homes or worked part-time. By 1860 the number of people employed in shoe factories was second only to the textile industry. Men are shown working in an unnamed factory in Lewiston or Auburn in 1916. Courtesy, Lewiston Public Library

In March 1937 a dispute within the Maine AFL led to the most massive and violent strike the state had witnessed. The Textile Workers Union left the AFL and joined the newly forming, far more aggressive Congress of Industrial Organizations (CIO), and the emboldened CIO pushed its organizing effort within nineteen shoe factories in the Lewiston-Auburn area. The owners adamantly refused to negotiate. A strike was called. An estimated 4,500 of 6,400 workers went out.

All over the country that year, people were striking. Throughout New England, thousands of workers were putting down their tools. Chrysler and General Motors were affected in the Midwest. There was labor violence in Kansas. Not far from Lewiston-Auburn, at Hathaway Shirt in Waterville, a strike was brewing.

Maine workers no longer had a sympathetic ear in state government. Democrat Louis Brann had been replaced by Republican Lewis Barrow. Picketers were arrested. The State Supreme Court through one of its Justices issued an injunction against the Lewiston-Auburn strikers, ordering them to stay 500 feet from factory entrances.

When the same Supreme Court Justice then issued an injunction against the strike, itself, the union leaders defied him. They called a mass meeting in Lewiston, after which 1,000 angry workers marched toward the twin city of Auburn. At the bridge over the Androscoggin River separating the two communities, they were met by state troopers and Auburn police, wielding billy clubs and firing tear gas. The union members flung back rocks. Injuries occurred on both sides. Governor Barrow called out the National Guard. Steel helmeted troops, bayonets fixed, enforced an uneasy peace.

Had it not been for the U.S. Supreme Court's decision on the Wagner Act, violence might have erupted again in Lewiston-Auburn with far more dire results. This legislation, which required employers to allow union elections, supervised by a National Labor Relations Board, saved the day. The workers, at least under federal law, could have a union if a majority of them voted to do so.

Madison native Louis J. Brann was elected governor in 1931, cheered on by boxing hero, Jack Dempsey, who appeared in Maine on his behalf during the campaign. Brann spent most of his professional life in public service, first as mayor of Lewiston in 1925 and then as Governor of Maine from 1933–1937. Courtesy, Maine Historical Society

MADAME SECRETARY FRANCES PERKINS

The U.S. secretary of labor in the 1930s, in charge of implementing the National Labor Relations Act, had strong Maine ties. Much of the early life of Frances Perkins was spent at her grandmother's home in Newcastle, Maine, and her parents both were natives of the Pine Tree State. Her grave is in the family plot at Newcastle and bears the simple headstone engraving:

FRANCES PERKINS WILSON, 1880–1965
SECRETARY OF LABOR OF USA, 1933–1945

Left out, first of all, is the historic fact that before Frances Perkins, who always went by her maiden name, no woman had ever headed a department of the U.S. federal government and served in a president's cabinet. She was a ground-breaker in many ways, starting in New York State when Governor Al Smith employed her on the New York State Industrial Commission. Here, she met Franklin Roosevelt, who appointed and reappointed her as chair of that commission. When president, he selected her to run the Department of Labor. Offered that job by FDR, she initially turned it down, not on the grounds that she would be a pioneer female in the federal bureaucracy, but that she wasn't from organized labor. The famously persuasive FDR could not convince her to accept. However, the advice she remembered from her Maine grandmother could. Cynthia Otis Perkins advised her granddaughter: "If anybody opens a door, one should go through it."

Frances Perkins always credited this "extremely wise woman" from Newcastle with continually inspiring her in her career. In a biography of Perkins, she is quoted, explaining, "Scarcely a week goes by that I don't find myself saying: 'As my grandmother used to say,' and then repeating something that has been a guiding principle all of my life."

Perkins not only implemented some of the New Deal's most revolutionary legislation; she also helped draft such measures as the National Labor Relations Act, the Walsh-Healy Government Contracts Act and the Fair Labor Standards Act. The blockbuster among all these new laws was the Social Security Act and it was to Secretary Perkins that FDR entrusted the awesome responsibility of masterminding that effort.

In 1945, the year FDR died, Frances Perkins resigned her position in the Labor Department. President Harry Truman convinced her to stay in government for almost another decade by making her a member of the Civil Service Commission.

At age seventy-seven she went to Ithaca, New York to teach at Cornell. There, her Maine roots resurfaced. In addition to the intellectual talents she brought with her, she is still remembered "high above Cayuga's waters," for the lobster dinners she used to give.

CREATIVE ARTISTS OF THE PERIOD

JOHN FORD

It may seem a stretch of imagination to link John Wayne and Hollywood Westerns to Maine, but the tie exists. The famous motion picture director John Ford was born in Maine and played football for Portland High School before heading to California and building his career as one of the greatest movie-makers of all time.

He did not begin life as John Ford. One of thirteen children of Irish immigrants, he grew up on Munjoy Hill, a section of Maine's biggest city where those Gaelic newcomers had congregated. By some accounts, he was Sean Aloysius O'Feeney; by others, John Martin Feeney; in any case nicknamed "Bull," for his ferocious toughness on the gridiron, playing sixty minutes two ways: as a defensive tackle and running back.

Sean Aloysius O'Feeney or John Martin Feeney as a name didn't quite fit in Hollywood, so he became John Ford, just as his protégé John Wayne, a football star, himself, at the University of Southern California, changed his name from Marion Morrison. Ford's first fame in Hollywood did not come from a Western. It was a 1935 Academy Award for *The Informer*, starring Victor McLaglen, a film set in the Irish rebellion against the British. Another Oscar came in 1940 for *The Grapes of Wrath* and yet another in 1941 for *How Green Was My Valley*. Ironically, his only Oscar for a John Wayne movie was *The Quiet Man*, 1952, not a Western, either. The picture in which Ford first directed John Wayne in a starring role, *Stagecoach*, called by many the greatest Western ever made, did not win the 1939 Academy Award for Best Picture because *Gone With the Wind* eclipsed it.

Ford served in both World War I and in World War II. He put his directorial talents to work for the U.S. Navy, making battle films. Two of these also won him Oscars, *Battle of Midway* and *December Seventh* a documentary short film. He retired from active service as a rear admiral.

Success in Hollywood never allowed him to forget his native state, particularly its veterans. Even before Pearl Harbor, he donated money to an American Legion Post on Peaks Island, a part of Portland where he had been a theater usher in his youth. In 1948 a VFW post in Portland gave Ford and his wife lifetime memberships.

This renowned son of the Forest City is now remembered by a statue at a large intersection of five streets known as Gorham's Corner, which was the traditional heart of the Irish community in Portland. It shows him in his director's chair, surrounded by stone blocks, bearing the names of his prize-winning films.

John Ford (1895–1973) was born in Portland as Sean O'Feeney. He graduated from Portland High School, attended the University of Maine briefly and went on to direct many major films including, The Quiet Man, How Green Was My Valley *and* The Grapes of Wrath. *Courtesy, Maine Historical Society*

KENNETH ROBERTS

One adventure movie in the 1930s that John Ford didn't direct was *Northwest Passage*, starring Spencer Tracy. It was a story of the French and Indian Wars taken from the best-selling historical novel by the Maine-born writer Kenneth Roberts. Of the numerous books of this genre penned by Roberts, three were turned into motion pictures. Most of his inspiration came from incidents in Maine's history, especially that of the Kennebunk area,

where he had grown up and returned permanently to live in 1938.

While he was away, Kenneth Roberts worked as a reporter and regular correspondent for the *Saturday Evening Post*. The skills he honed as an investigative researcher were then directed to fiction. His first historical novel, *Arundel*, was published in 1930, to immediate acclaim. The opening volume of a trilogy, it told the story of Benedict Arnold's ill-fated expedition through Maine to capture Quebec City during the Revolution. *Northwest Passage*, the book often considered his masterpiece, dealt with an earlier expedition, the commando-like raid by Roger's Rangers on the Indian encampment at St. Francis in Canada in the 1750s.

Roberts strongly believed that history was "most effectively told in the form of fiction." His works were meticulously correct in their use of historical facts; they often appeared on nonfiction lists.

He was also an early Maine environmentalist, albeit with a touch of snobbery. Billboards were a *bete-noir* for him. He wanted them banned in the state, which they now are. Likewise, he heaped praise on the York Harbor "rusticators" when they established Maine's first zoning law to keep a trailer park from expanding into their midst and averting, as Roberts put it, the "danger of being almost completely swamped by young ladies in shorts, young men in soiled undershirts and fat ladies in knickerbockers. . ."

For his literary accomplishments, Kenneth Roberts was recognized with a special Pulitzer Prize citation in 1951, shortly before his death.

MOLLY SPOTTED ELK

In the late spring of 1940, a Penobscot Indian woman from Maine was in the small city of Royan in southwestern France, north of Bordeaux. The Nazi occupation had just begun. Molly Dellis Nelson, dancer and movie actress, married to a Frenchman, wrote in her diary: "Everywhere there are Germans. . .There remains only one thing for me: to go home."

Born Marie Alice Nelson at Indian Island on the Penobscot River, she had always been known by the way her people pronounced the first two names—Molly Dellis. Her marriage had added a surname of Archimbaud and her six year old daughter in 1940 had been given the same *prenom* as her father: Jean. With the northern part of France overrun after the surrender to Hitler, Molly's husband, a scoutmaster and former Paris journalist had fled south into the Vichy territory the Germans had let remain as a free

puppet state.

Molly soon took little Jean and fled in the same direction. She and her child crossed the Pyrenees and reached Spain, then Portugal, before traveling to the still-neutral U.S. Her trek through the Pyrenees had a certain irony. She and her husband had long planned to write a novel about another Maine Indian woman, Molly Mathilde, daughter of the Penobscot chief Madockawando, married to an eighteenth century Frenchman, the Baron de St. Castin. His family's property and heritage had been in these same Pyrenees, near the city of Pau, where Jean Archimbaud was to seek refuge before his death from a heart attack in 1941.

Molly had initially gone to Paris a decade earlier with the United States Indian Band, to perform at the 1931 Colonial Exposition. She was billed as "Princess Spotted Elk." Her previous professional life included a stint as a featured dancer in one of the famed Texas Guinan's speakeasy nightclubs in New York City and then a starring role in the movie *The Silent Enemy*, which was a fictionalized portrayal of the Ojibwa tribe, shot in the Canadian north.

Prior to her "show biz" career, Molly had briefly dabbled in some anthropological work at the University of Pennsylvania, thanks to Professor Frank Speck, the noted authority on the Penobscots. There, her roommate was a Mohegan Indian girl from Connecticut, Gladys Tanta-quidgeon. Despite both being Americans, the two women had to live at International House, an illustration of how Native Americans were then regarded as foreigners. In 1937 Gladys Tanta-quidgeon, working for the Federal Bureau of Indian Affairs, visited Maine and reported on the Passamaquoddy and Penobscot tribes for her superiors.

Remaining in France after the Colonial Exposition ended, Molly Spotted Elk benefited from the French fascination with American "exotics," such as that for the African American dancer, Josephine Baker. Despite the general French tolerance on racial matters, Molly's marriage to Jean Archimbaud was not appreciated by his family. Pregnant, Molly went back to Indian Island to have her child, but shortly before World War II, she returned with her daughter to her husband. Their separation in 1940 was unhappily permanent. The love story they were writing of the Baron de St. Castin and Molly Mathilde had been promised publication by a French company, only to have the war intervene. Their own story, somewhat parallel to the eighteenth century romance, was finally told in 1995 by writer-anthropologist Bunny McBride in "Molly Spotted Elk, A Penobscot in Paris."

MARSDEN HARTLEY

Maine has always been a magnet for painters. Although classed as a member of the Hudson River School, Frederick Church received as much inspiration from Maine scenes as he did from the natural beauty of New York State. His depictions of Mount Katahdin and Mount Desert helped spur tourism in Maine. Winslow Homer, a born Bostonian, settled at Prouts Neck in Scarborough, where he painted most of the watercolors and oils that have made him one of America's most renowned artists. In the 1930s, N.C. Wyeth, illustrator extraordinaire, moved to mid-coast Maine and started a dynasty of world-class artists—his son Andrew and his grandson Jamie, with the family's strong connection to the Knox County area around the small town of Cushing.

In 1939 a Maine-born artist, after studying, painting and exhibiting in Europe, returned to the U.S. and settled in another small Maine coastal town, Corea. Marsden Hartley, a Lewiston native, had actually worked in a local "shoe shop" before going to Cleveland to live with a sister and attend the Cleveland School of Art on a scholarship. Summers, he returned to Maine.

His cubism-influenced work originally received a better reception in Europe than in the U.S. For thirty years, he spent most of his time abroad. During the 1930s, he had shows in Berlin, London, Paris, Dresden, Vienna and Munich.

A year after his final return to Maine, he gained

Newell Convers Wyeth (1882–1945), known as N. C. Wyeth, was the first in a multi-generational family of Maine artists that included Andrew Wyeth and Jamie Wyeth. A noted illustrator, Wyeth's work appeared in a number of magazines and books. He illustrated several classic books, most notably, Treasure Island, Last of the Mohicans *and* Robinson Crusoe. *Courtesy, Library of Congress*

more American recognition by winning the J. Henry Scheidt Memorial Prize from the Pennsylvania Academy of Arts for *End of the Hurricane, Lane's Island, Maine*. Poetry was another of his interests and a book of 500 of his poems was published after his death in Ellsworth, Maine in September 1943.

Dow Air Field, formerly Dow Air Force Base, in Bangor was named for James Frederick Dow of Oakfield. Dow was killed in a training flight in 1940 at Mitchell Field in New York. Dow Field was in operation from 1940 to 1968, closing briefly after World War II and reopening for the Korean War. Courtesy, Bangor Public Library

Also after his death came a greater appreciation of his art. In 1944 the Museum of Modern Art in New York City held an exhibition of his works. Five American museums, including Portland's museum, hung his works in the 1960s; once they had toured Europe. By the 1970s his pictures were in constant demand on both sides of the Atlantic. A major Marsden Hartley retrospective was held in New York City's Whitney Museum in 1980. "He is best known for his paintings of Maine people and scenery," states one of his encyclopedia biographies.

WORLD WAR II

Like a storm, World War II swept across Maine, concentrating the energies of its people for nearly half the decade of the 1940s. As in some previous conflicts, Maine was forced to think of its own security, as well as adding to the nation's war effort. The long Maine coast was perceived as vulnerable to infiltration and the state's shipping and fishing industries seen as a possible prey for German U-boats. These latter, on occasion, could be glimpsed in battle with Allied vessels from the Maine shore, which was dotted with hastily constructed observation bunkers. Despite the best efforts of the defense unit watchers, two German spies did manage to land in November 1944 at Hancock Point from a U-boat that snuck undetected through Frenchman's Bay. However, a local high school student, driving home from a Saturday night dance spotted what he thought was a suspicious-looking pair. The Hancock County Sheriff was alerted and he called the FBI. Kept under surveillance, these would-be saboteurs were tracked to New York City, where the U.S. authorities apprehended them.

Maine's geography gave it a strategic importance. The Pine Tree State was the closest American soil to Europe. Two major airfields were rushed into operation downeast. One was at Presque Isle in Aroostook County, where a former fairground was converted to a major Air Force facility and the other was Dow Field at Bangor, which became a central transit point for aircraft flying to the European Theatre. At Brunswick, a Naval Air Station, still in existence, was created to search the surrounding waters for enemy subs. Even before the U.S. entered the War, Portland Harbor had been fortified under President Franklin Roosevelt's "preparedness" program. Parts of Casco Bay were ringed with anti-aircraft batteries, sealed-off by anti-submarine nets and provided with a huge fuel depot and barracks on several of its islands. When FDR, in August 1941, left to meet Winston Churchill at sea off New-

In 1932 Bath Iron Works began to build destroyers again after a fourteen-year hiatus. The company quickly geared up for war and grew to employ 12,000 men and women for the duration. The shipyard turned out vessels at an amazing rate of one nearly every seventeen days, and launched a record eight ships on August 16, 1942. Painting by Carroll Thayer Berry, 1943. Courtesy, Maine Historical Society

Opposite page
A Civil Air Patrol (CAP) crew is shown during morning calisthenics in June 1943. The CAP had two air bases in Maine during World War II: the one shown here, located in Trenton in Hancock County, and the other in Portland. CAP was founded in 1941 to defend American coastline during World War II, and now serves as civilian auxiliary to the U.S. Air Force. Photo by John Collier for the Office of War Information. Courtesy, Library of Congress

During World War II women served prominently in civil defense efforts in their home communities. The Federal Civilian Defense Agency relied on women to participate in and spread the word about civil defense practices, but most often utilized them in traditional ways that stressed their homemaking and nurturing skills. Women also became block wardens to manage home security in their neighborhoods or air raid wardens using binoculars to scan the skies for enemy planes. Courtesy, Bethel Historical Society

foundland to sign the Atlantic Charter, he sailed from Portland on a U.S. Navy vessel.

Before December 7, 1941, too, other elements of the "preparedness" effort had been underway in Maine. The Bath Iron Works (BIW), started by Civil War general Thomas Hyde in the 1880s to build ships, had already doubled its work force by the summer of 1941. Constructing destroyers, the company would triple its number of employees to more than 12,000 prior to the end of World War II.

Its first destroyers were on the small side—1,630 tons. Soon, Bath was making ships of more than 2,000 tons. The *Nicholas*, the prototype for this class, fought for thirty-three months in the Pacific and helped escort the battleship *Missouri* into Tokyo Bay to receive the Japanese surrender in 1945.

The size of the Bath-built destroyers continued to grow during the War—2,200 tons next and then 2,250. Of the former, one was named the *O'Brien* after Maine hero Jeremiah O'Brien, from the Revolutionary War naval battle off Machias. Among the latter was the *Frank Knox*, honoring FDR's Republican secretary of the navy, who had died in 1944.

At its home base in Bath, itself, BIW built eighty-three destroyers, plus four cargo vessels and a private yacht that was turned over to the Navy. Further activity went on in South Portland, where the company had teamed up with the Todd Shipyard of California, initially to build freighters for the British merchant marine, starting in 1940, and then American "Liberty" ships. At the twin yards they established, thirty vessels were built for the British and 244 for the U.S. Ten percent of all the Liberty ships used to transport supplies for the Allied forces were the product of these Maine facilities.

When it came to building submarines, Maine was also a major producer. Between 1939 and 1945, eighty-five of the undersea craft rolled off the ways at the Kittery-located shipyard that bears the official name of the Portsmouth (New Hampshire) Naval Shipyard. Why that official name exists, when the facility has been determined by the courts to be in Maine, is allegedly the result of a promise President Chester A. Arthur made to a Republican Women's Club in the New Hampshire city. The Treaty of Portsmouth, brokered by President Theodore Roosevelt in 1905, ending the Russo-Japanese War, was signed in Building 86 on the shipyard's grounds, so it could logically be called the Treaty of Kittery.

At its wartime peak, the Kittery yard employed more than 20,000 workers. Half the American subs built during the war were designed there. A record was reached on July 27, 1944 when four subs were launched on the same day. The massive Naval Prison at Kittery, where Spanish sailors and officers had been held at the time of the Spanish-American War, received the crews of German U-Boats, once they surrendered after V-E Day.

These were not the only German prisoners interned in Maine. Numbers of them, particularly from the Afrika Korps, were brought to northern Maine and put to work, cutting pulp for the paper companies and harvesting potatoes in the agricultural areas. The story is told of the camp at Houlton in potato country where the local authorities, in order to make their jobs easier, warned the Germans that the nearby woods were full of "wild Indians" who would scalp them if they tried to escape. Some of the American captors, stripped to the waist and wearing headdresses, actually paraded at the forested edges of the fields in constant sight of the prisoners. The ploy seemed to have worked, for few if any escapes were recorded.

Elsewhere, though, a German prison camp was actually located next to the Indian Township reservation of the Passamaquoddy tribe. Here, the problem was not so much escape as fraternization between these young Germans and Native American women. At least one little Passamaquoddy was born and bore his father's surname of Ritter.

By V.J. Day, the seeds of change had been planted in Maine by three and a half years of warfare. As Maine people wildly celebrated the ultimate end of hostilities, they probably weren't thinking of the postwar challenges. They were

Pictured are ships under construction at the East Yard of the New England Shipbuilding Corporation in February 1943. The company was started by Bath Iron Works and the Todd Shipbuilding Company to make Liberty ships for World War II. The company employed over 30,000 workers at the height of World War II and made 266 ships. Courtesy, Library of Congress

simply enjoying a great victory "pahty" in nice August weather. On Vinalhaven Island, a dynamite blast set off by celebrants broke over 100 windows and in the town of Paris, a ninety-six year-old man celebrated the way his family had on the Fourth of July since 1776. Old Percival Parris shot off the Revolutionary War musket that one of his ancestors had carried into battle.

Even then some of Maine's leaders, at least, were looking ahead. The very day in August 1945 in which the atomic bomb was dropped on Hiroshima, Governor Horace Hildreth, mindful that the War might end soon, was conducting a discussion of what to do about the state's 15,000 veterans. Three thousand of them had already come home. In conjunction with this future planning, he had received the positive news from Congresswoman Margaret Chase Smith that Bangor's Dow Field would remain active regardless. Little did the wealthy "Establishment" Republican chief executive imagine that within three years, he would be facing off in an election with that same female.

MARGARET CHASE SMITH

If anyone in Maine public life signaled that the tried-and-true ways of operating in Maine might not go on as they had, it was this former telephone operator from Skowhegan who had been in the House in Congress since 1940. That year her congressman husband Clyde Smith died of a heart attack, and she was elected to take his place. For a Republican, Clyde Smith was unusually liberal, staunchly pro-labor and a champion of shorter working hours and workers' compensation. He had been on the Labor Committee, but Margaret was not allowed to have the same assignment. Her first choice for committee was Naval Affairs, on which no woman had ever served, so to mask her ambition, she put it down as her second choice—after Appropriations. The GOP leaders were glad to dispense a second choice. The reputation she earned as a military and defense expert stood her in good stead after the war when she decided to try to move to the U.S. Senate in 1948.

Since Maine was solidly Republican in the late 1940s as it had been almost uninterruptedly since 1856, Congresswoman Smith's major problem was winning the Republican primary. Her three opponents were men, two of them formidable politicians—ex-Governor Horace Hildreth and Sumner Sewall, who had been an earlier governor. "Dirty tricks" in the form of vicious rumors surfaced in the campaign. One rumor stated she had broken up Clyde Smith's first marriage, although his divorce had happened seventeen years before they were married. Another was that she had a fatal disease and only wanted to hold the seat so Governor Burton Cross could have it when his term in Augusta ended. To try to get the anti-Franco vote, a third rumor was spread that

Chase wasn't her real name, but the French Chasse. The patent absurdity of such tactics combined with her straight-forward, independent manner and considerable charm led to an overwhelming victory. Margaret Chase Smith's 63,876 votes were more than those of her three opponents combined. Running against a Democrat in the fall, she took 71 percent of the vote.

Clearly change was in the air downeast.

Margaret Chase Smith (1897–1995) won election to the House of Representatives in 1940, taking her deceased husband's seat. She was elected to the United States Senate in 1948. Her long and distinguished career includes the Presidential Medal of Freedom, being the only woman to chair the Senate Republican Conference and most famously, her Declaration of Conscience speech in 1950 that challenged Senator Joseph McCarthy's and his heavy-handed anti-Communist campaign. In 1960 Democrat Lucia Cormier of Rumford challenged Smith, and they made history as the first time two women ran against one another for a seat in the United States Senate. Smith easily defeated her opponent. Courtesy, Maine Historical Society

9
MAINE A-STIR
(1950-1980)

Maine's Congressional Delegation in the early 1960s. From left to right: Stanley Tupper, Republican from Boothbay Harbor; Edmund Muskie, Democrat from Rumford; Margaret Chase Smith, Republican from Skowhegan and Clifford McIntire, Republican from Perham. Courtesy, Margaret Chase Smith Library

EDMUND S. MUSKIE

The year was 1954 and as Maine prepared for another gubernatorial election, the Republican hegemony in the state seemed assured. Although Margaret Chase Smith had broken the GOP's male hegemony six years before, no one foresaw any drop in the Republicans' overall mastery. Their preponderance in the 1952 Legislature had been overwhelming: 127 R's to 24 D's in the House and 33 R's to 2 D's in the State Senate—far above two-thirds in both bodies. There had not been a Democratic governor since the start of the Depression, more than twenty years earlier. Running in 1954 was the Minority Leader of those woefully outnumbered Democrats in the House, a fairly obscure lawyer from Waterville named Edmund S. Muskie. His opponent was the incumbent governor, Burton Cross.

Even Ed Muskie, himself, and the coterie of young Democrats now leading the ultra-minority party considered the race unwinnable. It was to be a warm-up for their efforts two years hence. Most likely the seat would be vacated because there was a tradition in Maine of no third terms for chief executives.

Since 1856 the few times the Democrats had won the governorship, the main reason had been splits in the Republican ranks. But as soon as the GOP came together again for the next election, the Democrats would be doomed. A split did occur in 1954. A bitter primary had been fought two years previously. One of the men beaten by Burton Cross—a Stockton Springs farmer named Neal Bishop—now openly supported Muskie.

However, much more than a party quarrel was at work. Maine, indeed, was a-stir, the change fueled by World War II, the veterans who had returned and a growing sense of stagnation in the State's public life and its total domination by one party.

Also, television was now available and the candidates could be seen by many more of the voters. Tall, Lincolnesque in looks, young, dynamic, different, Ed Muskie caught on. It seemed not to

matter any longer that he did not fit the Maine mold ethnically. Born in the paper mill town of Rumford, he was the son of Polish Catholic immigrants, his surnamed anglicized from Marciszewski. Yet he had worked himself up in the best American tradition, gone to Bates College, established himself as a lawyer, been elected to the Maine House from Waterville. Moreover, he was a fine, powerful speaker, his stentorian tones tinged by a faint but unmistakable Maine accent. Though it might have been unexpected, his victory sent up a signal that Maine would never be the same again, at least not politically. For the next four years—gubernatorial terms were then two years, and he was reelected—Ed Muskie had to use all of

Bates College in Lewiston was founded in 1855 by Oren Cheney as the first coeducational college in New England. The institution takes its name from Benjamin Bates who provided the funds necessary to open the school. George French Collection. Courtesy, Maine State Archives

his charm and political skills in dealing with a powerful Republican opposition. Republicans not only controlled the legislature with enough strength to override any vetoes, but they also had the Governor's Executive Council, which could block any of Muskie's appointments.

His astute politicking with the Republican leaders enabled him to build a record of accomplishment that included the creation of a Department of Economic Development, a Maine Industrial Building Authority, a four-year term for governor and the passage of highway and education bonds. This was a big step forward for a state accustomed to stand-pat administrations. As a result, Muskie had a respectable platform from which to run when he decided to try for the U.S. Senate in 1958.

His win in that election by an impressive 61,000 votes was helped the fact that his opponent, ex-Governor Frederick Payne was implicated in several scandals. A more important contribution to Muskie's win was a stealth buildup of Democratic strength in the Pine Tree State. Not only did Muskie triumph, but the Democratic candidate to succeed him as governor was victorious. The Democrats took two Congressional seats and increased their 1952 representation six-fold in the State Senate and more than double in the House.

Ed Muskie joined Margaret Chase Smith in Washington, D.C. as a colleague, and both politicians were to achieve widespread national fame.

MAJOR PROJECTS

One important change Ed Muskie initiated in Maine was the official attitude toward the environment. Later, he earned the title "Mr. Clean" for his efforts in that regard in Washington. In his two terms as governor, he worked hard to deal with the pollution in Maine's rivers—some of the most polluted in the country—and it was left to future chief executives and legislatures to finish this pioneering work of water protection. There were ups and downs in the fight, but never again in Maine would the environment be ignored.

In January 26, 1970 Newsweek *magazine named the Androscoggin River as one of the ten dirtiest rivers in the nation, as pictured in this photo taken by the Environmental Protection Agency in June of 1973. This image shows waste discharged into the River by the International Paper Company at Jay. Maine's Edmund Muskie was a major force behind the Clean Water Act in 1972 and since that time, industries along the Androscoggin and elsewhere within the State of Maine have made great strides in cleaning up the water. Fish and other wildlife are rebounding and the Androscoggin had dropped to number forty-three on the list of polluted rivers in the nation. Courtesy, National Archives*

THE ALLAGASH

Earlier in Maine history it would have been unthinkable to make a public fuss about preserving the wilderness condition of a river and its woodland surroundings. The Allagash, a tributary of the much bigger St. John, had in fact already been tampered with during the nineteenth century logging days. Its direction had been changed and its flow directed into the Penobscot. Otherwise, it was still a wild body of water and a favorite location for extended canoe trips away from the sight and sound of civilization.

One of the canoeist's was U.S. Supreme Court Justice William O. Douglas. In November 1960 he wrote to Percival Baxter, asking if the Allagash waterway could possibly be made a part of Baxter State Park. Douglas was worried about rumors that the area was to be made into a national park, and he feared its character would be changed unless the State took control.

From that suggestion, plans developed for a separate state protective entity, given impetus by a report from the newly-formed, private, nonprofit Natural Resources Council of Maine. Momentum for the idea increased when, in 1964, the Democrats captured both bodies of the Maine Legislature, thanks to Lyndon Johnson's landslide victory over Barry Goldwater. Paradoxically, the primary opposition to saving the Allagash came at this juncture from a group proposing "public power" for northern Maine. They had plans to build the huge Cross Rocks dam on the St. John, which would flood a large area including most of the proposed wilderness waterway. Many Democrats in Aroostook and other northern counties were for public power. Then, an ingenious counter-argument developed. If it looked like Cross Rocks might go through, the Federal government would take the Allagash area by eminent domain to save it and no one wanted the Feds around. In the end, Cross Rocks was rejected. At the very last session of the Democratic 102nd Legislature, a $3 million bond issue was passed to create the state-owned Allagash Wilderness Waterway. Canoe trips continue on its pristine although sometimes crowded waters to this day.

Ripogenus Dam forms Chesuncook Lake, part of the Allagash area, now Maine's third largest lake after Moosehead and Sebago. The dam is shown here in 1905. This wooden dam is now under water. Fishing enthusiasts flock to the area for some of the best salmon fishing in Maine. Collections of Maine Historical Society

DICKEY-LINCOLN

Senator John F. Kennedy is shown here campaigning for president in Portland in 1960. He gave a press conference at WGAN in Portland on September 2, where he spoke about Russian leader Nikita Khrushchev, the revival of the Passamaquoddy Project and trade protection for New England Industries. He praised Maine Senator Edmund Muskie and talked about Atomic Power as a way to clean up the nation's polluted rivers. Courtesy, Library of Congress

For a while, another proposal to build a massive dam on the St. John River was called "a conservationist's dam." This was the Dickey-Lincoln project, named in part for a much-revered Democratic politician of the nineteenth century from nearby Fort Kent, William Dickey, and an adjacent location on the stream bank where a Lincoln School had been in existence. The conservation aspect of this huge public works development grew out of the fact that it would not flood the Allagash. Since it was also to produce "public power" under the control of the Federal government, Maine Democratic supporters of Cross Rocks transfered their allegiance to it.

The origin of Dickey-Lincoln lay in the election of John F. Kennedy in 1960. With prodding from northern Maine Democrats to help bring industry to an impoverished "downeast," the idea of reviving the long moribund Quoddy power project was raised. But experts decreed that the tidal dam could not economically stand alone and so a new scheme emerged: Quoddy would be tied in with a dam at the Dickey-Lincoln site on the St. John and together they would produce enough base and peaking power to attract industries to northernmost and easternmost Maine.

Initially, the plan had a bipartisan approach. Maine's two U.S. senators, Margaret Chase Smith and Edmund S. Muskie provided enthusiastic support in D.C. cost-benefit studies deemed that Quoddy, no matter how it was linked, would cost more than the value of the power generated. Therefore, the tidal phase ceased, while Dickey-Lincoln proceeded. For more than twenty years, the fight was waged in Congress. Planning funds were voted, then rescinded, then re-allocated. As early as 1965, the House of Representatives voted against any Dickey funding. A compromise a month later allotted $800,000. Dickey was declared dead in 1967 and alive again in 1969. In 1971 President Richard Nixon dropped Dickey from his budget. Two years later, Republican Congressman William Cohen urged Nixon to reconsider. Maine's new governor, the maverick Independent James Longley, pushed for Dickey-Lincoln in 1975. A year later, Miss Furbish's rare lousewort plant was re-discovered, providing another reason to kill the project. Before the decade was out, both Governor Longley and Congressman Cohen joined the opposition. Only in the 1980s was the last little bit of life was squeezed out of this once popular so-called panacea for an industrialized northern Maine.

Regalo and State of Maine brand potatoes for sale in the 1940s. George French Collection. Courtesy, Maine State Archives

SUGAR BEETS

A far quicker death was dealt to another "magic bullet" notion for dealing with Maine's north country, especially Aroostook County. In this case, it was actually put into effect and proved not to be feasible—at least in the manner in which it was carried out.

Potatoes had been the economic lifeblood of Aroostook County since the early nineteenth century. However, the reliance on a single crop—prey to marketing conditions beyond the control of anyone in Maine—had created a situation of feast or famine. The farmers in "The County," as the locals call it, either prospered or starved, depending on prices; the cry for a second crop had grown ever louder over the years. John H. Reed, an Aroostook potato farmer, himself, was governor when a New Jersey entrepreneur, Fred Vahlsing, offered to start a sugar beet operation. Vahlsing already had plants processing potatoes in Aroostook. Now, he proposed to build a $14.5 million sugar refinery and the creation of a fresh business opportunity in Maine's far north.

In 1980 workers dismantled the unsuccessful sugar beet refinery that was supposed to have become the lifeblood of the Aroostook County economy. The venture failed and the multi-million dollar factory in Easton was auctioned at an equipment sale. Courtesy, Maine Historical Society

The politicians were supportive. In Washington, U.S. Senators Smith and Muskie procured an allotment through Congress for Maine's right to plant 33,000 acres in sugar beets. The Augusta side was taken care of by Republican Governor Reed and the Democratically-controlled 102nd Legislature. The situation became a bit more dicey when Vahlsing insisted he would have to pollute a small body of water, the Prestile Stream, to get his sugar refinery up and running.

The debate in the State Capitol was acrimonious. Finally, Vahlsing won out. The water classification of the Prestile Stream was lowered from B to D. Basically, this classification turned the stream into an open sewer.

The Vahlsing refinery was built, covered by loan guarantees from the state and the federal government. More than 20,000 acres of beets were planted. This major experiment in large-scale agriculture seemed to be on its way to success.

Then everything fell apart.

Citizens in neighboring New Brunswick dammed the Prestile Stream and drew international attention to its horrendously smelly waters. Worse still, "Freddie" Vahlsing stopped paying the Aroostook farmers for the sugar beets they brought him. Subsequently, few were planted. The refinery went bankrupt, with the State of Maine mostly left responsible for the default. The press and politicians indulged in an orgy of finger-pointing. Sugar-making never became a Maine industry.

OIL REFINERIES

"Non-trend development" was a favorite term used by Maine's Democratic governor, Kenneth M. Curtis, who came into office in 1966 at the age of thirty-five. He was non-trend himself: the youngest governor in the country at the time, a progressive in the Kennedy mold and a strong proponent of shaking up Maine's economy with large scale projects that did not fit the traditional downeast pattern. Oil refineries on the beautiful Maine coast were unmistakably non-trend. Existing federal law accounted for the opportunity. To Americans today, it may be unthinkable that the U.S. did not always import oil, or, rather, that companies could not import oil unless they held a federal permit. Some oil companies had these lucrative contracts; others did not. Occidental Oil, owned by famed entrepreneur Armand Hammer, wanted to import oil from Libya. Occidental and the Curtis administration struck a deal whereby a free trade zone would be set up at Machiasport and a refinery built there to receive the product from giant tankers taking advantage of deep water close to the shore in this easternmost section of the Maine coast. Once the announcement was made, fierce opposition developed—from oil companies with import permits, to environmentalists, summer residents and fishermen. The latter were aghast at the idea of a major oil facility and the threat of pollution it posed to the entire Gulf of Maine.

The battle was not as protracted as that involving Dickey-Lincoln, but, if anything, even more furious. Before it was over, other oil projects were brought forward for the area, including one by Atlantic Richfield and several more for other parts of Maine. All came to naught. The concept of oil and the Maine coast was simply frightening, in spite of the fact that Portland was then, and still is, the second largest oil port on the U.S. east coast. All of the oil consumed by the city of Montreal and its several million people is received by tanker in Portland and pumped to the Quebec Province metropolis.

Ironically, two of the major lasting accomplishments of the eight years that Ken Curtis governed Maine can be traced to this oil refinery fiasco. Under his leadership, two landmark pieces of legislation, the first of their kind in the country, were passed into law. One was a "Site Selection" law, establishing a state agency, the Bureau of Environmental Protection, to vote on whether or not the State should allow any impacting projects over a certain size and, if so, under what conditions. The second law taxed the Montreal pipeline and other oil importers so much per gallon to create and maintain a cleanup fund to be used in the case of spills.

One more major project credited to Governor Curtis was in the fiscal category. He successfully pushed for the implementation of an income tax for Maine. Astoundingly, he was reelected after doing so and retired at the end of his eight years in office as one of the most popular governors the state has ever had.

attention of the president of the United States and the highest echelons of Maine's political leadership. This was the Maine Indian Land Claims controversy, which has had persistent repercussions.

Of the many Native American groups in Maine prior to contact with the European world, only four remain. Two of these are the southernmost representatives of essentially Canadian tribes, located in Aroostook County—the Houlton Band of Maliseets and the Aroostook Band of Micmacs. In neighboring Washington County, two reservations of the much more numerous Passamaquoddy tribe exist and the Penobscot Nation maintains its growing population at its ancient home of Indian Island, Oldtown, not far from Bangor. All told, there are approximately 13,000 Indians in Maine.

Heirs of the survivors of seventeenth and eighteenth century warfare that drove large numbers

of the original natives to Canada, killed them off in the fighting or decimated their ranks through unwittingly imported germs have not always been well treated. The Penobscots, Passamaquoddies, Maliseets and, to an extent, Micmacs fought on the American side during the revolution. Undoubtedly, this is the main reason they are still in Maine today. But both before and after the War for Independence, they lost much of their land to white settlers and large-scale speculators. Treaties they signed were violated with casual impunity. As part of Massachusetts, and one of the thirteen colonies, resident Indians came under state control downeast, not federal, once the U.S. was formed. When Maine broke away in 1820, the new entity assumed responsibility for its Indians and frequently did not exercise it fairly. Beginning in 1794 and continuing until 1833, hard bargains were driven by agents of the state of Maine, stripping most of the desirable Indian lands away from their communal owners.

These dates are critical because of subsequent events. It's key that these major land deals took place after 1790, when a federal law was passed at the instigation of Secretary of War Henry Knox and President George Washington declaring that such state-Indian transactions henceforth had to be approved by Congress. Those treaties, completed in Maine after 1790, never were submitted to D.C. In fact, they were forgotten for the next 182 years.

The 1960s brought a wave of change to the U.S. that reached to its farthest corners, including downeast Washington County, Maine. Among other programs of President Lyndon Johnson's

Maine Native Americans are shown here in 1979 at a rally at the Maine State House in Augusta. The Maine Indian Land Claims case was finalized just a year later, awarding three of Maine's four tribes $81.5 million in an out-of-court settlement. A 1972 lawsuit claimed 12.5 million acres of land was taken from Maine's Indian tribes in violation of national treaties. Courtesy, Maine Historical Society

"Great Society," free legal help for the poor was included. Aggrieved Passamaquoddies, suspecting that land of theirs had been illegally taken, suddenly found hippyish lawyers willing to help them, one of whom, young Thomas Tureen, just out of George Washington University Law School, had an intriguing notion. Learning about the 1790 federal "Non-Intercourse Act" and how Maine had ignored it, he asked himself, "Are those transactions valid?" His belief was that, in the language of the act, they were null and void. If so, the implications were enormous. Two-thirds of the land area of the state of Maine might still belong to those two major tribes, the Passamaquoddies and Penobscots.

When Tureen took the matter to court, the idea seemed so preposterous that it wasn't taken seriously. Even after the prestigious federal judge Edward Gignoux ruled that the 1790 law did apply to Maine and that the U.S. Department of Justice had to act as the Indians' lawyer, there still was not much consternation.

It took several years before Judge Gignoux's appealed decision was upheld. By then, James Longley had become Maine's governor. Neither he, nor Joseph Brennan, the new attorney general, later to become governor, agreed the claim had any merit.

Then, in September 1976, Ropes and Gray, a Boston bond counsel, declared they could not approve municipal bond issues in the disputed territory because all land titles there were now clouded. Maine people in two-thirds of the state suddenly feared losing their property.

From that moment on, the clash was like warfare. Goaded by Governor Longley's inflammatory statements, homeowners rushed out to buy guns. The chief executive had to be warned he was fomenting violence. The fearful Indians hurriedly issued a promise they would never take any individual's home or small landholding. Efforts were made in Congress to extinguish the Indians' claims legislatively—efforts that failed. President Carter stepped in and appointed a mediator. His compromise plan was hollered down by both parties. Another negotiating arrangement followed and finally a deal was struck. The Indians, instead of demanding the $21 billion the land was worth, agreed to accept $81.5 million for the two principle tribes, with a $900,000 grant going to the Houlton Band of Maliseets.

Opposition to even this attenuated package from those who did not want to compensate the Indians was initially fierce. Wiser heads prevailed; the state, with its new governor, Joe Brennan, feared going back to court and possibly losing, while the Indians, who had opponents in their own midst, dreaded the impending arrival of President-elect Ronald Reagan, who might not give them anything. The agreements were put into bill form and passed by both the Maine Legislature and the U.S. Congress. Just before going out of office, President Jimmy Carter signed the measure, flourishing an old fashioned quill pen.

The prime political casualty of this fight was U.S. Senator Bill Hathaway. Prior to his reelection campaign, he had urged a negotiated settlement. Ads attacked him for "Giving the State of Maine Away" and he was defeated by his Republican opponent, a young Congressman William S. Cohen, who had made a name for himself as a member of the Nixon Impeachment Committee.

STEPHEN KING

In a book about Stephen King written by one of his writing professors at the University of Maine, the statement is made that "the landscape of terror Steve King reigns over was created in tribal times..." That the world's most famous practitioner of horror literature not only is Maine born and bred but also explicitly uses Maine as the locale for many of his stories must say something about the subconscious ambiance of the state. Normally, Maine is thought of as bucolic and beautiful and eminently peaceful, with the lowest murder rate in the nation. Yet, its past has seen plenty of violence. One can also look perhaps to the land's own tribal antecedents, particularly in the myths of the Native Americans, where supernatural happenings

Author Stephen King and child film star Drew Barrymore during the world premier of King's Fire-Starter a film starring Barrymore. The premier was held in Bangor, King's hometown, to benefit OMBAT, a consumer organization.
Courtesy, Maine Historical Society

and evil grotesqueries are plentiful. King's wife Tabitha, too, comes from Old Town, home of the Penobscots, and shares some of their ancestry.

King, himself, has stated, "I write about small towns because I'm a small town boy." The town in which he grew up, Durham, Maine, is typical of rural Maine, although closer to the industrial center of Lewiston than the countryside. Its culture, however, derived mostly from the Anglo-Saxon settlers who first populated it and the people who had their own particular wild and imaginative gothic tales to tell. Combine these elements with the chilling fantasies produced by the modern media, as Stephen King has, and he becomes, in one critic's words, "the first hugely popular writer of the TV generation."

King's popularity began four years after his graduation from the University of Maine with the publication of his shocking novel, *Carrie*, which, to no one's surprise was later adapted into a successful movie.

Next came a steady stream of more and more best-selling novels: *Salem's Lot, The Shining, The Stand, The Dead Zone*—winning him international

fame and, in time, a fortune that allows him to be equivalent to a major industry in Maine. His word processor never seems to stop. The volume of Stephen King's work is enormous, and he has won literary prizes for it. It takes all forms: screenplays, teleplays, radio drama scripts, even works self-published exclusively on the Internet—an innovation that was not continued. King and his wife have owned two radio stations in Maine, one specializing in sports, the other in Rock and Roll music. They are fans of high school and college women's basketball in Maine to the extent that Tabitha King, a fine writer herself, wrote a novel about it. Above all, they are ardent followers of the Boston Red Sox. One of Stephen's later novels, *The Girl Who Loved Tom Gordon*, bears the name of a one time relief pitcher for the Fenway Park team.

Stephen and Tabitha were both brought up poor in Maine and they are exceedingly generous to their native state, funneling millions of dollars into projects that benefit a state still counted as the poorest in New England. They live in Bangor, with a summer home in the lakeside town of Lovell and, like many Mainers, also have a winter residence in Florida.

179

MARGUERITE YOURCENAR—A MOST UNUSUAL "MAINE" AUTHOR

If Stephen King is the quintessential Maine small town boy turned world-famed writer, Marguerite Yourcenar can be seen as the exact antithesis, although an internationally renowned novelist, herself. Belgian born, raised in France, she did not come to Maine until 1948, one year after Stephen King was born. Moreover, she had not grown up poor, but in a chateau in Flanders and, upon her father's death, had become independently wealthy through the inheritance she received.

Her real name was Marguerite de Crayencour; she made up the pen name of *Yourcenar*, an anagram of *Crayencour*, when her first book was published in 1929. Nine years later, she left France with her companion and translator, a young American student named Grace Frick. Together, they migrated to Maine, once Marguerite had become an American citizen. It was in a charming New England homestead on Mount Desert Island at Northeast Harbor that the two women spent the rest of their lives.

Marguerite's literary career blossomed in 1951. This was the year that her masterpiece, the *Memoirs of Hadrian* was published, originally in French, drawing widespread acclaim. A fictional study of the noted Roman Emperor in his retirement, the work made Marguerite Yourcenar one of the most important French women writers of the day. Then, after other of her books had won literary prizes she became, in 1980, the first woman ever to be accepted into the ultra-prestigious *Academie Francaise*, or French Academy—the highest honor any French language author can receive. Those admitted to its ranks are known popularly as "the Immortals."

All the while, Marguerite Yourcenar, American citizen, continued to live at "Petite Plaisance," the home she and Grace Frick had established in Maine. Grace died in 1979, but still Marguerite continued to live and write in the same Maine surroundings in which she received word of her momentous

Belgian born novelist Marguerite Yourcenar (1903–1987) moved to the United States after World War II and made her home on Mount Desert Island after 1950. Her most popular work, Memoirs of Hadrian, *tells the story of the Roman emperor who built the famous wall that marked the boundaries of Roman Britain. In 1980 she became the first woman to be elected to the Academie Française. Courtesy, Maine Historical Society*

French Academy honor. Previously, the Royal Belgian Academy had similarly honored her with a membership.

Unlike Stephen King's writings, Maine never became a milieu for Marguerite Yourcenar's fiction. But it was her home for almost forty years. She died at the Mount Desert Hospital in December, 1987 and her ashes are buried in the nearby Somesville Cemetery. "Petite Plaisance" has become a museum that can be visited from the middle of June to the end of August by appointment.

There is a memorial to her in France, as well, at Mont Noir in Flanders, where she spent her girlhood.

RACHEL CARSON

Yet another world-famous writer with a strong Maine connection was neither born in the state nor lived there permanently. Rachel Carson, after the enormous success of her book, *The Sea Around Us*, finally had the financial wherewithal to do things she had always wanted to do. As one of her biographers wrote, "Her first extravagance was the purchase of a very fine binocular microscope. Her second luxury was the summer cottage on the Maine coast."

The cottage was located on Southport Island, adjacent to the much larger tourist center of

Boothbay. She spent every summer there from 1952 until 1963 when she was too ill from cancer to make the trip. The following year, she died.

Rachel Carson's winter home was in Silver Springs, Maryland. For the better part of her life, she had worked for the federal government in the U.S. Fish and Wildlife Service. In one of her first jobs for the agency, she wrote a radio show, *Romance Under the Waters*, was also a junior biologist and ended her career as chief editor of all their publications.

While *The Sea Around Us* and its sequel, *The Edge of the Sea*, were runaway best-sellers, her most important—and most controversial—book was *Silent Spring*. Her attack on pesticides brought a

Author Rachel Carson (1907–1964) is shown here testifying before a Senate subcommittee about the results of spraying pesticides in 1963. She spent her early professional life working for the U. S. Fish and Wildlife Service, but she also published a number of popular books about ecology and the environment. She published her controversial, but influential book Silent Spring *in 1962. The work criticized the use of synthetic pesticides and she is credited with being one of the founders of the modern environmental movement. Courtesy, Library of Congress*

vicious industry rejoinder down upon this quiet, scholarly maiden lady, ended the use of DDT and revolutionized the thinking of many people and organizations about dealing with insects and other natural pests. This one publication, which appeared in 1962 two years before her death, had a monumental impact worldwide.

The Bates College Library in Lewiston, holds a collection of letters between Rachel Carson and Dorothy Freeman, her closest friend in Maine. The Freemans, Dorothy and her husband Stanley Sr., were also summer people, but with family roots in Southport dating back to the 1880s. In the summer of 1951, they read *The Sea Around Us* aloud to each other and, learning that Rachel Carson was building a place close to theirs, Dorothy wrote to her as a welcoming neighbor. The next summer, the two women met and started "a profound and intimate friendship" Dorothy was fifty-five, Rachel forty-six. *The Edge of the Sea* was dedicated to the Freemans and it was left to Dorothy Freeman to scatter her beloved friend's ashes following Rachel's death, which occurred only four months after Stanley Sr. had passed away.

The letters were collected and edited by Dorothy's granddaughter, Martha Freeman, who is currently the director of the State Planning Office in Maine government.

Other memorials to Rachel Carson in Maine include the Rachel Carson National Wildlife Refuge that stretches from Kittery to Scarborough, a distance of some forty miles, encompassing many valuable wetlands in the southernmost and fastest growing area of the state. There is a Rachel Carson Greenway, maintained by the Boothbay Regional Land Trust. Also, a major conference in honor of Rachel Carson's memory has been held each year for the past three years at the Spruce Point Inn in Boothbay Harbor. It is sponsored by New-Cue, Inc., an organization of nature and environmental writers and college and university educators.

Rachel Carson has plainly left her mark on Maine, just as Maine and its struggles to maintain environmental quality left its mark on her.

SKIING in the East

THE BEST TRAILS and **HOW TO GET THERE**

A GUIDE FOR WINTER SPORT FANS

$1 50

Describing over 1000 *TRAILS* in 216 *LOCALITIES*

MAINE, NEW HAMPSHIRE, VERMONT, MASSACHUSETTS, CONNECTICUT, NEW YORK, NEW JERSEY, PENNSYLVANIA,

AMERICAN GUIDE SERIES

WPA FEDERAL WRITERS' PROJECT
110 KING STREET • NEW YORK CITY

WPA FEDERAL ART PROJECT DIV 4

10

UP TO THE PRESENT (1981–2006)

Enthusiasm for winter sports has a long history in Maine, attracting visitors and locals alike for over 125 years. There were ski clubs in towns like Portland and snowshoe clubs in places like Biddeford. Winter carnivals in the 1920s featured ski jumping demonstrations, ice skating and hockey. Local people cut trails into the woods on nearby hills and mountains, or just took off overland right out the back door. These days skiing is big business with Sugarloaf alone serving over a million skiers per year. Courtesy, Library of Congress

PAYROLLS AND PICKEREL

For a very long time, Mainers have talked about the choice, as they put it in their distinct lingo, between "payrolls or pickerel." Even before Ed Muskie started his crusade to clean up local rivers in the 1950s or Rachel Carson stunned the world with information about harmful pesticides in 1962, the debate had been going on in the Pine Tree State. It could be said that until the 1970s, payrolls almost always won. The local industrial powers—pulp and paper companies and electric utilities got their way, whether it was dams they wanted to build or new generating plants or polluting materials they wished to dispose of cheaply in public waterways. When plagues of insects like the spruce budworm attacked the company lands, the state of Maine paid for the spraying, which included DDT. Only in a case, like the Quoddy Dam since it would have been government owned, did the big businesses object. Years later, attacking the Dickey-Lincoln Dam for the same reason, they had the now-growing Maine environmental movement as their ally. Aroostook County, consequently, remained with the pickerel.

It was a different story when a coalition of environmentalists went after Maine Yankee, the nuclear power plant in Wiscasset that the Central Maine Power Company and a consortium of other utilities had placed in "Maine's prettiest village" at an earlier time without too much resistance. Now, people in the surrounding area and throughout other parts of the state wanted it shut down. They were fearful of the mounting nuclear waste disposal problem and of the possibility of a catastrophic nuclear explosion or accident similar to Chernobyl in the Soviet Union. Twice, in 1982 and 1984, the question went to the Maine electorate in referendum and twice, by margins of about 55 percent to 45 percent, the plant was kept open. Then, finally, its owners shut it down themselves because it was getting too expensive to run, and no longer making a profit.

While Maine environmentalism grew tremendously and took leadership positions in defeating "non-trend" developments like oil refineries and a huge aluminum smelter, the state's economy also kept pace. During the Curtis years, the "sleeping giant," the term the governor used to characterize Maine, had awakened. More than 4,000 jobs were created in 1968; alone, tourism had grown by 15 percent; fifty-eight new firms had come in from "away;" and ninety-three existing ones had expanded. The new tax structure had begun paying dividends. The sales tax, always a measure of growth, while staying at essentially the same rate, went from bringing in $30 million in 1963 to $858 million in 2003. The income tax, which began in 1970, within fifteen years was bringing in more than the sales tax at a rate of 7.6 times above inflation. And federal grants had poured in, as well, rising from $42 million in 1963 to $1.7 billion in 2002. From 1975 to 2001 the total value of all taxable Maine real estate rose from $7 billion to $85 billion. The state's population increased, too, from less than 1 million to 1.3 million, despite periods of out-migration from the northern counties.

The payrolls-pickerel debate still continues in various guises. "Sprawl" is a word one hears constantly in the southernmost counties and all along

Maine Yankee Nuclear Power Plant in Wiscasset opened in 1972. Throughout the controversial life of the plant it faced protests and efforts to shut it down. In the end, the owners closed the plant in 1996 when they deemed it too expensive to continue operation. Courtesy, Maine Historical Society

In 1984 the Margaret Chase Smith Federal Building in Bangor was dedicated. Flanking Smith are Edmund Muskie, William Cohen, George Mitchell and Joseph Brennan. Courtesy, Margaret Chase Smith Library

the coast. A "Grow Smart" movement has begun, seeking governmental changes to limit the phenomenon. At the same time, cries for more jobs continue from the "other Maine"—rural areas where local industries have closed. Severe changes are occurring in the pulp and paper industries and having a profound effect upon the character of the Maine North Woods. Land Trusts are sprouting everywhere, with plans for saving natural areas. One controversial proposal calls for a 3.5 million acre national park. Major industrial project ideas also crop up, not as frequently, but with great controversy, like a liquid natural gas port development, proposed for several seacoast sites and rejected at most of them. Likewise, an outsized Indian casino proposal roiled the state until it was defeated.

THE NORTH WOODS SITUATION

More than half the land area of Maine is practically uninhabited. The "Unorganized Territories" is the official name for a large collection of "townships," each of 23,000 acres, that were plotted out by surveyors in the nineteenth century, but never organized into "towns." Here the government is the state of Maine. There is an Augusta-run school system for the Unorganized Territories and a zoning system called the Land Use Regulation Commission. Yet, for the most part, these millions of acres are not state property. They are owned by private individuals and corporations, although tradition and local pressure has kept them open to public use, primarily for hunting, fishing and other recreational activities.

Until recently, this made for a tidy arrangement. A case in point was Millinocket, the town built almost overnight in the Maine wilderness by the Great Northern Paper Company (GNP). The people who worked at the GNP mills were paid some of the highest wages in Maine. They were able to afford sporting camps in the nearby woods and lakefronts; some even took winter vacations in the South. Great Northern was a paternalistic employer but treated its workers well and projected

This is Millinocket in May of 1939 with Mt. Katahdin in the background. Formed in 1901 as a company town for the Great Northern Paper Company, Millinocket was the king of the papermaking world. That early GNP plant made 240 tons of newsprint per day. Courtesy, Maine Historical Society

an image of financial and political strength that would seemingly last forever.

This was not to be.

The tale of Great Northern's demise can stand as a prime example of the changes that have overtaken that way of life developed in the Maine woods since at least the start of the twentieth century, when industrialization arrived.

One of the company's historians, Paul McCann, has written, "For Great Northern, the 1980s ended with a company that had been a money-maker for its first fifty years and was now a loser month after month."

He was complaining about Great Northern's merger with a Wisconsin company that owned woodlands businesses in the South and the competition GNP now faced within the overall Great Northern Nekoosa operation. Since southern trees grow much faster than trees in Maine, this put the northern company at a disadvantage.

Other problems arose too. Even more damaging than the devastating spruce budworm infestations on thousands of GNP acres was a hostile takeover by the Georgia-Pacific Company. Then, there was the element of foreign competition, companies from really "away" entering the U.S. forest products market. Before anyone knew it, an English company headquartered in South Carolina, Bowater Corporation, bought out Georgia-Pacific's Maine assets. All too soon, Great Northern's two mills and 2 million acres of forest went on the auction block and Bowater, with an eye on increasing its stock value, sold to a Quebec outfit, Inexcon, and before long the new owners put its Great Northern division into bankruptcy.

The loss of jobs, staggering as it was, provided only part of the turmoil. Suddenly, land was being exchanged in many parts of the state and in vast quantities. One of the first of what seemed like moves in a giant game of Monopoly was the sale in October 1998 by the SAPPI company of 911,000 acres of its Maine timberlands. This company whose acronym stood for South African Pulp and Paper Industries, epitomized the aspect of

Located between Route 1 and the St. Croix River, this is the Georgia-Pacific paper plant in Woodland as it looked in 1973. As of 2000, the Woodland mill had potential of 125,000 tons of premium and business papers, but successive layoffs in the 1990s led to the eventual sale of the mill in 2001 and its closure in spring of 2005. Courtesy, National Archives

Changing shifts in at the Georgia-Pacific paper mill in Woodland in 1973. Courtesy, National Archives

globalization during this time. They were successors to a long-time-in-Maine branch of a national company, Scott Paper, which had absorbed an original Maine-developed pulp and paper firm, Hollingsworth and Whitney.

The shock wave from SAPPI's action related to the ultimate fate of the land. They had been using it to feed wood to their mills. What would happen now that it was being sold to a high-end real estate development group specializing in selling off choice lots to millionaires?

Environmentalists were particularly concerned. The effort to create a 3.5 million acre national park, strongly resisted by local people, was already underway. But the idea of the gentrification of the Maine North Woods, with gated communities and private hunting preserves, also met strong opposition. A way of life had now been threatened on a second front.

Increasingly, land kept coming on the market. International Paper, which was founded in Maine, offered 125,000 acres of wilderness, albeit cut-over, on the upper St. John River to the highest bidder. The buyer turned out to be the Maine chapter of the Nature Conservancy, paying $50 million for the land, which it borrowed from its national organization and then proceeded to raise by itself—the most money at that time ever spent by this major conservation group for a piece of property. They announced they would keep the integrity of the land and even allow it to be logged. An anti-environmentalist, much in favor of more aggressive clear-cutting, responded snidely, "Yes, they'll be practicing wine and cheese logging."

Several referendums to ban clear-cutting had already been held in 1996 and 1997 and ended in a stalemate—no ban and no real change in forest cutting practices.

Currently, there are various attempts to contend with the changes in the North Woods' economy. The national park idea still seems stalled, but one Mainer, Roxanne Quimby, who sold her home-grown "Burt's Bees" cosmetic business for millions, has bought thousands of acres with her own money

and the apparent intent of emulating Governor Percival Baxter on an even larger scale. Land trusts have formed throughout the region hoping to raise funds to preserve huge parcels of land and put together "corridors" where quantities of wildlife, including someday restored wolves, can roam. Attempts to revive the pulp and paper industry also continue. Yet, as of 2004 the International Paper Company, owners of a major mill in the town of Jay and another at Bucksport, has announced its intention to sell all of its Maine lands. The situation in the Maine North Woods remains entirely fluid.

Making all-natural, honey-based personal care products and bees wax candles, Burt's Bees started manufacturing in an abandoned schoolhouse in rural Maine. Now they are a multi-million dollar, international business. Courtesy, Burt's Bees

THE INDIAN CASINO

The Great Northern Paper Company had just gone bankrupt when in March 2002, the announcement was made of a plan that would help Maine make up for those lost jobs in the north, and then some. No less than 10,000 new jobs were projected and the financially hard-pressed state government would receive, over and above an abundant amount of ancillary taxes, a direct payment of $100 million a year.

The two major Indian tribes, the Passamaquoddies and Penobscots, in conjunction with their lawyer in the Land Claims Settlement, Tom Tureen, revealed that they would be seeking approval to build a mammoth casino and hotel complex in

Maine has a long history of horse racing and many towns once had trotting parks that have since disappeared. Today, you can see races at a number of fairs in the fall, and at the Bangor Raceway and Scarborough Downs. Courtesy, Maine Harness Racing Commission

southern Maine. It would rival the highly successful Foxwoods Casino in Connecticut and was slated for Kittery, the entrance to the state.

Tureen had already been involved in the formation of the Foxwoods endeavor, as the lawyer for the Mashuntucket Pequots, the tiny tribe that established the largest single gambling operation in the world. Their start, in fact, through running high stakes beano, also called bingo games, had been originally bankrolled by Maine's Penobscots with money they received from the Land Claims Settlement. The Pequots paid back the Penobscots and then went into slot machines and a full array of gambling games, all packed into a glitzy Las Vegas-style palace.

The reaction in Maine to the idea of large scale gambling was surprisingly negative, despite the fact that the state ran a lottery, allowed horse-racing and off-track betting and had permitted their own Indian tribes to conduct high stakes beano for many years and give prizes in the thousands of dollars.

Although there was intial support in the legislature, with a bill for the casino in the offing, and most of the gubernatorial candidates saying it was an idea worth considering, the tide soon turned. The existing governor, Maine's second Independent chief executive, Angus King, said he would fight it tooth and nail. Grass-roots opposition quickly formed in the southern area around Kittery, calling itself "Casinos-No." The area, too, Maine's fastest growing section, was already fighting new developments of any kind. The notion of 10,000 new workers, a huge tourist complex drawing people all year and endless traffic added to existing gridlock problems had seemed more than they could bear. Anti-Foxwoods officials and residents came from Connecticut and fanned the flames with horror stories of the impacts on their rural neighborhoods.

Since the Maine Indians had said they wouldn't locate where they weren't wanted, they had to vacate Kittery as their desired site when the town voted overwhelmingly not to accept the casino.

New sites were soon sought by them, with promises of large annual payments in lieu of taxes to any community that agreed to house their gambling complex. Finally, they won a vote in the town of Sanford. But because they needed a change in state law and Governor King would veto any legislation, even if they could get it passed, the casino forces sought a statewide referendum. Buoyed by polls showing them with a commanding lead, they acquired the necessary signatures and the question went on the ballot in November 2003. By that time, however, Casinos-No had done an effective job of demonizing the project, claiming, in particular, that it would bring large scale crime to a state with one of the lowest crime rates in the U.S. The pro-casino proponents, relying on out-of-state advertisers and advisors, concentrated only on the jobs and money aspects and never overcame the doubts Maine people had. Thus, the casino was voted down overwhelmingly.

The fact that, on the same ballot, voters approved another referendum measure to allow slot machines at horse racing tracks in the state led to accusations of racism from certain Indian leaders as a cause of their defeat. Strong disappointment and bitterness among the Indians resulted in their withdrawal from the Maine Tribal-State Commission, set up during the Settlement as a venue for working out differences. Echoing their sentiment "Why are we the only Indians in the country not allowed to have a casino?," they have begun making known their desire to undo the Settlement Act of 1980, which they are now holding responsible for their lack of sovereignty.

THE SOMALIS

Outright racism was to enter into another incident in Maine that drew world-wide attention when fringe American hate-groups became involved.

The setting was Lewiston, Maine's second largest city. It began in October 2002 after Mayor Laurier T. Raymond sent a letter that had explosive repercussions. The recipients were a group of elders of a fast-growing concentration of Somali refugees recently migrated to Lewiston, whose population since the 1870s had been dominated by French Canadian immigrants.

As his first name of Laurier implied, "Larry" Raymond was of Franco-American descent. Later, he complained bitterly that charges of "racism" against him due to the tone of his letter were misplaced in that his own daughter had adopted two black children. What he had written was a plea for the Somali elders to ask their fellow countrymen to stop coming to Lewiston, which had seemingly become a mecca for these exiles from the horn of Africa. In that more than 1,000 Somalis had arrived from all over the U.S. in the past eighteen months, Mayor Raymond exhorted the community to "exercise some discipline and reduce stress on the city's limited finances and generosity." Lewiston needed "breathing room," he wrote, and is "maxed out financially, physically and emotionally."

His statements were interpreted as racist, implying that the Somalis, who are black and Muslim, weren't welcome. Not only did the Somalis make this charge in a press conference where they called upon Raymond to apologize and retract his message, but others in the state joined in—most notably, the Portland newspapers, in a city with an even larger Somali population. They editorialized that, if nothing else, his statements would fortify racism.

In a demonstration organized by local Lewiston-area churches, 300 supporters of the Somalis marched in protest from the Calvary United Method Church to a mosque on the city's main street. Trying to diffuse the situation, Governor Angus King said he was looking for funds to help Lewiston and did not believe Mayor Raymond was

This Somali woman was part of a group of 1,000 recent immigrants who moved to Lewiston in 2002. The group had been refugees to Atlanta from Somalia but were attracted to Lewiston because it is a smaller, safer city. By the time they moved to Lewiston, the Somalis were no longer refugees, but full-fledged U.S. citizens looking to make a new start in Maine. Courtesy, Bates Magazine

These Lewiston High School students attended the rally in support of the 1,000 Somali Americans who moved to Lewiston in 2002. Courtesy, Bates Magazine

a racist. The mayor, himself, announced that he was sorry for any misunderstanding, but he didn't disavow his letter.

Then, some real racists entered the picture. One group of white supremacists from West Virginia, the National Alliance, came to Maine and distributed their hate literature and created a Web site to try to recruit local members. Another strongly anti-Semitic group, the World Church of the Creator, next applied to hold a rally in Lewiston.

First amendment considerations forced Lewiston officials to allow the World Church to proceed with their meeting. Its goal was to urge Lewiston to expel all of its Somali residents.

The leader of the World Church, Matthew Hale, however, never made the trip to Maine. He was arrested and held in jail for conspiring to murder a federal judge—a crime for which he was later convicted—shortly before he was to leave Illinois.

About two dozen of his followers showed up for the "rally."

Simultaneously, a "counter rally" was held in Lewiston, organized by a group that called itself "Many and One." Assembling at Bates College, more than 4,500 people demonstrated their support for the Somalis, including Maine's newly elected governor, John Baldacci, the state's congressional delegation, many legislators and the mayor of Portland.

But not the mayor of Lewiston. Larry Raymond was in Florida that January day, "on vacation." "*Ou est le Maire?*" one Franco-American attendee had printed on his sign. "Where is the mayor?"

This protest rally was acknowledged as one of the most massive in Maine's history. The handful of bigots slinked quietly away once they had finished their ranting in a different location.

Mayor Raymond issued a statement saying he had stayed away to minimize the attention that might be given to the World Church. Five months later, he revealed that he would not run for re-election.

Governor John Baldacci was born in Bangor in 1955. He went from Bangor city counselor to the Maine State Senate to the U. S. legislature. He became governor of Maine in 2002. That same year he attended a rally to support Maine's newest citizens, the 1,000 Somali immigrants who moved to Lewiston from Atlanta. Courtesy, Bates Magazine

THE POLITICAL SCENE

Back in the days of James G. Blaine, Hannibal Hamlin, Thomas Brackett Reed and others, Maine strode large on the Washington, D.C. scene. That level of influence seemed to return with the careers of Edmund Muskie and Margaret Chase Smith. This influence continued with their successors Republican William S. Cohen and Democrat George J. Mitchell.

Both men, despite their party differences, had much in common. Both were Bowdoin graduates. Both came from poor families of immigrant origins. Cohen's father was Russian Jewish, his mother Protestant Irish. Mitchell's father was Catholic Irish, his mother an immigrant Lebanese Maronite Christian.

This clever message was sent to Senator Bill Cohen in 1985 by a worker from the Hallowell Shoe Company. Workers were worried about cheap shoe imports and their affect on the Maine shoe industry. Very little is left of this once-thriving industry as jobs were sent overseas to take advantage of cheaper labor. Courtesy, Maine Historical Society

Bill Cohen entered Maine's political scene in 1972 with an unexpected win in his first major race, capturing the Second District congressional seat. His only previous office had been mayor of Bangor, to which he had been elected by his fellow city council members. Young, photogenic, a basketball star at Bowdoin, he had borrowed the idea of a "walk" through his district from Senator Lawton Chiles who had done it in Florida and the tactic gained him significant recognition.

Assigned to the Judiciary Committee, it was Cohen's good fortune to become part of the Nixon impeachment process, giving him tremendous exposure on television. His vote, as a Republican for Nixon's impeachment, resonated well in Maine. Six years after his initial election, he went after the seat of the man he had replaced in Congress, U.S. Senator William Hathaway and handily defeated him.

Military matters were one of his main interests and he became a member of the Senate Armed Services Committee. In 1986 when a Select Senate Committee was appointed to investigate the Iran-Contra scandal, Cohen again faced the television cameras as a member and one of three Republicans to hold President Ronald Reagan responsible. Senator George Mitchell was also a member of that panel. He and Cohen collaborated on a 1988

book, *Men of Zeal*, about their experiences.

By then, Senator Cohen had published a number of books, starting with a volume of poetry, then a novel, *Double Man* written with Senator Gary Hart of Colorado and another work of fiction, a mystery, entitled *Murder in the Senate*.

While already having begun his campaign for reelection in 1996, Cohen stunned Mainers by announcing without warning his withdrawal from the race and retirement from the Senate. But a year later, this moderate Republican went to work for Democratic President Bill Clinton as secretary of defense. Despite pressure from his party to resign, he stayed during the impeachment process and remained in that post until the end of the Clinton Administration.

George Mitchell's career followed a similar pattern. At the height of his achievement in Washington, serving as majority leader, the number one position in the Senate, he too resigned abruptly, having already started a campaign he was bound to win by a landslide. He also went on to other triumphs after leaving elected office, especially in his role as a special mediator on the international scene. President Clinton sent him to Northern Ireland to try to broker a peace between warring Protestants and Catholics, a feat that he accomplished to an extraordinary degree. Following that effort, he took on the even more difficult task of trying to bring together the Israelis and Palestinians, also enemies, and made significant progress at the time.

George Mitchell had entered the political arena as an assistant to Senator Ed Muskie. His first attempt for Maine public office was a three-way gubernatorial race in 1974. Independent James Longley unexpectedly won, and the conventional wisdom downeast was that Mitchell's career was finished before it had even started. He then held two nonelected jobs: U.S. attorney for Maine and U.S. district judge, a lifetime appointment. Yet he gave up this sinecure in 1980 when Governor Joseph Brennan selected him to fill the U.S. Senate seat that Ed Muskie vacated to become secretary of state.

The office was only guaranteed to Mitchell for two years before he faced reelection. His opponent was a popular Republican congressman, David Emery. Early polls showed Mitchell losing to him by more than thirty points. As it turned out, Mitchell won by thirty points. Nor was his popularity confined to Maine. His fellow Democrats made him chair of the Senate Campaign Committee. He led them to victory, winning back control of the Senate from the Republicans. His next stop was Senate majority leader, where he served from 1989 to 1995.

Following his retirement from the Senate, in addition to his negotiating duties, he has pursued

an active legal career and is a member of numerous corporate boards, among others that of the Disney Company where he was elected chairman. A major activity for him in Maine is with the Mitchell Institute, which he founded. The Institute provides college scholarships for Maine students who otherwise couldn't afford higher education—one each year from every high school in the state. In establishing this goal, Mitchell attempted to combat a notorious set of Maine statistics. The state has one of the highest percentage rates of high school graduates in the country, but ranks among the lowest whose students go on to higher education.

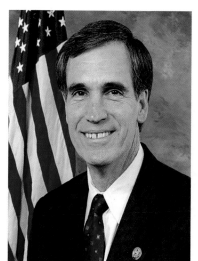

Portland native, Tom Allen serves in the United States Congress. A Rhodes scholar and former mayor of Portland, Allen was first elected to Congress in 1997. Courtesy, Office of Congressman Tom Allen

Senator Olympia Snowe, Senator William Cohen, White House Chief of Staff Leon Panetta, Labor Secretary Robert Reich, and Representative John Baldacci in Panetta's office May 7, 1996 for the announcement of a Department of Labor contract award to Training Development Corporation of Bucksport to run the Job Corps Center at Loring, Maine. Courtesy, University of Maine, Special Collections

Succeeding Cohen and Mitchell in the U.S. Senate were two Republican women, Olympia Snowe and Susan Collins, who have been building distinguished careers in the tradition of Margaret Chase Smith. The state's two congressmen are Democrats, Tom Allen, serving his fifth term, who was a Rhodes scholar at Oxford with President Bill Clinton, and Michael Michaud, in his second term, the first Franco-American to be elected to major office in Maine. Michaud succeeded longtime Democratic congressman John Baldacci, who went on to become the state's governor. His predecessor was Maine's second Independent governor, Angus King.

United States senator Susan Collins was first elected in 1996. She grew up in Caribou where both of her parents served as mayor. Senator Collins currently serves on three committees: the Committee on Armed Forces, the Special Committee on Aging and the Committee on Homeland Security and Government Affairs. Courtesy, Office of Senator Susan Collins

SPORTS HEROICS

Maine, with only 1.3 million people and whose biggest city is Portland, population 64,000, metro area 230,000, is fanatically sports-minded, but obviously too small to host major professional sports franchises. However, it does have two important minor league teams: in baseball, the Portland Sea Dogs, a Boston Red Sox farm team and the Portland Pirates, an American Hockey League affiliate of the Washington Capitals.

Although the University of Maine, with 14,000 students, has competed in college baseball world series events in the past, it is in hockey that the state university won its only NCAA Division 1 National Championships.

The first came in the 1992–1993 season. When the University of Maine Black Bears, under their legendary coach Shawn Walsh, became national champions. They compiled an extraordinary forty-two to one to two record and capped their performance by beating Lake Superior State five to four. Paul Kariya, an eighteen year-old Canadian from North Vancouver, British Columbia, was not only their biggest star, but he also won the Hobey Baker Award, making him college hockey's best player of the year. Soon afterward, he turned pro, joining the Anaheim Mighty Ducks, and excelled as one of professional hockey's highest paid superstars.

All Maine was agog over this unprecedented sports victory. A huge billboard was erected on the Maine Turnpike, advertising and extolling the triumph. The players were honored with a cer-

emony in the Rose Garden by President Clinton in Washington with Senators Cohen and Mitchell in attendance.

But the following season, trouble plagued the Maine champions. Coach Walsh was accused of using an ineligible player, suspended for five weeks and the team was forced to forfeit three of the games it won that year. The Black Bears also were not allowed to compete in the Hockey East Division league playoffs.

University of Maine hockey star, Paul Kariya during the amazing 1992–1993 season in which the Black Bears won the NCAA Division 1 title. Courtesy, University of Maine Athletic Department

The Portland Sea Dogs are the Double-A affiliate for the Boston Red Sox. The team was formed in 1994. By 2000 they already had the seventh highest attendance record in the Eastern League which was formed in 1923. Maine, by and large, is Red Sox territory, and while the Dogs did well as part of the Florida Marlins system, their popularity has skyrocketed since being acquired by the Red Sox. Courtesy, Portland Sea Dogs

During the 1994–1995 season, Maine was allowed to play and made it to the NCAA Championship finals. Before the year ended, worse problems arose. An NCAA investigation uncovered other violations. Since some involved the use of ineligible players in the 1992–1993 season, Maine was in danger of having its championship revoked. Nevertheless, in the end, the NCAA Executive Committee decided not to invoke such dire punishment. The university was banned from competing in post-season games and lost five scholarships. Despite calls for the firing of Coach Walsh, he was kept on and returned in December 1996. Three years later, Maine was back at the top in big-time college hockey, beating Clarkson to get into the NCAA's "Frozen Four" finale.

They were led by Steve Kariya, Paul Kariya's younger brother. Beating Boston College in the semi-final, the team then faced arch-rival New Hampshire. The game was played in Anaheim and Maine pulled out a squeaker three to two victory in sudden death overtime.

This second national championship was seen as a vindication for Shawn Walsh. Soon, he had a bigger challenge to face. Still in his forties, he was diagnosed with a rare form of liver cancer. Able to coach in 2000, he gained another championship for Maine, this time of their Hockey East Division. It was the last great triumph for a coach who was one shy of 400 wins and had coached two Hobey Baker award-winners and twenty-six other All-Americans. A stem cell transfer from his brother failed and Shawn Walsh, age forty-six, died in a Bangor hospital on September 24, 2001.

Earlier in 1984, Maine and the rest of the nation had thrilled to the sight of a woman athlete from the Pine Tree State, running alone into the Olympic stadium in Los Angeles. Thin, petite, almost frail-looking Joan Benoit from Cape Elizabeth, Maine, was on her way, well ahead of her nearest rival, to winning a gold medal in the first ever female marathon run as an Olympic event. She had previously won the Boston Marathon twice and in order to make the U.S. Olympic team, had had to

Maine's three champions from the 1984 Olympics: Joan Benoit, Billy Swift and Holly Metcalf. The Olympians were greeted in Portland by cheering crowds, Governor Joe Brennan and Senators George Mitchell and Olympia Snowe. Courtesy, Maine Historical Society

In 1999 the residents of Bethel decided to make the world's tallest snowman and named it in honor of Governor Angus King. "Angus, King of the Mountain,"

made it into the Guinness Book of World Records and attracted worldwide attention as morning news show crews showed up to film the event. Governor King is shown here giving a statement about his namesake. He joked that "Willie Melt" might have been a better name. Photo by Barry J. Hough, Sr.

enter qualifying heats after painful knee surgery. Her Olympic record, two hours, twenty-four minutes and fifty-two seconds, was still standing in 1999, the same year that *Sports Illustrated* placed her twentieth in their list of 100 all-time top women athletes. Although diagnosed with Parkinson's disease in 1996, she has kept on running. At age forty-six, she was competing in the Honolulu Marathon and still won the Portland Half-Marathon.

Not only does Joan Benoit Samuelson, a mother of two, enter races, she also has been instrumental in starting one in Maine that has instantly become an international classic. With the proceeds donated to charity, the Peoples Beach to Beacon race, sponsored by her employer, the Peoples Heritage Bank, draws upwards of 4,000 contestants every year. The ten kilometer race ends at her hometown of Cape Elizabeth and in its second year already drew three of the top ten male runners in the world and three of the top five women.

As late as 2000 "Joannie" was aiming again for the Olympics at age forty-two. She finished ninth in the trials, notwithstanding the pain of a slipped disk in her back.

Four years later, she was participating in a ten kilometer all-female road race, saluting U.S. Olympians.

To young women track athletes the world over, Olympian gold medal winner Joan Benoit has been and continues to be an inspiring example of courage and dogged persistence.

THE REAL MAINE

In Maine, you will hear a lot about the "Two Maines." This is a fairly new phenomenon and derives from the significant economic growth in southern Maine and the problems of the economy in northern and western Maine. While there are pockets of prosperity in northern Maine, there are likewise areas of low employment and poverty in the south. The two designations are neither cut and dried nor mutually exclusive.

Image terms like these about the Pine Tree State exist in other forms, as well. One that surfaced in recent years was "The Real Maine," of gritty poverty presumably opposed to "The Ideal Maine," as posited by the tourist industry with pictures of rockbound seashores, glossy lakes, colorful forests and the nice, outdoorsy folks who inhabit this pleasurable land.

In 1985 a work of fiction quite unlike any other about Maine made a national splash and helped start that talk about "The Real Maine." Its title was *The Beans of Egypt, Maine* and the author of this first novel was Carolyn Chute, who had been living a life of extreme rural poverty until publishing her novel. It was said that she and her husband bought their first automobile with the royalties she received.

Ironically, the section she describes and in which she lives is in York County, the state's southernmost and fastest-growing area, not far from the "Gold Coast" of towns like Kennebunk, Kennebunkport, York and Ogunquit. The particular country Chute writes about is in the foothills of the White Mountains and so scenic that it has been dubbed Maine's "Little Switzerland." Yet, this somewhat forgotten corner of the state offers atrociously hard living to many of its inhabitants.

About her maiden effort, she has made the following mordant comment, "This book was involuntarily researched. I have lived poverty. I didn't choose it. No one would choose humiliation, rage and pain." *The Beans of Egypt, Maine*, a short work, was followed by *Letourneau's Used Auto Parts*, a longer novel, in 1988 and *Merrymen*, even longer, 695 pages, in 1994.

More recently, Carolyn Chute has gained considerable attention outside of her writing by organizing a highly unusual "militia" group in her rural enclave. Rather, there seem to be two connected entities: the 2nd Maine Militia, operating statewide, and the Border Mountain Militia, confined to her region. She calls it a "No Wing Militia" and emphasizes that it is pro-gun, but anti-big business. Its essence is redneck, working class and tribal class, and she elaborates, "The working class person values place, interdependence, cooperation and the tribe." Her own terminology for herself is "an uneducated redneck novelist."

It could be argued that Stephen King, also from a poor Maine small town background, exemplifies this same "Maine realism," yet his Maine world essentially always turns phantasmagoric. In her latest novel, *The Snowman*, Carolyn Chute also heads in this direction, indulging in political fantasy that backs her views.

One other example of "Maine realism" in contemporary literature is the novel by Richard Russo, *Empire Falls*, that won the Pulitzer Prize in 2002. Russo, who taught at Colby College before he left to write full-time in his coastal Maine home, zeroes in on Maine's blue collar workers. The fictional Empire Falls, Maine is representative of a number of small Maine cities deserted by manufacturing industries. Waterville, where Colby is located, and not-too-far-off Lewiston could serve as models. In Russo's words, the place he writes about "never recovered from the migration of textile jobs." Grim as this may be, the author describes himself as a "comic novelist." Russo has also been likened, in his depiction of main street, America, to Sherwood Anderson and Sinclair Lewis. A highly acclaimed made for TV movie of *Empire Falls* starring Paul Newman and his wife Joanne Woodward was produced in 2005. Russo, himself, has written TV plays and movie scripts, one of them for an earlier novel of his, *Nobody's Fool*, also made into a film.

MAINE HUMOR

Despite, or perhaps, because of the economic difficulties of life in such a gorgeous state as Maine, a singular type of humor has developed and even provides a good living for some of its comedian practitioners.

A sample might be in the tag some Mainers have tied on Carolyn Chute's redneck rifle-toters: the "Wicked Good Militia," tossing a bit of tongue-in-

The Maine accent is often the centerpiece of humor in the state and Tim Sample has made full use of his. One of his early books was How to Talk Yankee. *It included loads of helpful hints on Maine language for the non-native. He is a popular author and performer, and as he advertises on his website, he's done, "SIX books, TEN albums, and TEN videos! Some of 'em million-sellers! (still got a million of 'em in the cellar)." Courtesy, Tim Sample*

cheek Maine lingo into the mix. Maine people don't always take things too seriously or too pompously.

"Wicked good" is an expression popularized by a man who might be called the dean of Maine humorists. At least Tim Sample achieved a national audience when he was recruited by Charles Kuralt in 1993 to appear as a regular on the CBS program *Sunday Morning*. His stint on the show was billed as "Postcards from Maine," a name taken from one of his many books and records. Other works of his include titles such as *Lobsters, Laughter and Lighthouses* and *Tourist Huntin' in Maine*, blurbed as "Tim interviews tourists about natives and natives about tourists" and "The results are hilarious."

A good deal of Maine humor revolves around tourists, most of them considered dumb, or "numb," to substitute a more common Maine word. "Number than a pounded thumb" Mainers will say of someone who is not too bright. The tourist, with questions that the locals invariably conceive of as "numb," bears the brunt of the gibes. Examples:

The tourist who asks the farmer by the roadside: "How do I get to Dexter High School?" Answer, after a thoughtful pause: "Waill, I guess you got to start in the first grade."

Or in the same vein:

A tourist motorist facing a fork in the road, inquiring of a native: "Does it matter which route I take to Bridgton?" "Not to me, it don't" is the dead pan answer.

Tim Sample is a master of this type of repartee. One of his books, recently reissued, is *Saturday Night at Moody's Diner*, a very real and popular restaurant on Route 1 in Waldoboro, with an introduction by none other than that "wicked famous Maine author Stephen King." Writes King about Sample: "He's funny if you come from Augusta, Maine. He's just as funny if you come from Augusta, Georgia."

Humor goes back a long way in Maine writing, probably even before Seba Smith who was doing political satire in the 1820s. One of the nation's first famous humorists—and Abraham Lincoln's favorite—was Artemas Ward, the stage name of Maine-born Charles Farrar Browne. Tim Sample gives full credit to two of his predecessors for reviving the art in the 1970s—Marshall Dodge and Bob Bryan, the perfectors of the "Bert and I" series of piquant dialogues. Dodge died tragically in 1982, killed by a hit and run driver while riding his bicycle during a Hawaiian vacation. By then, new practitioners had begun appearing on the scene.

Washington County native Kendall Morse was among them. One of his favorite stories involves not a hopeless tourist but a bald old downeaster named Uriah Boardman, standing outside the famous Helen's Restaurant in Machias. While he and Boardman are talking, a seagull flies by and poops on Boardman's bare skulltop. As Morse describes it, "He just stood there, looking numb, he's good at that." Morse quickly offered to run and get some toilet paper. Boardman shook his head. "What's the use o' that?" he asked. "By the time you get back, that gull'll be a mile away." One of Morse's books, incidentally, is called *Sea Gulls and Summer People*.

Others who do Maine humor include Mark Easton, with his character Hugh Maine, Moose Ranger, featuring stories of *Siberia*, an actual section of the actual town of Patten, in a remote area at the northern gateway to Baxter State Park and the Allagash.

Gary Crocker, from the Augusta region, who works at the legislature on occasion, no doubt, finds plenty of humor there. He also has a pet pink flamingo lawn ornament he has named Filbert and does an early morning. radio show called *Morning in Maine*.

Joe Perham, occupant of Trap Corner in West Paris, where the famed Indian wise woman Molly Ockett hung a bear trap in a tree to indicate the site of her buried treasure. Perham will also do Abraham Lincoln's humorous stories.

Robert Skoglund, the "Humble Farmer," hosts a regular radio program on Maine Public Broadcasting Network. For over twenty years, "Humble" has brought his listeners jazz mixed with yankee wit—an unusual and entertaining combination. Courtesy, Robert Skoglund

Robert Skoglund, from mid-coast St. George, has had his own show, *The Humble Farmer*, on Maine Public Radio for twenty years. He always refers to himself as "Humble," and speaks with an unbelievable Maine accent, both on and off the air.

This humor is genuinely a form of Maine culture, reaching up from a depth in the soul of the state that is every bit as real as anything Carolyn Chute or Stephen King or Richard Russo has put into prose

It is timeless, too.

Witness these examples from a long list of equivalents in Maine lingo—and from a Maine perspective—for present day computer language terms.

Dot matrix = Old Dan Matrix's wife

Software = The dumb plastic knives and forks at McDonald's

Mouse = What makes the holes in the Cheerios box

Network = Mending holes in the gillnet

Netscape = What haddock do when you don't do your network

Download = Getting the firewood off the truck

Floppy disk = What you get from downloading too much firewood

LOBSTERIN'

Finally, as an undying symbol of Maine, there is the lobster (*homarus americanus*), two-clawed and bright red when cooked. Thanks to air transportation, its delicious flesh is now enjoyed all over the country and around the world—a delicacy whose trademark is always "Maine Lobster," even if it came from Massachusetts, and priced right up there with rare goodies like caviar and foie gras. Within the state, some Mainers living away from the coast have disputed its dominance as the state's image. During a debate in Augusta over what symbol to put on Maine's license plate, the lobster, while a favorite, drew spirited opposition. The state flower, which is the pine cone and tassel, was proffered, as was the potato, the blueberry and the moose. To no avail—*homarus americanus* won out, but its reproduction on the metal plaque was so poorly done that many Maine people revolted against what they said looked like "a boiled cockroach." The next set of plates sported a chickadee, the state bird, on a pine cone. Yet a lobster plate is back, now with a handsome likeness of the incomparable crustacean. This plate comes at an extra cost, but the money helps fund marine research.

In an age of overfishing and concern about exhaustion of the oceans' resources, the Maine lobster fishery represents an object lesson in conservation.

Lobster catches, unlike most fish landings, have not declined, despite continued increases in the number of traps in the water. Indeed, in the twenty-first century so far, they are said to have "exploded"—double and often triple the number of pounds taken from 1950 to 1990. Even in 2003, when the catch was down by about a third from

2002, it was still triple what it had been in 1991. And 2002 had set an all time record: 57.2 million pounds, with a value of $188.5 million.

Why is this so? The question is often asked by alarmed conservationists who fear the resource is being overexploited, despite these good results. One answer comes from the lobstermen, themselves. Although they have the reputation of being extreme individualists, they band together to maintain the regulations they need to ensure future supplies of marketable lobsters and see that these laws are obeyed. Minimum and maximum lobster sizes, a ban on catching females, limiting the number of traps and, more recently, the number of lobstering licenses, are measures that help keep the fishery healthy. The state of Maine has gone a step farther, too, by allowing the lobstermen to police themselves. The state is now divided into seven lobstering zones and the license holders in each form regional councils that set the local rules and see they are enforced with the help of the wardens of the Department of Marine Resources.

This system was modeled in part on a tradition established voluntarily 100 years ago by the year-round residents of the island of Monhegan. There, on Trap Day, December 1, the lobstermen at this remote location far offshore in Penobscot Bay put their traps in the water simultaneously. Trap Day is sometimes later, if the weather is bad or one of the lobstermen is incapacitated. No traps will be set until everyone's trap can be set. It is a community project and all of the townsfolk pitch in to assemble the traps, even those who don't lobster.

No summer in Maine is complete without a lobster meal. Whether you boil it, bake it or cook it in seaweed over hot coals, lobster is a delicacy associated with the Maine summer. Clams, too, are a part of that meal— and add an ear of corn and you have the perfect Maine cuisine. This photo was taken at the Yarmouth Clam Festival, a sure place to sate your seafood cravings. Photo by Michael Leonard

Blueberries and apples are two of the Maine agricultural products that rely on migrant workers to harvest a good part of the crop each year. Latino and Jamaican workers travel to Maine to work in the orchards or barrens, but there has always been a certain number of seasonal workers who come in from Canada, too. Both apples and wild blueberries are traditional Maine crops, and blueberries are the state's fifth largest agricultural product. Courtesy, David Yarborough, Maine Cooperative Extension Service

Also, this lobsterin' is done in the winter, when most other Maine lobstermen do not venture out to sea. The rationale on Monhegan is that this leaves the lobsterman to do other work in the summer when there is a lively tourist and summer resident trade.

Responsible management is not the only reason given for the remarkable condition of lobsterin' in Maine. The demise of groundfishing in the Gulf of Maine is offered as another consideration. Cod, haddock and other market fish eat young lobsters. The plummeting of these stocks means a rise in surviving juvenile lobsters. The availability of a plentiful supply of edible food in the form of lobster bait in the traps and the minimum size rule has made Maine's lobster "pot" filled waters like a "lobster free-lunch delicatessen," in one downeaster's words. A Gulf of Maine Research Institute researcher also credits Maine lobstermen's choice of herring as bait. Lobsters grow 16 percent more on herring than on other baits, he discovered, and Maine lobstermen use 220 million pounds of herring a year.

Investigations of what author Trevor Corson called "The Secret Life of Lobsters" in his 2004 book by that title are continually underway at various Maine institutions. There are many varia-tions to the mysteries of lobster abundance and decline. Some ground-breaking studies deal with lobster larvae and their disbursement in the Gulf of Maine and why and how these free-floating entities settle on the bottom where they do. A new wrinkle in this lobster work is the collabora-tion between Maine scientists and lobstermen, exchanging the intellectual knowledge of academics and the experience of those whose livelihoods depend on intuitively learning the ways and habitats of these creatures.

When the first settlers came to Maine in the early 1600s, lobsters were plentiful. They could be picked up on the beach and speared in shallow water. Because they were so common—and cheap—a colonial ordinance decreed that you were not allowed to feed your servants lobster more than three times a week.

Such incredible abundance has not yet returned as far as present lobster populations are concerned. But almost 400 years later, they are still teeming in the offshore Maine waters, bringing millions of dollars in revenue every year. Additionally, the lobsters put smiles to millions of faces of people from "away" whenever Maine is mentioned and memo-ries arise, both visual and mouth watering, of those

Eleven miles off the coast of Maine, Monhegan is a ruggedly beautiful place. The island is only a mile long, but walking several trails lead to fabulous views. As if there wasn't enough natural beauty, Monhegan is also home to several artists who open their galleries to visitors. Courtesy, Maine Historical Society

famed red-shelled seafood dinners that taste so wicked good.

CONCLUSION

The timeless and sustaining lobster population in Maine waters is possibly a more appropriate symbol for ending this story of the Pine Tree State, in which the once-majestic stands of white pines are no longer dominant. Maine changes and yet, withal, remains its eternal and *different* self. That says something about its gorgeous geography, especially the flinty underpinnings of its rock-strewn soil, as well as the character of its people which is strong, stubborn and yet absorptive and tolerant. Over the years Mainers have transmitted their hominess and sense of humor, infused solidity to the generations populating the land, whether home-born or arrived from"away," even from as far *away* a place as Somalia.

Tucked in the farthest northeastern reaches of the United States, between Canada and New Hampshire, the State of Maine, an independent entity since 1820, has played well its part as one of the stars on the field of blue in our nation's flag. It has given the U.S. outstanding leaders, environmental inspiration and a place to relax and refresh in a hectic, globalized world. It has preserved an air of kindliness and measure and good common sense in an age of hype. And yet Maine is no *stick-in-the-mud*—it keeps up with the times, swings in its own catchy way and maintains its very real if not quite definable "mystique" through the ever-changing years.

Red's Eats in Wiscasset is a classic roadside attraction on the coast of Maine. Everyone has a favorite—with low-key meals served on paper plates and eaten out back at the picnic tables. You place your order at the counter and wait for your number to be called, all the while smelling the delicious fried clams and lobster rolls that mean summer in Maine. Photo by Stephanie Philbrick

Old rock walls still snake through fields and woods around Maine. The walls marked property boundaries, but they also made use of the many rocks farmers had to remove when they cleared land for farming. Autumn in Vienna, Maine (pronounced Vy-enna). Photo by Scott Landry

In the 1600s, there were nearly 200 people living at the village of Pemaquid in New Harbor. Though it was destroyed during King Philip's War in 1676, extensive archaeological study has given us a good view of life in the village. Nearby is a cemetery with stones dating from the seventeenth and eighteenth centuries. Photo by Stephanie Philbrick

Below left
The dome of the Maine State House in Augusta. Photo by Stephanie Philbrick

A maple tree in full fall glory at the Cumberland Congregational Church. Photo by Michael Leonard

Marshall Point Light sits at the entrance to Point Clyde. Photo by Michael Leonard

Opposite page top
Wild blueberries are native to the region of Maine and maritime Canada. They are called wild because the plant spreads itself naturally as opposed to being planted. Blueberries constitute the fifth largest agricultural crop in Maine and cover over 60,000 acres. Photo by David Yarborough. Courtesy, Maine Cooperative Extension

Fort Point Light in Stockton Springs. Built in 1836, the brick tower was commissioned under President Andrew Jackson. Photo by Michael Leonard

Previous page far left
Casco Bay Lines offers passenger ferry and mailboat service to Peaks, Long, Cliff and the other islands of Casco Bay. Collectively owned by the people who live on the islands, CBL serves over 977,000 passengers each year. Photo by Stephanie Philbrick

Previous page right
Brownstones on Deering Street in Portland. Photo by Nancy Noble

Above
Almost 7 percent of Maine's 19,750,000 acres are devoted to agriculture. Photo by Michael Leonard

Top
Fishing and pleasure boats crowd a Maine harbor.
Courtesy, Camden-Rockport Chamber of Commerce

Above
Seagulls circling a lobster boat off Camden. Courtesy,
Camden-Rockport Chamber of Commerce

Left
The lobster industry works very hard at regulating
itself and maintaining the stocks in Maine waters.
While observing size regulations and returning all
egg-bearing females to the water, lobstermen still
send 14.2 million pounds of lobster to market each year.
Courtesy, Camden-Rockport Chamber of Commerce

Above
Big and small boats at Bar Harbor. The windjammer St. Croix at the pier and kayaks on shore. Courtesy, Bar Harbor Chamber of Commerce

Left
For nearly fifteen years Lewiston has been host to the Great Falls Balloon Festival. Colorful balloons dominate the skyline, but carnival rides, parachutists and fireworks round out the festivities. Courtesy, Lewiston Sun Journal

Opposite page
Burnt Island Lighthouse near Boothbay Harbor. Photo by Michael Leonard

Above
The HMS Rose *off of Portland Head Light in Casco Bay. Over 400,000 people toured the historic tall ships during Opsail 2000. Photo by Michael Leonard*

Right
Rockport from the harbor. Photo by Rodd Collins

Above
Most tourists see this popular and often photographed tourist attraction in the summer. Portland Head Light in Cape Elizabeth is equally beautiful in winter. Photo by Michael Leonard

Left
Rock Beach at Frenchboro. Photo Rodd Collins

Above
The great thing about Nordic or cross country skiing is that you can head out the backdoor whenever there is snow. Snowmobile trails do double duty and provide great, groomed trails for skiers. Photo by Moe Dubreuil

Right
With plenty of snow and 13,000 miles of trails, Maine is a snowmobiling paradise. Photo by Scott Landry

Above
From 2002 to 2004 Bangor was host to the National Folk Festival, a government-sponsored festival featuring music, crafts and culture from around the world. Bangor has continued the tradition with its own American Festival on the waterfront. Pictured is the festival in August 2005. Photo by Stephanie Philbrick

Left
L.L. Bean is one of Maine's top tourist attractions, but Freeport is also home to over 170 shops and boutiques. Over 4 million visitors come to the shopping mecca each year. Courtesy, Freeport Merchant's Association

Opposite page top
Sugarloaf USA ski resort started in the 1950s with a few trails hand-cut through the woods. Since then the "Loaf" has grown to over 130 trails and over a million skiers per year. In this picture taken in the spring, the ski slopes are still visible. Photo by Stephanie Philbrick

Opposite page bottom
Fox Islands Thoroughfare near Vinalhaven. Photo by Rodd Collins

219

Above
In 1873, looking for a way to protect his ears while skating, Chester Greenwood, a native of Farmington, invented earmuffs. Each December, locals don their "ear protectors" and pay tribute to Greenwood with a parade. Photo by Scott Landry

Above right
A quiet Boothbay Harbor in the off-season. Photo by Stephanie Philbrick

Right bottom
Holiday spirit on the Maine coast. Photo by Nancy Noble

Below
Golf at the Sugarloaf Golf Club in Carrabassett Valley. Photo by Scott Landry

Top
Christmas lights on Nubble Light in York. Photo by Michael Leonard

Left
Aerial view of the Kennebec River. Photo by Stephanie Philbrick

Above
Lupine bloom on roadsides and in fields throughout Maine each summer. Deer Isle celebrates the favorite flower with a Lupine Festival each June. Courtesy, Rangeley Chamber of Commerce

Aerial view of Portland Harbor. An oil tanker is at the Portland Pipeline terminal. The oil storage tanks in South Portland are located where the World War II shipbuilding yards used to be. Photo by Stephanie Philbrick

11

CHRONICLES
OF LEADERSHIP

Fishing first brought Europeans to the shores of Maine. Well, not exactly at first. The fishermen who came from the Basque country in Spain, Brittany in France and in later years the "West Country" of England, were leery of the Indians on the mainland. So, when they landed to dry and salt their catches before bringing them back home for sale, it was on the islands off the Maine coast.

Several of these areas became beehives of activity for the English—Damariscove Island, Richmond's Island and Appledore Island, among the Isles of Shoals, whose ownership today is split between Maine and New Hampshire. Contact with the Indians was imminent, particularly after settlements started to spring up in the 1630s. The Pilgrims at Plymouth swapped corn they grew with the Maine Indians downeast and up the Kennebec River, receiving furs in return. The prime fur was beaver, much sought after in Europe for the manufacture of men's hats.

As settlement spread north of the Piscataqua River (the boundary between Maine and New Hampshire), so did agriculture. Farming then, and well into the 19th century, was mostly for home consumption, although animals were often walked from southern Maine to a major livestock market in Brighton, Massachusetts.

Fishing continued, but in a different fashion. The vessels went out of Maine; the catches were consumed there, not in Europe. Salted cod, however, was shipped to the West Indies and the southern part of the U.S. to be used as cheap food for slaves. Merchant shipping developed and handled exports of lumber and pork; imports of sugar and tea from the tropics and luxury items from the Orient. Maine also became a shipbuilding center. Soon, Maine sea captains were roaming as far as Asia, from which one of them, Captain Samuel Clough, brought back a type of cat, now popularly known as the Maine Coon Cat.

On another of his voyages, this time to France, Clough was supposed to bring back ex-Queen Marie Antoinette, who was fleeing from the revolutionaries who had overthrown her husband. But she dallied too long on the way to the ship, was recaptured and all that arrived in Maine on Clough's vessel was her furniture.

Large scale commercial agriculture commenced in Maine with the potato, allegedly brought by Irish refugees escaping the "Potato Famine." Primarily, the tasty spuds were grown in Aroostook County, all of which became part of Maine following the Webster-Ashburton Treaty of 1842. Manufacturing did not set in fully until after the Civil War, but during that conflict Maine turned out 5 percent of all the gunpowder used by the Union Army. The chief postwar manufactures were initially in the textile fields, as the immigration of French Canadians provided low cost and reliable workers. Shoe production followed. This combination of shoes and cloth was of major importance to the Maine economy until recent years.

As the most heavily forested state percentage-wise (95 percent), Maine was a center for creating lumber early on. Indeed, in the 1830s Bangor was the "Lumber Capital of the World." Once a technique had been devised to turn wood pulp into paper in the late 19th century, the emphasis changed to paper-making. International Paper Company and Great Northern Paper Company were giant complexes that originated in Maine. Until very recently, pulp and paper was the number one industry in the state. That honor has since been bestowed on tourism.

Tourism really grew in Maine at the close of the Civil War when the few private homes that had been receiving visitors as boarding rooms were replaced by large hotels in certain localities, especially on the coast and at inland lakes. Some spots became extremely fashionable for the wealthy of the big eastern cities—places like Bar Harbor, York Harbor, Prouts Neck, Poland Springs and Mount Kineo. The growth of the Interstate Highway System and Maine's own Turnpike (initiated in the 1940s) has simply accelerated the trend of converting Maine into what its license plate proclaims it to be: VACATIONLAND

The "new economy," dependent upon high technology, electronics and educational excellence has also reached into Maine. However, traditional skills are still at work. Lobstering remains big business, wood products are still important, potatoes are still grown and ship building and repair continues on a large scale. A return to craftsmanship is evident in the state. As always, Maine is a magnet and inspiration for artists and writers.

BROWNE TRADING COMPANY

Rod Browne Mitchell embodies the soul of a Maine fisherman, just like his grandfather. Through his time spent with his older relative, Earl Browne, Mitchell learned about the fish that inhabited the rivers of Maine and the Atlantic Ocean. In turn, Mitchell thirsted to know everything about sea life and pursued a degree in marine biology from the Southern Maine Technical Institute in South Portland. Knowledge in hand, Mitchell created a leading wholesale seafood business, offering the best catch from the North and South Atlantic, the Hawaiian Pacific and European waters. His expertise in what makes fresh seafood "fresh," along with his masterful entrepreneurial skills, have made him and Browne Trading Company the seafood wholesaler of choice for many of the country's top chefs and restaurants.

Before he went into the seafood business, Mitchell was a wine connoisseur. In 1979 Mitchell met a local wine importer who taught him everything he knew about wine. Mitchell grew almost as passionate about fine wines as he was about fishing, enough so that he opened his own gourmet wine and cheese shop in

The Browne Family with a Kennebec River sturgeon, circa 1946.

Camden. There, in the early 1980s, the legendary French chef, Jean-Louis Palladin, shopped during his New England vacations. At the time Palladin, who is considered one of the culinary geniuses of the 20th century, had just opened Jean Louis at the Watergate at the Watergate Hotel in Washington, D.C. Frustrated with the quality of American seafood, Palladin asked Mitchell to find him fresh scallops. Armed with his knowledge of the local waters and experience as a scuba diver Mitchell went in search of the perfect scallop. As a result, Palladin introduced the now classic "Maine Diver Scallop" to American cuisine. Since then, master chefs have been coming to Browne Trading for the best and also the most exotic the sea has to offer. These include Peekytoe (named by Mitchell from the name "picked toe" used by the cottage industry of Maine crab pickers) and Piballes (glass eels).

In 1991 Rod and his wife Cynde established the Browne Trading Company. They opened their business on Merrill's Wharf in the heart of the working waterfront, steps away from the local fisherman's landing. The reputation of the company's seafood grew as did their selection of fish. In addition to native New England fish purchased daily from the Portland Fish Exchange and other local sources, their menu of fish expanded to include imported high quality Turbot, Daurade and Loup de Mer from Europe; John Dory from New Zealand; Hawaiian Opah and many other species from all over the world.

Browne Trading is now a leading supplier in the United States of an exemplary selection of farmed and sustainable caviars. Caviars are imported from France, Italy, Germany, Iran and former states of the Soviet Union, as well as a selection of North American roes. The company's selection of caviar includes the private stock designated and reserved for the renowned former executive chef of Le Cirque, Daniel Boulud, who is the owner and master chef of the cel-

Browne Trading Company's American Spoonbill caviar with their signature handcrafted smoked salmon.

Browne Trading offers a wide selection of fresh seafood, exquisite caviars, wines, cheeses, local Maine produce and a variety of gourmet culinary items such as oils, vinegars and salts.

ebrated Daniel in New York and several other restaurants, bistros and cafes around the country.

The company also sells its own line of caviars under the Browne Trading label including their exclusive Caviar Astara, from the pristine deep waters of the southern Caspian Sea.

Browne Trading is also the sole producer of "Chef Daniel Boulud Smoked Scottish Salmon" and their signature label "Scotch Cured Smoked Scottish Salmon," both of which are produced in the Browne Trading smoke house under the direction and care of their dedicated smoke master.

Following the 2001 death of Chef Palladin, with whom the Mitchells enjoyed a twenty year relationship, the Jean-Louis Palladin Foundation was formed in 2002 to preserve his memory and continue his legacy of passionate cooking. Part of the foundation's mission is to educate young chefs about the sources of high quality seafood.

As a member of the Founding Board of Directors, Mitchell formed the Rod and Cynde Mitchell Internship. This week-long "Trade Internship" allows the awardee to experience first-hand how fish and caviar are selected and handled and to work with the dayboat fisherman and scallop divers

off the coast of Maine during the height of the winter diver scallop harvest.

In 2000 the company expanded to include the Browne Trading Market, a retail shop located in the same Commercial Street property. The gourmet store offers locals and visitors alike the same gourmet caviar it sells to many of the nation's top chefs, as well as an excellent selection of fresh fish, a variety of breads and cheeses made by local and regional artisans, local produce, daily fresh soups and an array of common to exotic cooking oils, vinegars and salts. The retail store also offers the largest wine selection in Portland.

The fish cases at Browne Trading Market on Commercial Street in Portland showcase the daily selections of fresh fish and shellfish from Maine and around the world.

"Browne Trading Market enjoys being able to fill a very special niche in a city like Portland that has such a wonderful heritage of fishing and a working waterfront," said Rod Mitchell. "This heritage has cultivated a great community that appreciates a number of nationally acclaimed restaurants as well as households that love being able to shop for local and exotic foods in one place."

Many of those Maine restaurants and their chefs are customers of Browne Trading Market, including Rob Evans of Hugo's, Melissa Kelly of Primo, and Clark Frasier and Mark Gaier of Arrow's Restaurant.

For both Cynde and Rod Mitchell, being able to offer their neighbors the same quality products they sell to the famed chefs and restaurants of Boston, New York and Chicago was a key reason for establishing the retail market.

"Portland has a unique blend of sophistication and small city appeal. While it supports some fine restaurants, it also needed a source for fresh ingredients where customers can try things that aren't found anywhere else. It has always been a great pleasure for us to interact with our customers and share the joy of some great food and wines," said Cynde Mitchell, chief executive officer of Browne Trading Company.

Browne Trading also has a thriving retail mail order business and ships throughout the continental United States and as far away as Alaska and Hawaii.

To learn more about Browne Trading Company and its wholesale, retail and mail order businesses visit them online at www.browne-trading.com.

CITY OF AUBURN

As the son of second-generation French Canadians who were proud of both their foreign heritage and their American homeland, Normand Guay, mayor of Auburn, didn't always fit in. His mother Anna struggled to raise her two sons after Norm's father died when he was only five years old. But his mother instilled in him a spirit of public service and a feeling of obligation to make the world a better place. Unbeknownst to young Norm, he was to become the city of Auburn's first Franco-American mayor and play a leading role in the city's most dramatic growth and revitalization in nearly forty years.

Together with its neighboring city of Lewiston immediately across the Androscoggin River, Auburn comprises Maine's second largest metropolitan area. It is the largest city in land area, having more than sixty-five square miles, and is the county seat.

Mayor Normand Guay.

Auburn was first settled in 1786 and founded as a city in 1869, although it was populated with American Indians long before that. Auburn has a long history as a farming, wood milling, industrial and manufacturing community. This progressive community has been a leader in innovation throughout its history.

The factory system of making shoes originated in Auburn in 1835. During the Civil War, Auburn was considered the shoe manufacturing center of Maine. This may account for the use of shoes in the design of the city seal. The city understood early on that transportation was critical for the future growth and economic development of the area. Together with its neighbor Lewiston, the cities built a railroad in 1849, street cars came about in the 1870s and the city established an airport in 1928. In 1917 Auburn was the first community in Maine and the second in the U.S to adopt the council-manager form of government.

The city is proud of its history and heritage, but the focus and vision is for its future. This notable trait of the people of Auburn and their leaders is proclaimed in the city's Latin motto: *Vestigia Nulla Retrorsum*, which means "No Step Backwards."

The most recent transformation occurred in the past decade. During the early 1990s, Auburn, like the rest of Maine and the country, was in the throes of a recession. Thanks to the leadership of the mayor, city councilors and the city manager, this period when economic activity came to a standstill and businesses were closing was used to lay the ground work for the coming economic turnaround.

In this period, Auburn planned for the future, including developing an industrial park. It

Main Street, Auburn.

was successful at getting state and federal matching funds to build an industrial park that would provide construction jobs initially and attract businesses that would bring quality manufacturing and skilled labor positions. By the time this project was off the ground, the city and the region started to come out of the recession and additional projects that it had been working on began to take shape. These included the Maine Intermodal Facility, an innovative truck-to-rail transportation project that with its double-stacking capability would move goods and supplies from Canada to Maine to the Northwest and on to the Pacific rim and Asia. This project made Maine businesses competitive in the global market. Whereas Maine was traditionally considered at the "end of the line" in the economic chain, the intermodal facility made obsolete the old saying about Maine: "You can't get there from here."

During the recession, Mayor Guay served as a city councilor and encouraged these planning efforts in order to adapt to the changing economy. Along with his predecessor Mayor Lee Young, they championed the most visible and complete rebirth of the city's downtown which, like many central cities throughout the U.S., had fallen on hard times with the advent of malls and the attraction of suburbia. With the city's industrial and manufacturing base fully secure, Mayor Young, and then-Councilor Guay and fellow councilors, they turned the community's focus to the downtown. They embarked on a comprehensive redevelopment of the downtown, including a citizen's committee which served as the sounding board, cheerleaders and advocates for a reinvigorated downtown. In 1997 the city council accepted the blueprint created for the development of the downtown, called Auburn Downtown Action Plan for Tomorrow (ADAPT).

The Great Falls Balloon Festival. Photo by Russ Dillingham

The combination of the leadership of the local elected officials and the ADAPT plan was a powerful combination which resulted in an array of development based on public-private partnerships. These include the improvement of the Riverwalk, a pedestrian loop which hugs the banks of the Androscoggin River and connects Auburn and Lewiston; building the city's only downtown hotel, the $10 million Hilton Garden Inn which opened in 2002 and expanded in 2006 due to its success; the renovation and expansion of a downtown landmark into a restaurant, shops and offices which created an attractive and welcoming gateway to the city and its

downtown; the $7 million expansion of the historic 1904 public library; Auburn's first bed and breakfast inn; the renovation and expansion of Auburn Hall into combined municipal school offices; two new parking garages; a proposed 200,000-square-foot office and retail complex and plans for a regional performing arts center.

The city of Auburn also takes pride in its collaborative and "can do" attitude. No other community in Maine engages more in delivering services jointly than Auburn and Lewiston. From its earliest joint ventures—the Lewiston-Auburn Railroad (1872) and the Auburn-Lewiston Airport (1936)—to its groundbreaking tax sharing agreement, the cities have done things jointly when it made sense for the taxpayers. Most recently, Mayor Guay and his brother Mayor Lionel Guay of Lewiston, have led the way for expanding the cities joint services by establishing a citizens commission that reviewed existing city services and made recommendations to the twin cities' mayors and the city councils regarding the next level of partnership that they should reach—up to and including merging the two cities into one.

Mayor Guay does not take any credit for the community's growth, its new improved image, its twenty-first century rebirth or the other successes during nearly fifteen years of elected leadership. He attributes that to his fellow elected officials and the mayors who preceded him. Upon his retirement, it will be remembered that his common man approach to leadership spurred a community to believe in itself and achieve.

CITY OF LEWISTON

First elected to government office at the age of twenty-one in Lisbon, Maine, James A. Bennett has been a catalyst for unique, positive change for the past two decades. The only difference is that now, the City Administrator is leading a notable revitalization in Lewiston, his hometown, currently the second largest community in Maine. With a strong background in financial planning, economic development and municipal leadership, he brings the experience of several positions to his current job, which includes a strong focus on the city's newest venture. His perspective, energy and ability to get things done have guided Lewiston through difficult times and ignited a spark that has set the city on fire with a project that could inspire any small town that has fallen on hard times.

With a long list of awards for his own and his community's accomplishments—Bennett claims his first win was due to name recognition, as his mother had been highly involved in the community. He was believed to be the youngest selectman elected

City Administrator James A. Bennett.

in Maine's history. At age twenty-six, he became the town manager of Dixfield, Maine. He then moved to several town manager positions—New Gloucester for almost three years, then seven years in Old Orchard Beach, a beach community that is heavily populated in the summer. After six years in Westbrook, he brought his vital experience home to Lewiston about five years ago.

Located in south-central Maine, Lewiston had been known since the 1800s primarily for its production of textiles and footwear and for being a rough, worn-out and unsophisticated

mill town. Large brick mills constructed near the Androscoggin River housed these industries and fully utilized the river as a power source. Immigrants came to work in textile mills and, notably, made Civil War uniforms.

Over time the river became polluted and neighborhoods, eyesores. As sometimes happens in areas where blue collar workers live and work, Lewiston's image suffered. Outsiders looked down on the city and its inhabitants. People exiting the turnpike into Lewiston saw a neglected city.

When Bennett came on as city administrator, he recognized what Lewiston was missing and took action. "I focus on the good things in every community," he said. "If you can help people be proud of where they are, the image changes. My goal was to do that in Lewiston."

His plan was twofold. First, aware that television, newspapers and magazines are primary sources of information, Bennett worked with the media to focus on positive stories about the area and its people. Second, he convinced the community to acknowledge that the aesthetic people traveling through major arteries downtown saw, as well as entering Lewiston from the turnpike, a city of daytime drunks, hookers and dilapidated neighborhoods. To change how people perceived the town, Lewiston had to physically alter its appearance. "We needed to create windshield wow," Bennett said.

At the time, a former Lewiston city administrator was in charge of development; a former city manager of Lewiston's sister city, Auburn, was director of the Lewiston's Chamber of Commerce. "When I told them I wanted to relocate them to this historical building that was designated to be torn down, they thought I was out of my mind. They saw our efforts

A view of the new Andover College and a section of the new Pontiac garage. The college is currently completing a $400,000 expansion after only two years of being established in the Gateway.

as trying to move them into a slum," Bennett recalled. Convincing these two people to move to the Southern Gateway was a major hurdle for his plan.

Bennett also knew of three businesses that were looking to relocate. To encourage them to move into the Southern Gateway, he designed a special deal. "We convinced each of the businesses that if they moved to this neighborhood, the others would move, too." Those three business pioneers were Oxford Networks, which provides fiber optics to Lewiston-Auburn; Northeast Bank, which moved into its corporate headquarters and VIP Auto Parts, an auto supplier. Knowing a refusal from one would kill the deal with the others, Bennett breathed a sigh of relief when all three agreed. In turn, Andover College opened its second Maine campus in that area. The move has been so successful that an additional building has also been renovated to accommodate them. Also, the Public Theatre has campaigned to renovate its performing arts venue. "We built a parking garage for the area and made street improvements," Bennett said. Once these were made, private sector investment

A view of the left side of the Southern Gateway, heading into downtown Lewiston, shows the new Northeast Bank corporate headquarters and the new Oxford Networks Fiber Optic Telecommunications building.

began. "The Chamber of Commerce was able to raise $600,000 from members to be paid over a three-year period to pay for one floor of the reconstructed four-story building there. They raised this money in about ninety days. This was a place no one wanted to go to before!" Bennett said. Now there are many other community-wide renovations planned, including healthcare facilities and a former church that has become a second home to the Mid-Coast Symphony Orchestra. "Once you get a couple of things going, they become a giant, unstoppable snowball rolling down the hill."

Jim Bennett understands that people do not always recognize what they have in their community and sometimes underestimate what is there. Bennett feels it often helps to have someone from the outside look at things locals may take for granted—someone who sees them a bit differently.

"I was surprised how quickly it happened, but I'm not surprised that it has been hap-

pening. The people who work for Lewiston city government care about what they do. For a long time, city organization was based on financial accountings and structured paperwork, but I'm a big picture person," Bennett said. "I like to figure out what's needed, let people in charge of their departments do their job, while honoring ethical and moral standards. We have talented department heads who know how to do the impossible with few resources. The challenge for any high-performance organization is to get talented managers to focus on working together toward the community's mission. We do a lot of team building. I could disappear for weeks, and they would still get the job done."

Bennett's greatest satisfaction comes from knowing that people are no longer embarrassed about their hometown. "When I run into a local citizen who says thanks for making me proud of where I live—that makes me proud."

The Southern Gateway's 400-car Pontiac parking garage opened in 2005.

DAY'S JEWELERS

Day's Jewelers, a rare combination of style, quality and innovation, has been in business in Maine for over ninety years. They have achieved this longevity by becoming the jewelry store Mainers rely on to celebrate their most precious events and occasions. Their history has intertwined two Maine families devoted to carrying on the Day's tradition. It is a true testament to this passion for their work and customers that Day's Jewelers has achieved the same timelessness as its one-of-a-kind pieces.

Day's Jewelers was founded in 1914. Captain Harry Davidson, a Russian immigrant, provided the entrepreneurial foundation. He had retired from life at sea due to ill health, but that didn't keep him off the ocean. Captain Harry would go down to the Portland harbor and row his little boat out in the water. He offered watches and chains straight out of his vest pocket to those on ships in port.

His sons, David, Sidney and Herman Davidson, picked up a thing or two about business from their father. In 1914 they opened shop at 489 Congress Street in Portland. They chose the name Day's, abbrevi-

This wooden sculpture graced Day's store window for fifty years, draped in jewelry and drawing the attention of passers-by. Sidney Davidson considered her the luckiest thing in the company—after he bought her, the company grew and grew.

Day's Jewelers in Caribou, the northernmost store in Maine, circa 1948.

ating their last name to compete with stores with unwieldy monikers like Sears Roebuck and Montgomery Ward.

They also conspired to get Captain Harry to join them in the store. Concerned about their father's daily jaunts to the cold harbor, they came up with a plan to inspire Captain Harry to give up the water. The brothers must have smiled when Captain Harry appeared, newly divested of his boat, and declared, "Some fool offered me twice what my boat is worth!"

Captain Harry became Day's original greeter. He could be found in a chair at the front of the store, welcoming customers. He was well known for always sporting a fresh white boutonniere.

At that time, Day's sold far more than just jewelry. The Davidson brothers knew that they would need to be creative in order to compete in the marketplace. Day's sold fine jewelry as well as refrigerators, house wares, even custom-ground eyeglasses.

The Davidsons were forward thinking in other ways as well. Day's was one of the first stores to offer credit accounts to its customers. This was long before the mass use of the modern credit card. The program allowed many to make purchases they would not otherwise been able to make. Many Mainers to this day credit Day's with giving them their first opportunity to build credit.

The cyclical energy the Davidson family put into motion has reverberated throughout Maine. In a funny way, they assured the passing of their torch to the next generation. In 1937 a ten year-old boy named Robert Corey began sweeping the steps at the store on Congress Street. Little could he have known that one day his own two sons would own Day's Jewelers.

Day's may have stayed a relatively small chain but for larger world events. At the end of World War II,

Day's had three stores in Portland, Bangor and Lewiston. But federal laws were passed which required employers to hire back any returning GIs that had previously been in their employ.

Jeffery Corey, current owner and CEO of Day's, estimates that somewhere between fifteen and eighteen previous Day's employees came back for the war needing jobs. One was his father Robert Corey, then nineteen years old.

Day's didn't have room for more employees at the three established stores. So they decided to expand operations. Robert Corey was sent up to Caribou, a small town near the Canadian border, to manage a new Day's location.

Caribou proved a success in more ways than one. Not only did the new location do well, but Robert's personal luck was going strong. He met Enid Sleeper, the woman who would become his wife, partner and mother to their seven children.

The new Mrs. Corey encouraged Robert to branch out on his own. He did, opening Robert's Jewelry in Madawaska, Maine, utilizing his experience at Day's to build his own store—a traditional family business, where each of the seven children apprenticed in turn. It was an experi-

Day's owners Jeff Corey, Kathy Corey, Jim Corey and Mark Ford were responsible for leading Day's Jewelers into the 21st century.

ence that inspired each of the three sons and four daughters, most of whom are still in the jewelry business.

As a young man newly out of college, Jeffery had dreams of opening his own jewelry store and starting a family, just as his parents had. He shared this with a young woman upon their very first meeting on a December night in 1979. Though she was in the middle of earning her bachelor's in nursing at the University of Southern Maine, she entertained the romantic conversation. It would be nice to get married, have a family and own a business that could bring something special to the lives of others.

A fanciful conversation at the time, but in 1984, Jeffery and the beautiful nursing student, now Mrs. Kathy Corey, were making those dreams a reality. After searching Maine for another community like his beloved Madawaska, Jeff and Kathy launched Jeffery's Fine Jewelers in Waterville.

The store was sold by none other than the remaining Davidson brothers, Sidney and David (Herman

passed away in 1973). Now eighty-five and eighty years old respectively, they were reluctantly letting go of the stores they had built and loved. The Corey's purchase of the Waterville store began a cordial relationship with David Davidson. Once he and Sidney had sold twenty-one of their twenty-two locations, David called Jeff and Kathy Corey. He and Sidney couldn't bear to see the legacy die. Feeling that the Coreys would do justice to the Day's name, David Davidson offered to sell them the final Day's store in Westbrook.

They teamed up with Jeffery's brother, James (Jim) Corey, who holds a Graduate Gemologist degree from the Gemological Institute of America, and Mark Ford, a cousin-in-law of the Corey brothers, who was also an accounting and finance specialist. The four new owners committed themselves to the four core values that had sustained Day's Jewelers over the years.

First was value. The Day's philosophy was that a customer should get a

Day's Waterville store, circa 1940. On the left side of the building, a war bonds advertisement is painted.

wonderful piece of jewelry at the best price. There would be no cleverly positioned, inflated prices at Day's. Specials and sales designed to lure people in would not be necessary. Customers would know that whenever they needed or wanted a special piece of jewelry, they would be able to find the best value at Day's.

Second was equal opportunity. "[The original owners] believed in providing the opportunity for everyone to own fine jewelry," Jeff Corey explained. "Day's had liberal credit programs and a huge inventory of jewelry at every price." Allowing everyone to share in the fine jewelry experience was important to the Day's legacy.

The third value was fostering an environment of trust among employees, vendors and especially customers. This was achieved by never selling, but serving. Each Day's Jewelers location has on-site goldsmiths and trained gemologists, not just salespeople. There are even custom designers ready to work with customers to create completely unique pieces. By consistently providing the very best experience, Day's has come to earn the respect of its customers. It is no small coincidence that each Day's Jewelers routinely wins Market Surveys of America's "Best of the Best" award for top local jewelry store.

Finally, the Day's philosophy embraced an understanding of the sentiment behind jewelry purchases. This was something all of the new owners connected with. "Our belief is that our people are like matchmakers," Mark Ford explained. "They have to understand the context to figure out the right piece of jewelry for the person and the occasion." Jeff Corey elaborated further. "A $10 piece of jewelry could be as valuable to a person as a $1,000 piece to another." The true value lies in the sentiment, and the emotion attached to the item.

David Davidson receives recognition from Sunbeam corporation in 1964. With twenty-two stores throughout Northern New England, Day's became one of the largest Sunbeam appliance dealers in America.

In addition to taking over the Westbrook location, Jeffery's Fine Jewelers was officially converted to a Day's Jewelers. It may never have come to be if the Davidsons hadn't employed young Robert Corey and sent him away to Caribou. This open-door atmosphere went far beyond the Corey family. Employees have always been valued and in turn served loyally. Arthur Childs began at Day's when he too was just ten years old. He remained with the company for nearly sixty years. Five other employees were with Day's for over fifty years.

Day's Jewelers also believes in its employees, and their power to better themselves and their community. When employees wish to further their education, Day's reimburses them fully for tuition upon successful completion of each course. Many employees have been able to take professional and college courses, with one em-

ployee recently earning her master's degree through this program. Day's also boasts the highest percentage of Diamondtologists on staff, as defined by the Diamond Council of America. Jim Corey counts the development of their people as a definite point of pride.

Day's Jewelers has now expanded to five locations throughout Maine and one in New Hampshire. When Jeffery's Fine Jewelers opened in 1984, five employees assisted Jeffery and Kathy Corey. Now the Day's roster tops 135 employees.

Day's leaves an indelible impression with it customers. In fact, Jeffery Corey is approached on a regular basis by people with stories to tell about how Day's touched their lives. Everyone at Day's feels the responsibility to maintain this esteem in their communities. It is what people have come to expect from their favorite fine jewelers.

Jim Corey, owner of Day's and manager of the South Portland location introduces his newly remodeled store. Day's South Portland is Maine's largest jewelry store with over 100 showcases of fine jewelry and watches. The store centerpiece is a hand inlaid marble ball with cascading water weighing nearly 1,000 pounds.

DOWN EAST COMMUNITY HOSPITAL

The foundation for Down East Community Hospital (DECH) was laid in 1957 when a group of dedicated citizens studied the feasibility of establishing a new medical facility in their rural community.

First, they tried simply inviting physicians to settle in the area, but without a local hospital in which to treat patients, few doctors answered the call. The region of 15,000 had only about six general practitioners to serve the area of Washington County. At the time, statistics showed that while in most of the United States there was one doctor for every 752 people, Maine had one doctor for every 914 people. In Washington County the figure was an astounding one doctor for every 3,000 patients.

The citizens created a questionnaire about healthcare or the lack thereof and distributed it to the citizens of the county. The response was overwhelmingly in favor of building a hospital in the area. The group used the responses to encourage citizens in the surrounding towns to form a nonprofit corporation whose goal was to begin the planning of their own community hospital. The group officially incorporated on January 5, 1960.

In March one citizen, C. Alton Bagley, who was president of the Machias Savings Bank, donated fourteen acres of land on Court Street for the new hospital.

The cost of the proposed facility was $800,000. Through the Hill Burton Act, the hospital would receive $360,000 in federal funds for the project. The board had already received nearly $170,000 in cash and pledges from members of the local communities. By 1962 the trustees of the Machias Savings Bank voted to participate in the hospital's first mortgage of $100,000.

The 1962 signing of the mortgage agreement. Seated: DECH board members James Baily, Gilbert Hanson and Arthur Handscom. Standing: Machias Savings Bank board members.

The corporation then employed a professional fundraising company to raise the local financial share of the project. Additionally, an auxiliary was formed by Adelaide Higgins and Mabel Small who, with a group of women, went door-to-door collecting donations for the new hospital.

Construction began on the new facility April 29, 1963. By the fall of 1964 the Down East Community Hospital officially opened its doors with a medical staff of seven licensed physicians and twenty-one nurses. The one-story hospital with thirty-six beds and ten bassinets welcomed their first patient on December 2, 1964.

In 1975 the hospital added to its physical plant—the first of three expansions—allowing extra space for the X-ray, laboratory, and patient examining rooms. Other additions and renovations included a new emergency area in 1989, a special care

When DECH opened its doors in fall of 1964, the employees proudly posed in the entryway of the new hospital.

unit in 1996 and a new operating suite in 1999.

In 2001 and 2002 the hospital faced serious financial and operational issues. Under such conditions, another facility might have sold out to a medical corporation or closed its doors, but the downeast community was determined to save and strengthen the hospital. The board instituted sweeping changes in 2003, including a corporate reorganization.

Susan West, a local business owner and financial services expert who had sat on the board since 1995, stepped up as the board's new chairperson to help ascertain what course of action would be taken. At the same time, a new CEO, Wayne Dodwell, was hired for his acumen for creative solutions and talent for implementing complex plans for the hospital's revitalization and success.

The board, medical staff and administration worked together to steer the organization out of those troubled waters and onto a successful path. This included instituting a corporate reorganization which included the formation of the Down East Health System (DEHS) under which fell Down East Community Hospital, Sunrise Care Facility and the newly formed fundraising subsidiary, the Down East Health Trust. This reorganization resulted in a reduction of operating expenses by 7 percent.

During this period, Dodwell and the Board devised a new campaign to make their intentions clear: "Stabilize, revitalize, and publicize our way to good health." A number of town hall-type meetings with the community and an extensive newspaper, radio and television blitz, provided avenues to inform the community about the important new directions the hospital were taking in order to preserve this important community resource.

Part of the hospital's new plan was to expand and diversify its services.

Wayne Dodwell, president and CEO of Down East Health System joined the team in September of 2002.

In 2003, as part of the corporate reorganization, DECH renewed its commitment to the Sunrise Care Facility, a twenty-eight bed nursing home located in Jonesport, a nearby community. This provided a continuum of care for patients needing skilled nursing care. The philosophy was that Down East Community Hospital should reach out to service the community beyond its four walls and so it made sense that the mission include managing a nursing home operation. The organization also renewed its commitment to the Milbridge Medical Center, a multi-physician practice located in the town of Milbridge, twenty-four miles south of Machias.

The reorganization was followed by the opening of the hospital's first digital X-ray facility, which included one of the first digital mammography units in the state. That same year a hospital helipad was constructed, making emergency care available to a wider range of people, and a Sleep Lab was opened.

The year 2005 brought together a historic partnership with the Maine Veteran's Home to construct a $12 million, private nonprofit thirty bed residential care facility attached to Down East Community Hospital. This project was a boost for the community-at-large as it brought in many construction jobs helped to reduce unemployment in the area.

The property on Court Street as it looked in the Spring of 1963. At that time, the construction on the hospital had just begun.

The collaboration with Maine Veteran's Home gave the hospital the opportunity to complete one of the hospital's major capital investments, a 10,000-square-foot connector building that joins the original hospital structure and the new Maine Veteran's Home. The facility includes a new reception and waiting area, private registration rooms, a café, gift shop, library and additional clinical space. By 2007 it will include a new interfaith chapel.

In August 2005 DECH officially received its "Critical Access Hospital Designation" with twenty-five beds available under that assignment. This strategic move has been part of the major reorganization under Dodwell's leadership. This assignment meant an additional $1.4 million in Medicare and Medicaid reimbursements for the hospital.

In 2005 and 2006 DECH aggressively sought out and hired a number of new physicians specializing in

The construction of the building that connects the hospital to Maine Veteran's Home was completed in 2006. A portion of the connector building is pictured above.

pediatrics, emergency medicine, family practice, internal medicine, obstetrics/ gynecology, pulmonary/critical care, neurology, urology and orthopedics. These additions brought the total DECH medical staff roster to twenty-nine physicians. By the end of 2005 the hospital realized a $1.6 million operational surplus.

A new waiting area, gift shop and hallway are part of the 10,000-square-foot connector building, as well as a café and private registration rooms which are not pictured.

Current plans for the hospital include expanding and improving patient care units, the emergency department and the diagnostic service facilities. As healthcare continues to advance, the hospital remains committed to evolving to meet the emerging needs of the community.

Down East Community Hospital is a shining example of what private citizens and medical professionals can do when they work together for the common good. The result of their hard work is a model hospital that has successfully overcome adversity and that is meeting the challenges of the twenty-first century with strength, compassion and professionalism.

You can learn more about the Down East Community Hospital and the DEHS by visiting their Web site online at www.dech.org.

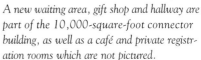

THE JACKSON LABORATORY

Could a mouse be a model for finding the cure for cancer and other human diseases? Clarence Cook Little, founder of The Jackson Laboratory, thought so. While attending Harvard as an undergraduate from 1906 until 1910 under famed geneticist William E. Castle, Little began to mate brother and sister mice in order to develop a genetically uniform strain of mouse, known as DBA (dilute brown non-agouti), that would produce reliable research data. He was studying the genetics of mouse coat color inheritance, work he later pursued as a graduate student at Castle's Bussey Institute.

By 1913 Dr. Little started to investigate the inheritance of tumor susceptibility in mice. Inbred strains, such as the DBA type, were developed in part to determine whether cancer has a genetic predisposition. Little's involvement in these experiments was inspired in part by his father's death due to leukemia. Today, The Jackson

Mount Desert Island native Muriel Davisson, Ph.D., is director of genetic resources at The Jackson Laboratory. Her distinguished career includes developing the world's most widely used mouse model for Down syndrome (shown).

Dr. George Snell (left) shared the 1980 Nobel Prize in Medicine or Physiology for his work in understanding the immune response. His work led to the later success of organ transplantations.

Laboratory is using these inbred strains to identify new cancer genes and to determine which of these genes cooperate to induce cancer, a requisite step for developing combinatorial therapies for treating human cancer.

In the 1920s Dr. Little convinced industrialists Edsel Ford and Roscoe B. Jackson, head of the Hudson Motorcar Company, to support a new cancer genetics research laboratory. With funds from Jackson's will and a land endowment, the Roscoe B. Jackson Memorial Laboratory was founded in 1929 in a small two-story building in Bar Harbor, Maine.

Cancer was the driving force that carried mouse genetics through its first five decades and greatly influenced the development of the mouse as a genetic system. One of the first research projects at the new laboratory was investigating the strikingly high incidence of mammary tumors in the inbred mouse strain known as C3H. The researchers crossed C3H mice with mice from a strain in which mammary tumors were rare. They noticed that females' susceptibility to mammary tumors didn't follow the

normal pattern of inheritance, but rather depended on which parent was from the high-incidence strain. In 1933 the journal *Science* published "The Existence of Non-chromosomal Influences in the Incidence of Mammary Tumors in Mice," the first-ever research paper published with group attribution and credited to the Jackson Laboratory staff.

The Jackson Laboratory was one of the first institutions in America to be designated a Cancer Center by the National Cancer Institute in 1983, and still funded to conduct basic research in the genetics of cancer. About 70 percent of all Jackson Laboratory research has relevance to understanding cancers.

The immune system, another area of research at the Laboratory, provides a major line of defense against infectious microorganisms. However, immune defenses can also attack normal tissues, resulting in autoimmune diseases such as lupus, rheumatoid arthritis or rejection of a transplanted organ. Dr. George Snell (1903–1996), who joined The Jackson Laboratory in 1935, is acknowledged for laying the foundation of modern immunological research. In 1944 Dr. Snell began studying the genetics of tumor transplantation, and by 1947 had discovered the group of genes that would become known as the major histocompatibility complex. Dr. Snell shared the 1980 Nobel Prize in Physiology or Medicine for this groundbreaking work.

In the 1940s Dr. Elizabeth Russell undertook the laborious process of "characterizing" many of the inbred strains maintained at The Jackson Laboratory. This involved recording physical attributes and disease susceptibilities—the foundation for today's giant genetics databases. Dr. Russell has also been credited for her groundbreaking studies of pigmentation, blood-forming cells and germ cells, instrumental in defining the field of red blood cell biology. By the early 1960s Dr. Russell and Dr. Seldon

Clarence Cook Little founded The Jackson Laboratory in 1929.

Bernstein had demonstrated the first successful bone marrow transplants to cure a type of anemia in mice. Since that time, the list of diseases and conditions with treatment potential from a bone marrow transplant has steadily increased. Today, people with immune deficiency disorders may also benefit from bone marrow transplants.

In 1981 the first mouse embryonic stem (ES) cells were isolated from normal embryos, but ES cell research got its start in 1952 at The Jackson Laboratory when Dr. Leroy Stevens conducted what is considered the groundwork for all ES research today. In the March 2000 issue of *The Scientist*, it was noted that "Leroy Stevens is truly the unsung hero of stem cell research."

Embryonic stem (ES) cells are now hailed by researchers and patient groups alike as a future source of new treatments for human diseases. Other kinds of stem cells (such as blood-forming cells in bone marrow), investigated early on by Dr. Russell, are already in therapeutic use. And investigators at The Jackson Laboratory are studying mouse stem cells to understand the powerful developmental

World-renowned geneticist Richard Woychik, Ph.D., came to The Jackson Laboratory as director in 2002, with a background in both academia and industry.

mechanisms involved in creating a blood cell, heart muscle or neuron.

In 1950 Dr. Margaret Dickie and research associate Priscilla Lane found very fat mice in a Jackson colony; the mutation causing the obesity in those mice was designated obese (ob). Then, in 1966 animal care technicians noticed some young mice that were much fatter than their siblings, with symptoms of diabetes, known as diabetes (db) mutant mice. Dr. Douglas Coleman of The Jackson Laboratory, a member of the National Academy of Sciences, conducted a series of experiments that in 1973 led him to propose the existence of a "satiety factor" (later identified as leptin) that the obese mice fail to produce and that the diabetes mice produce but do not respond to.

Back in the 1940s approximately 100 mouse gene locations were known, and to keep track of them The Jackson Laboratory's Dr. Margaret Green had started an index card file. This file grew into the Mouse Locus Catalog. Technological and scientific advances in the 1980s, including the advent of molecular biology, allowed genes to be identified much more quickly. Computer power grew fast enough to keep up with all the new genetics data. Thus, a new scientific field was born: bioinformatics, the application of computer technology to the management of biological information.

The Encyclopedia of the Mouse Genome launched in 1989 was The Jackson Laboratory's first interactive genetics database. The Laboratory was awarded a $1.7million federal grant in 1992 to merge all Jackson databases into a single Mouse Genome Informatics program. Information "mining" of large genomic regions from different primates and non-vertebrates has led to identifying functions for parts of the human genome already explored in mice. This would not be possible without

Dr. Shaoguang Li, an oncologist-turned-researcher, is making strides in developing new treatments for chronic myelogenous leukemia and other cancers.

The Jackson Laboratory is located on Mount Desert Island, adjacent to Acadia National Park.

The Jackson Laboratory's repositories of genetically defined mice, and its compilation and curating of the resulting Mouse Genome Database and other informatics resources.

Scientists the world over now have access to the single largest collection of publicly available information about the laboratory mouse, The Jackson Laboratory's Mouse Genome Informatics Web site (www.informatics.jax.org). In its first year the site logged 6.5 million "hits" from investigators in search of gene locations, physiological data, research publications and other essential information.

Today Clarence Cook Little's belief that mice were the ideal model for human genetic diseases has been fully vindicated. Study of mouse and human genomes have demonstrated that the two species share the overwhelming majority of their genes. This means that mice get the same diseases as humans, for the same reasons.

The potential of the mouse to help scientists unlock the secrets of the genetic mechanisms of normal development and disease began to be dramatically fulfilled in the 1990s. In addition to the many discoveries by

Jackson Laboratory investigators, cutting edge research progressed in several areas, including osteoporosis (a major public health threat for more than 28 million Americans, 80 percent of whom are women); glaucoma (a major cause of human blindness often associated with elevated intraocular pressure); heart-related conditions (including heart disease, hypertension, HDL-cholesterol levels and cholesterol gallstone formation) and epilepsy.

The Jackson Laboratory makes more than 3,800 varieties of genetically defined mice available to researchers around the world. The Laboratory was one of the first institutions to embark on a program of cryopreserving, or freezing, mouse embryos in the 1970s, and today most strains are now permanently "archived."

The Jackson Laboratory has grown into one of the world's most prestigious research labs with more than 1,300 employees. The campus is located on 147 acres on Mount Desert Island, adjacent to Acadia National Park.

Most of the Laboratory's research, office and production buildings—today totaling about 700,000 square feet—occupy a sixty acre area and in 2005 operated on a budget of $146 million.

The original values, established by Clarence Cook Little when he brought University of Maine biology students to Mount Desert Island as early as 1924 to conduct field studies with wild mice, are carried on by Dr. Richard Woychik, the current director. A world-renowned geneticist whose distinguished career includes contributions in both academia and industry, Dr. Woychik professes that his own interest in the biomedical field began in his early school days studying biology. Realizing the great importance of early introduction to science can have on creating tomorrow's scientists, Dr. Woychik puts great emphasis on the Laboratory's expanding educational offerings.

The importance of The Jackson Laboratory's educational programs is clearly indicated in the story of Drs. David Baltimore and Howard Temin, who shared the 1975 Nobel Prize for Medicine or Physiology. They also spent their summers working at The Jackson Laboratory and have credited the laboratory for launching their careers in science.

With its rapidly growing roster of courses, conferences and education and training programs, which draw more than 2,000 students and established scientists each year to Bar Harbor, The Jackson Laboratory continues to build on its history of training the next generation of scientists. Programs include a week-long bacteriology course for local second-graders, taught by Jackson Laboratory scientists and other staff members, K-12 school visits to The Jackson Laboratory and outreach by Laboratory scientists to schools throughout Maine.

For aspiring science teachers, The Jackson Laboratory offers the "Mas-

The Laboratory was one of the first institutions in the world to receive a 4Pi confocal laser scanning microscope. The instrument, shown here with physicist Joerg Bewersdorf, is part of the Institute for Molecular Biophysics, a joint program of the University of Maine, University of Heidelberg and Maine Medical Center Research Institute.

tering Science" teacher training program, in which candidates for a Master of Science in Teaching degree at the University of Maine spend time in a research setting at The Jackson Laboratory to learn experimental methods that can be taught in the classroom. There is also an interdisciplinary, interinstitutional Ph.D. program in Functional Genomics, supported by faculty from the University of Maine together with The Jackson Laboratory and the Maine Medical Center Research Institute, and a postdoctoral training program offering recent Ph.D. awardees the opportunity to conduct independent research projects under the supervision of seasoned, independent investigators.

The laboratory was recently awarded large federal grants to create major centers for the study of complex genetic traits and aging "We are proud to say that we uniquely enable research worldwide even as we conduct our own ground-breaking investigations in search of cures, treatment and someday even prevention of diseases that cause human suffering," said Dr. Woychik, the director of The Jackson Laboratory. "These Center programs illustrate the unique value of The Jackson Laboratory: research excel-

lence paired with dynamic, creative approaches to supporting research worldwide. As the twenty-first century progresses, it is clear that the Laboratory will continue to play a major role in improving the health and well being of all humanity."

An essay in the journal *Nature* states "At least seventeen Nobel prizes, two major scientific tools (monoclonal antibodies and gene-targeted strains), profound scientific insights into the immune system, retroviruses, oncogenes, cancer, the inheritance of complex traits and countless scientific experiments have flowed from Dr. Little's inbred, or 'isogenic', strains...When diseases such as cancer and AIDS are eventually conquered, isogenic mice and the understanding of oncogenes will have played an important part in the battle." This is Clarence Cook Little's gift to millions of people he will never know.

KENNEBEC SAVINGS BANK

Kennebec Savings Bank is a $607 million state-chartered mutual savings bank with seventy-six employees and offices located in Augusta, Waterville and Winthrop. It has been serving the people of the Kennebec Valley communities for more than 135 years. Established not only for the successful wage earners and seamen of the time, it was also created as a savings outlet for people outside of mainstream business, such as women who wanted to safely grow their modest life savings. This mutually beneficial institution, which still nobly serves its strong and established community, is an integral part of Augusta's history; its roots reaching back to the post-Civil War era of the late nineteenth century when times were more uncertain.

In the 1800s dominating influences in the new state of Maine were railroad transportation, the Civil War, fires and floods. Even the year the bank opened, the town of Augusta suffered one of its most devastating floods in its history; 160 feet of the Kennebec dam was swept away. Despite its share of ups and downs, Maine grew and prospered and Augusta

Kennebec Savings Bank's main office at 150 State Street in Augusta, Maine.

Mark L. Johnston, president and CEO of Kennebec Savings Bank.

established its place in commerce being a city which occupied both sides of the vital Kennebec River.

Years prior to the bank's incorporation in 1870, Augusta was already on the move—known as a great publishing center as well as a manufacturing hub for cotton, wool and paper. By the mid 1800s the general population began earning wages that enabled them to save money. The check became a common medium of payment for business affairs by 1865. Banking became a new phenomenon, and the number of banks in Maine increased from fourteen to forty-three during the 1860s.

In order to provide a savings outlet for Augusta citizens, Kennebec Savings Bank was formed and was incorporated March 7,

1870 by an act signed into law by Governor Joshua L. Chamberlain. The governor was a prominent general in the Civil War known not only for his great leadership, but also for his part in accepting the surrender of General Robert E. Lee in Virginia.

Governor Chamberlain was very passionate about the need for a mutual savings bank and heralded the importance of Kennebec Savings Bank for the individuals of Augusta and the surrounding communities. He had this to say in his 1870 address to Maine's Legislature: "The moment he has money in the bank, the humblest feels a bracing up of his self-respect and whole moral force. From that moment springs an incentive to industry, frugality, temperance, enterprise; to all, in fact, which constitutes good citizenship, and advances the character and condition of men. Anything, therefore, which tends to discourage deposits in savings banks, should be scrupulously avoided."

The bank opened for business on April 1, 1870 "occupying rooms" within Freeman's National Bank at 192 Water Street. The first treasurer (CEO) of Kennebec Savings Bank was Joseph L. Adams. The first customers were Mrs. Priscilla P. Hallett and Mrs. Emma J. Adams, both of Augusta and Mr. John Dunphy of Gardiner. Total deposits for the day were $410. Total assets at the end of 1870 were $84,571.

In 1884 Freeman's charter expired. The bank closed, and Kennebec moved its office to 237 Water Street with Augusta National Bank. In 1902 Augusta National Bank liquidated but Kennebec Savings remained at that location until 1918 when Kennebec moved to 292 Water Street, the southwest corner of Market Square at Granite Block. The bank remained at this location until 1945. At that time there were only two employees. Bank assets in 1945 were $2,493,377.

In 1945 Kennebec Savings Bank changed its address to 288 Water Street when a new entrance was added to the Capitol Theater. By this time there were three employees. The bank remained at the 288 Water Street location until 1959 when, at this point in Augusta's history, the center of business activity was expanding in all directions from Water Street.

The bank purchased property at 150 State Street in 1958. Kennebec Savings Bank turned the site into a then-modern banking facility which included a relatively new phenomenon—a drive up window. It is believed that Kennebec Savings Bank was the first in the area to have one. Bank assets at the end of 1959 were $6,587,584. The only type of deposit accounts being offered remained savings accounts until certificates of deposits (CDs) began being offered in November 1969. In November 1975 the bank began offering checking accounts.

Kennebec Savings Bank's Waterville office (post expansion) on 226 Main Street.

As Kennebec Savings Bank grew, it became necessary to look for additional space. In 1984 the Park Circle Office Building, also known as the Tappan-Viles House, at 154 State Street was purchased. The structure is a unique blend of three magnificent architectural styles—Federal, Italianate and Colonial Revival. The year 1985 marked Kennebec Savings Bank's first year of profits exceeding $1 million. In 1988 the bank began a two-year construction and restoration project to connect the Tappan-Viles House to the existing bank building, creating the modern banking facility that exists today.

Since the early 1800s, Kennebec Savings Bank has continued to serve its customers and evolved into one of the oldest and most important depositories for peoples' savings in all of Maine. True to the commitment to community, the staff and board members are involved in community projects and fundraisers creating parks and raising money for important causes. Additionally, Kennebec Savings Bank invests hundreds of thousands of dollars annually to local non-profit organizations and projects, from sponsoring a small fundraising event to playing a leadership role in the community by donating, in a significant way, to local capital campaigns.

Kennebec Savings Bank is committed to operating as a profitable, conservative mutual savings bank that serves the banking needs of customers and is dedicated to positively contributing to the quality of life in the Kennebec Valley communities.

Kennebec Savings Bank's Winthrop office at 84 Main Street in Winthrop, Maine.

THE LEWISTON-AUBURN ECONOMIC GROWTH COUNCIL AND THE ANDROSCOGGIN CHAMBER OF COMMERCE

The CEO of Acorn Products remembers watching a televised NASA mission in the 1980s and spotting one of the crew members wearing his company's slippers. He couldn't believe genuine Acorn slippers were in orbit. Two decades later, these once-Lewiston-Auburn manufactured slippers, along with most other footwear, are made overseas.

With the exodus of traditional manufacturers in the 1980s and 1990s, local officials knew the economic outlook for the twin cities Lewiston-Auburn (L-A) was about to change. Keeping in mind a galaxy of possibilities for development, plans were put in the works for revitalization projects.

Diversifying the economy to include high-precision manufacturing, healthcare, printing and graphics, financial services and transportation and logistics allowed L-A to survive the rise and fall of its textile and shoe industries. With a wave of Somali and Togolese immigrants in the early 2000s, L-A became increasingly diverse. Meanwhile, local college enrollments were up, companies were relocating to the area, industrial parks were full and transportation projects were underway—including an expansion at the state's only double-stack Maine Intermodal

One of the cornerstones of Lewiston-Auburn's renaissance is the Bates Mill Complex. Once home to one of New England's preeminent textile mills, the redeveloped complex now houses bank operations centers, office and retail space, a museum and upscale eateries, including a fresh seafood restaurant and a brick-oven pizzeria.

Bates College, consistently ranked among the top liberal arts colleges by U.S. News and World Report, has a quintessentially New England-feel to its campus. Pictured is the tower atop Hathorne Hall.

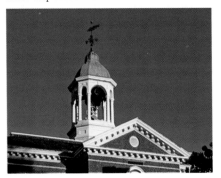

Terminal. In addition to these improvements, unemployment was at record lows. Auburn was now the site of a U.S. Customs Port. Local arts programs and festivals were growing. Everything from local law enforcement programs and tax assistance initiatives to citizen participation efforts were winning national recognition from trade associations and industry groups. The enthusiasm seemed contagious.

An important turning point in the renaissance of Lewiston-Auburn was the implementation of the Auburn Downtown Action Plan for Tomorrow (ADAPT), approved by the Auburn City Council in 1999. ADAPT was led by former Mayor Lee Young to transform Auburn's downtown into a vibrant, modern and attractive destination for business and leisure. City officials met with hundreds of business and community leaders to gather input for the collective vision of Auburn's downtown. Within five years, they saw the results: a new 110-room Hilton Garden Inn, a performing arts space called Festival Plaza, a new Riverwalk that capitalized on the beauty of the Androscoggin River, a library expansion/renovation and new office and retail space built downtown.

Meanwhile, the City of Lewiston was calling for faster and additional renovation of mill space, new downtown office, retail, arts venues and streetscape improvements as well as the transformation of a former music hall into the new district court building.

By the turn of the new millennium, the press started reporting on the widespread changes too. In 2000 the tourist-focused *Downeast* magazine devoted their annual edition to coverage of the Twin Cities. Articles focused on its dynamic female mayors, unique companies, outdoor gems including Thorncrag Bird Sanctuary (the largest bird sanctuary in New England) and the magnificent gothic masterpiece of Saints Peter and Paul Basilica.

Not long after these developments, a showdown over the historic Bates Mill Complex took place at the voting polls. Certain residents were in favor of turning the complex into mixed use office/retail/ light manufacturing space, while others wished to tear it down. The pro-development contingent won. The mill is flourishing, with a new seafood restaurant, a brick oven pizzeria and several back-office operations.

In 1999 and 2000 another ideological battle was waged, this time, on the healthcare front. Lewiston's Central Maine Medical Center (CMMC) planned to create a modern cardiac care and catheterization center in Lewiston, to the dismay of competing hospitals in Southern Maine, who saw it as unwanted competition. Local hospital officials argued the area could sustain—moreover, they deserved—a world class facility, while naysayers, including local residents, questioned the need for such a facility. Ultimately, CMMC was victorious, and the Central Maine Heart & Vascular Institute was born.

A few years later, the City of Lewiston focused its attention on what was perhaps the community's most notorious eyesore: a major downtown entranceway known as Lower Lisbon Street, dotted with dilapidated buildings and outdated storefronts. Slowly, Lewiston gained control of this downtown land, demolished many decayed buildings, and created a welcoming entranceway city officials dubbed Lewiston's Southern Gateway.

In 2004 Oxford Networks, a telecommunications company, invested $20 million in upgrading local fiber optics and building a new headquarters and server housing facility in the Southern Gateway. That same year, VIP Parts, Tires, and Service, a Lewiston-based regional chain, opened the doors of its new flagship store there. The cavalcade continued. Andover College opened a new campus later that year. In 2005 a new city parking garage, an expansion at the equity theater called the Public

Balloons soar over the Androscoggin River during the annual Great Falls Balloon Festival, held in August. Photo by Russ Dillingham, Sun Journal

Theatre and the headquarters for Northeast Bank opened. The following year, a central Business Service Center for economic development and business service providers opened.

Perhaps the greatest sign of the area's economic sophistication came with a nearly 900,000-square-foot mechanized food distribution center for Wal-Mart Stores, Inc. Employing an estimated 450-500 employees at full capacity, the center is believed to be Maine's largest distribution center.

As housing prices continued to soar in nearby Portland, people began looking north for more affordable options. High-end housing and condo projects, including Chestnut Hill Estates and Colonial Ridge, offered luxury and convenience in L-A at a fraction of the Southern Maine market price.

Soon focus was brought to additional mill properties. In 2005 a local developer announced plans to transform the former Cowan and Libby Mills into a mixed-use retail, housing and office complex called Island Point. The waters of the Great Falls lap directly against its foundation.

Since 2002 the area's revitalization has drawn the interest of retail site locators as well, as stores including Kohl's, Lowe's, Home Depot, Best Buy and Longhorn Steakhouse have set their sights on the area, particularly Auburn's Mount Auburn Avenue.

Progress continues at a busy clip. A local image and awareness campaign, "L-A: It's Happening Here!," has produced a wellspring of community pride. In 2004 *Inc* magazine named Lewiston-Auburn one of the "Best Places for Doing Business in America," and has made the list ever since. In an international study conducted by KPMG International comparing the after-tax cost of start-up and operation of a business, Lewiston-Auburn fared better than many U.S. communities analyzed. Lewiston was named an All American City finalist in 2006, and the *Boston Globe* featured a lengthy story with a headline that read "Changes afoot in a hipper L/A." Though L-A manufactured slippers might not make another cameo in space, the Lewiston-Auburn area is making sure that the community is deserving of a spotlight right here on earth.

MAINE EMPLOYERS' MUTUAL INSURANCE COMPANY (MEMIC)

In 1992 Maine faced a serious threat to its economy. The state's workers' compensation system was collapsing, threatening employers with prohibitive costs and liability. Politicians fought to a stalemate, unable to arrive at a solution. The impact was potentially devastating for workers. Not only was the safety net created by workers' compensation in trouble but their livelihoods were threatened as employers left the state.

Maine Employers' Mutual Insurance Company (MEMIC) was born in, and of, these rocky times. Hardly a situation from which anyone expected greatness, one of the state's true economic success stories of the late 20th century was forged in this milieu.

The challenge of creating MEMIC put its incorporators in uncharted waters. However, this determined group, who set out to achieve its goals and with Yankee common sense and

MEMIC's office at 261 Commercial Street in Portland.

More than 500 MEMIC policyholders attend the annual MEMIC Comp Summit each November. Featuring well-known and challenging speakers, the free conference calls attention to important workers' comp and business issues.

hard work, navigated successfully when many doubted the endeavor would last a year.

To fully understand the scope of MEMIC's accomplishments and impact on the state of Maine, it is important to understand the circumstances that led to MEMIC's founding. Through the 1970s and early 1980s, the workers' compensation system had been in steady conflict. By 1992 the insurance

market in Maine was bleak. In that year, citing millions in losses, no fewer than twelve insurance companies withdrew entirely from providing workers' compensation in Maine. This left only five of a previous field of sixty insurers: four of those indicated they would withdraw by year's end.

Part of the problem was that there were simply too many injuries. Maine's injury rate was double the national average and work fatality rates were among the highest in the nation. The system itself offered no relief either. Benefit levels had risen over the years, making workers' compensation disputes a high stakes legal game. Lawyers became one of the biggest beneficiaries of the system. In the 1980s Democratic Governor Joseph E. Brennan famously remarked, "Maine doesn't have a workers' compensation system. We have a retirement system for lawyers."

By 1992 government action was vital. Yet the state legislature and Maine Governor John McKernan were at an impasse. McKernan refused to sign a budget until the Legislature voted

to reform workers' compensation. This led to the July 1992 shutdown of state government which garnered headlines across the country. Finally, the Legislature and the governor agreed to create the Blue Ribbon Commission on Workers' Compensation Reform. Fingers were crossed that a solution could be hammered out by the end of August 1992.

A distinguished but unlikely panel, only one of whom had experience in the insurance industry, fashioned an entirely new workers' compensation model. They adopted many elements of the Michigan workers' compensation system. But the key piece was the creation of a new, private mutual company, which would be open to every employer in the state of Maine.

Yet more political bickering ensued. The Legislature wished to amend the plan in various ways. The governor wanted legislators to vote on the plan as it was presented. Eventually, a com-

promise was struck: four proposed amendments would be sent to the Blue Ribbon Commission. If it approved, McKernan promised to support the legislation.

The Commission approved the amendments, and on October 7, 1992, the Blue Ribbon Commission's plan to overhaul Maine's system was signed into law.

While the politicians were finally finished, the real work was just

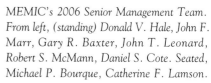

MEMIC's 2006 Senior Management Team. From left, (standing) Donald V. Hale, John F. Marr, Gary R. Baxter, John T. Leonard, Robert S. McMann, Daniel S. Cote. Seated, Michael P. Bourque, Catherine F. Lamson.

beginning for a group of determined employers and their representatives who were to become the incorporators of Maine Employers' Mutual Insurance Company (MEMIC). They convened for the first time in October 1992 and knew they were going to be put to the test immediately. MEMIC was slated by the governor and the state legislature to begin operation on January 1, 1993. This meant that the incorporators, all of whom held full-time jobs or ran their own businesses, had less than three months to organize a colossal undertaking.

The expectations were mile high. Tens of thousands of Maine employers and workers were counting on them. Yet as of October 1992, MEMIC existed only in theory. There were no offices, employees, supplies, nary even a business plan. The nine incorporators may have harbored misgivings— if they'd had the time to. Instead, they plowed forward.

MEMIC's 2006 Board of Directors. From left, M. Jane Sheehan, Jolan F. Ippolito, Katherine M. Greenleaf, Robert D. Umphrey (seated), Ward I. Graffam, S. Catherine Longley (seated), John T. Leonard, David M. Labbe, Vicki W. Mann.

They met very early in the morning or very late at night, also utilizing weekends to accommodate their own busy work schedules. It was exhausting and overwhelming on many fronts, yet they each had a strong, singular motivation: Maine's workers' compensation system *had* to be fixed.

This possibly naïve optimism coupled with the group's minimal understanding or acceptance of insurance industry standards gave the incorporators an out-of-the-box edge. The methods and practices of the industry had failed Maine before. This was the perfect, if slightly inadvertent, opportunity to bring fresh eyes and ideas to the table. They applied their own experiences as employers and employees to the framework of MEMIC.

The incorporators knew that merely insuring workers and paying

out claims would not solve the problem. MEMIC would have to exert some control over the number of claims made. MEMIC was therefore founded on a twofold mission. Not only would it provide workers' compensation insurance, it would take a proactive role in preventing workplace accidents. The safety of the average workplace would be improved while costs would be kept under control for claims MEMIC paid out. This cost-reduction would in turn be passed down to employers in the form of lower rates. All of these factors would ensure Maine's workers stayed healthy and so would the workers' compensation system.

To that end, the MEMIC Board included in the company's structure a strong and independent safety department which would focus its efforts on working in the field with employers and their employees. These safety specialists would become the face of MEMIC. The company hired experts in safety not from the insurance industry, but from the industries to which they would be assigned. This meant that construction industry

customers would be served not by pencil-pushing insurance people but by individuals who really knew the industry. This model helped the company develop instant credibility with its customers

More pressing to the company's formation was the need to build a capital reserve. Without the promised start-up loan from the Legislature, which never appropriated the money, an interesting concept was developed—a 15 percent policy surcharge, called capital contribution. The Board promised this would be paid back when the company hit its financial milestones. Not surprisingly, the plan was met with a grumbling response. Nonetheless, the incorporators continued to extol the virtues of the new system and promised to return the money once the company stood on a solid foundation.

After debating where the company should be located, the Portland area was chosen. A 6,000 square foot space on Larrabee Road in Westbrook was leased as the incorporators went to work hiring staff and determining a structure.

Some in the insurance industry thought MEMIC should operate mainly as a shell, outsourcing most of its operations to vendors. Why not let MEMIC be a storefront with subcontractors handling policies and claims? The incorporators, however, had bigger plans in mind. As soon as it could, MEMIC would be a fully operational insurance company. This was key to taking responsibility for making the Maine workplace safer. Besides, if everything was parceled out to the same people who had driven the old system to debt, Maine's problems would never be fixed.

Through a divine convergence of events, MEMIC opened for business on schedule. Eight employees, a twelve member board of directors and a temporary CEO were in place on January 1,

Andy Wood (right), MEMIC's manager of Natural Resources Safety, works with a group of brush cutters in the northern Maine woods. Wood helped lead MEMIC's efforts to require training which has helped make the logging industry in Maine much safer.

1993. Attorney Chris Howard of Portland law firm Pierce Atwood held the position of temporary CEO while the new board of directors, which included seven of the original nine incorporators, searched for the right candidate to lead MEMIC.

A match was soon made. John Leonard, an insurance industry veteran, was recruited and reported for work on February 14, 1993, which also happened to be his birthday. Soon after his appointment, it became clear that the right choice had been made. Leonard, who began his insurance industry career straight out of Siena College in New York, knew the business like the back of his hand. He also had the requisite desire to put the welfare of people first and foremost. For John Leonard, running MEMIC would not be just a job, not only a career; it would be his passion.

The company grew at an exponential rate. The first year of operation saw a deluge of policies being processed. Nearly 22,000 were issued almost immediately after MEMIC opened. The dream was taking shape.

The company took its campaign for workplace safety to the airwaves across the state with a television media campaign titled "The Partnership for Workplace Safety." Through these messages, the company helped both employers and workers understand their stake in improving Maine's economy by working safely. The advertisements told of employers and employees working together to create better results. These messages stood in stark contrast to the antagonism of the old workers' compensation system. Leonard himself appeared in the ads and became known around the state as the face of workplace safety.

Though MEMIC was off to a heady start, insurance premiums were still on the rise. This was much to the chagrin of many who had expected costs to decrease immediately. Leonard at-

Rod Stanley, director of MEMIC's safety services for construction, talks with a worker about safety standards on a job site.

tributed this to only having completed the first phase of the reforms. The next step, which entailed actively participating in safety programs and streamlined patient care for injured workers, was still in its nascent phases.

Creative ways of encouraging safety would need to be employed. In June of 1993 MEMIC unveiled three plans which rewarded employers for workplace safety with varying premium reductions. MEMIC was attempting to make a major shift throughout Maine. The company was going to have to convince an entire state to commit to safety.

MEMIC's charter provides that it is the guaranteed market in Maine. This means that MEMIC's insurance policies are available to every Maine employer. Though MEMIC must leave its door open to all who need insurance, it can require adherence to certain safe work practices. Refusal to participate in such programs can result in termination of coverage.

MEMIC's experience in curbing serious injuries and fatalities in the logging industry is one example of these efforts in action. Since forests cover nearly 90 percent of the state of Maine, logging is an important industry for the state. However, this industry also accounted for a significant number of serious and expensive injuries.

Late in 1993 MEMIC premiered a mandatory training course for logging industry employees. This comprehensive, forty hour intensive program focused on proper safety precautions and procedures for cutting and moving trees. Even veteran loggers felt that they had learned something from these techniques. More importantly, no logging fatalities were suffered by MEMIC policyholders in the years following the institution of the program.

MEMIC's efforts were paying off across the board: workplace injuries were significantly lower just one year after MEMIC opened its doors. This translated into dollars and cents. Based on these figures, premiums dropped in 1995 as much as 12.5 percent. Instead of representing the low end of U.S. statistical figures, a common occurrence where Maine and workers' compensation had been concerned, this figure was the top premium reduction in the nation.

MEMIC made other active efforts to contain costs. The company made inroads in changing the adversarial nature of the claims process. Limitations on attorneys' fees and other litigation costs helped force the system into more cooperative directions. Instead of fighting to avoid paying exorbitant legal fees, the emphasis became reducing the incentive to litigate.

MEMIC also began to closely monitor claims for fraud. Exaggerated and even patently false claims drove up premiums. Stamping out this abuse helped preserve the integrity of the system and keep costs down. In 1995 MEMIC successfully prosecuted the first workers' compensation insurance fraud cases since the reform. The offenders were fined and required to pay restitution. Fraud hurts everyone and would not be taken lightly.

By 1995 the policy surcharge was discontinued. Improved safety and lower claim rates were continuing to benefit policyholders. The next few years saw further premium reductions and improvement in services. MEMIC was fulfilling its mission "to improve Maine's economy by providing safety training services and the best workers' compensation insurance products at the lowest possible cost while promoting fair and equitable treatment of all workers." Overall costs for workers' compensation insurance were down by more than 30 percent, driven by a corresponding 30 percent reduction in workplace injuries.

The news spread across the country that Maine was "fixed" thanks to the work of MEMIC. This drew interest from the insurance market which came back to join in the improved system. By the late 1990s more than 200 insurers were again licensed to underwrite workers' compensation insurance in Maine. This competition led to even steeper price declines for some Maine employers.

The company began to earn accolades both in and out of Maine. Reacting to an editorial cartoon that announced yet another rate cut which helped to support Governor Angus King's premise that "Maine is on the move," King sent Leonard a note saying: "Thanks for providing the fuel!" During those years, the Greater Portland Chamber of Commerce and then the Maine Chamber of Commerce gave MEMIC their top awards for leadership in economic development. Additionally, Maine Businesses for Social Responsibility (MEBSR) gave

MEMIC *manufacturing safety specialist Henry Reynolds talks with a printing press operator about safety standards.*

MEMIC its "Eagle Feather Award" for socially responsible policies and actions.

Much credit must be given to those behind the scenes. The company now employed about 200 workers and had moved to a once-vacant building on Portland's waterfront. Under Leonard's leadership, employees were imbued with a sense of pride and responsibility. That sense of mission is credited by many as the backbone that helped the company succeed. In addition, the flat management structure encouraged a sense of teamwork and camaraderie. These factors have kept the company's turnover rate low.

By 1998, just five years into the company's history, finances were stable enough to lead the Board of Directors to make an announcement that most employers never expected to hear: MEMIC would begin to repay the capital contribution paid in earlier years. That set off a round of congratulations among Maine newspapers, including a commendation from a Portland *Press Herald* editorial calling MEMIC "the Maine Miracle."

The company began repayment by mailing 30,000 checks totaling $5 million to eligible employers. Over the next three years, the company committed to returning the entire $47 million that it had collected. This prompted great support from the company's independent agents and, in particular, its customers. By 2001 MEMIC was able to continue the tradition of giving back by paying its first dividend. All totaled, between 1998 and 2005, the company returned more than $59 million to its customers. Those savings came on top of the already reduced rates.

In early 2000 Leonard, the senior management and the company's Board of Directors set out to strengthen the company further through geographic diversification. While the business considered other strategies, including other insurance lines, it determined that MEMIC's formula for workers' compensation was its true mission. The company sought through the Maine Legislature, with support of then-Governor King, the ability to start a subsidiary company that could underwrite workers' compensation in other states.

The company applied to the New Hampshire Department of Insurance to start MEMIC Indemnity Company. The application received heated opposition from the insurance industry which claimed that MEMIC's Maine connection amounted to an unfair advantage. However, the New Hampshire insurance commissioner ruled in favor of the license finding no such advantage.

MEMIC Indemnity Company opened in September of 2000. By 2006 the new company was licensed in thirty-one states, though efforts remained focused in the Northeast. The MEMIC formula of safety training and compassionate claims management quickly earned the company a niche as a top flight insurer across New England.

In recent years, as Maine was affected by the fluctuations of the global insurance market, MEMIC has again proven up to the task. Today, its Maine market share remains at 65 percent. It has solid financial backing, with a strong surplus that allows it to weather difficult times. This means that Maine employers have a company they can count on, irrespective of the market conditions.

Nationally, MEMIC has earned a strong reputation as well. In November 2005 Leonard was featured on the cover of industry bible *Best's Review*. The story highlighted the company's strong performance in the difficult business of workers' compensation. The company is rated A (Excellent) by A.M. Best, the insurance industry's most respected bench-marking orga-

A seagull flies near MEMIC's headquarters on the working waterfront of Portland, Maine.

nization. In addition, from 2001 through 2006, MEMIC has been included in the Ward 50. This honor is given by Ward Financial Group, based in Cincinnati, Ohio, which reviews more than 3,000 property casualty companies. This selection is indicative of MEMIC's performance, which puts it among the top 2 percent of property casualty insurers in the U.S.

Today, workers' compensation in Maine is rarely in the news. With MEMIC leading the market, employers are confident that they are served by one of the nation's most respected workers' compensation specialists. This has helped to keep the issue out of the political fray in Maine. Since 1993 few changes have been made to the careful balance created by the Blue Ribbon Commission.

Furthermore, the company has received support from each of the three governors in Maine who have been in office since MEMIC was

formed. Republican McKernan, Independent King and Democrat John Baldacci have all helped by keeping workers' compensation out of the political arena. Leonard reinforces that fact, saying, "[Our] company *never* becomes political. We are a purely factual company."

MEMIC is now a strong business with hundreds of employees and assets growing toward $1 billion. Leonard is immensely proud of the enormous impact MEMIC has had on the state of Maine and beyond. By taking responsibility for the causes of injury and by managing the expenses, it has improved conditions for both employees and employers. Most importantly, it has significantly contributed to the betterment of the state's economy, a benefit every Maine citizen can enjoy.

MAINE EYE CENTER

From a one-man practice at the turn of the twentieth century, to the largest eye care facility in northern New England, Maine Eye Center has an impressive history in Portland, and has continued to thrive introducing advancements in eye care services throughout its history. Its practitioners are dedicated to providing the best possible care to their patients including participation in academic studies for new technologies and medical treatments.

Now the largest city in Maine, Portland was originally settled by the

The current Maine Eye Center surgeons, from left to right: Top Row: Jeffrey K. Moore, M.D., Curtis M. Libby, M.D., Jeffrey L. Berman, M.D., Peter S. Hedstrom, M.D., Frederick S. Miller, M.D., Walter B. J. Schuyler, M.D. Bottom Row: R. Samuel Cady, M.D., Natan D. Kahn, M.D., Frank W. Read, M.D., Richard A. Bazarian, M.D., Linda K. Morrison, M.D., Charles M. Zacks, M.D. Not shown in this photo: Stuart W. McGuire, M.D., and the optometrists Nirupama Aggarwal, O.D., Jill M. Amundson, O.D., Matthew A. Thees, O.D., and John L. Walters, O.D.

Maine Eye Center is located on Congress Street in Portland, Maine, conveniently off exit 5 of Interstate 295. Pictured above is the classic brick building which was built in 1907 to house a shoe factory. The seventeen providers at Maine Eye Center now practice on all four floors of the building.

British in 1632 and served as the state's capital from 1820 to 1832. The city has historically attracted and been home to talented people—from poet Henry Wadsworth Longfellow (1807–1882) to architect Francis Fassett (1823–1906) to today's artists in the Maine College of Art.

Moreover, after being nearly destroyed in the Great Fire of 1866, the city was rebuilt with concern for public health, an outlook which may have made it very attractive to the many physicians and medical students who would reside and practice medicine in Portland over the next several decades. Geo. J. Barney wrote in his *History of Portland, Maine*, published in 1886, that "good drainage and well-lighted streets, pure water, [and] excellent air" made Portland "one of the most desirable of cities for a home and business." During this period, the city became the center for healthcare in southern Maine. Meanwhile, changes were taking place in the way people thought about eye care. Although ophthalmology had historically been treated as just another aspect of general medicine, that perception was beginning to change.

These two facts combined —a new birth in the field of eye care and Portland's emphasis on healthy living—may have helped draw Sylvester "Judd" Beech to the city just after the turn of the century. Elegant, formal, and, according to Maine Eye Center's Frank Read, M.D., "probably without much of a sense of humor," Dr. Beech opened his own practice in 1907 on Congress Street, the city's main thoroughfare. It flourished there for nearly forty years.

Sylvester Beech, M.D., graduated from Harvard University as an EENT—an ear, eye, nose and throat specialist. He recognized the need for specialized eye care, and was an early officer of the American Academy of Ophthalmology, founded in 1896, which

promoted accurate testing standards for ophthalmologists beginning in the first half of the century and continues today.

Having practiced for nearly forty years, Dr. Beech was undoubtedly looking for someone to whom he could pass on his patients. Indeed, some of Dr. Beech's patients continue to be treated at the Maine Eye Center to this day. In 1946 Dr. Beech was joined by another ophthalmologist, Richard Goduti, M.D. Dr. Goduti went to Harvard for his undergraduate degree, and then he attended Tufts Medical School and did his residency at Massachusetts Eye and Ear Infirmary. Their practice thrived, drawing patients from throughout southern Maine. Eventually, Dr. Beech retired and left the practice in Dr. Goduti's hands. In response to an overwhelming need for quality eye care, Dr. Goduti moved his practice to Deering Street, then known as Doctor's Row.

Frank Read, M.D., has been with Maine Eye Center since 1971 and has played a large role in making the practice a fully comprehensive eye care facility.

Richard Goduti, M.D., was the second founding doctor of Maine Eye Center. He joined Judd Beech, M.D. in 1946 and ran a solo prctice after Dr. Beech retired. He then recruited Frank Read, M.D. in 1971, who still practices at Maine Eye Center today.

By that time, Dr. Goduti was a widely known and respected ophthalmologist. As such, he received many letters from young ophthalmologists eager to work with him, usually a few each month. Each time, he would respond to the hopeful writer that he was not interested. However, as time passed and his patient base continued to grow, Dr. Goduti seemed to have had a change of heart. In 1971 Dr. Frank Read wrote Dr. Goduti to offer his services, and for whatever reason, the famed ophthalmologist agreed.

"My letter just struck a chord with him," Dr. Read says, adding that he doesn't remember what he wrote that might have intrigued Dr. Goduti. "My letter came at a time when he was probably already thinking about getting someone. The practice was getting too big; he was getting older." Perhaps Dr. Goduti, having built up the practice alone, was looking for someone to whom he could pass it on. Dr. Read

joined the practice later that year. However, further changes were taking place in the field of medicine that would make his time there very different.

Dr. Read's primary reason for becoming a physician was to help people, and he became especially interested in ophthalmology in medical school. "When you do a cataract surgery operation on a grandmother, and she comes back the next day and tells you she just saw her grandchild for the first time in five years, that's when you know why you do it," he says.

Another thing that appealed to him about the profession was that he could be his own boss. "You can't do that today," he says. Dr. Read explains that the rules and regulations involved in medical practice today make it nearly impossible for a person to practice alone. Just after he joined Dr. Goduti, this situation became evident to them both. They began to take on a larger staff of practitioners and administrators to balance an increasing patient load with an ever-lengthening list of new rules. Soon they became not Goduti and Read, but Ophthalmology Associates. The solo practice had become unsustainable.

Yet the need for quality eye care seemed to be increasing at an ever higher rate. By 1981 the practice had grown so large that it had to be moved again, this time to 15 Lowell Street. The classic, four-story brick building is alternately known as "the old shoe factory" or the John Calvin Stevens Building. It has been home to the practice ever since.

When they moved there in 1981, the Ophthalmology Associates occupied only half of one floor. However, over the next twenty-five years, the practice grew faster than ever. By the time the name was changed from Ophthalmology Associates to Maine Eye Center in the early 1990s, it was already the largest and most comprehensive eye care practice in northern New England. Today, the office that once occupied half a floor in the building on Lowell Street has grown to fill all four floors. The practice that started with one man a century ago has grown to include seventeen practitioners and 130 employees.

Today, Maine Eye Center offers the broadest range of subspecialty eye care services in Northern New England. These services include LASIK laser vision correction, cataracts and multifocal IOL's, glaucoma, cosmetic and reconstructive surgery including BOTOX treatments, retinal disorders, macular degeneration, corneal disorders, pediatric ophthalmology, adult strabismus and routine eye care. Maine Eye Center also houses its own full service optical shop, which lets patients purchase their eyeglasses right at their doctor's office. Another convenience to Maine Eye Center patients is the on-site surgical unit. Maine Eye Center is the

Maine Eye Center has a full service optical shop located on the first floor in the lobby. This offers patients the convenience of purchasing their eyeglasses or sunglasses at the same location as their doctor.

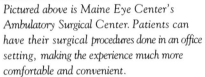

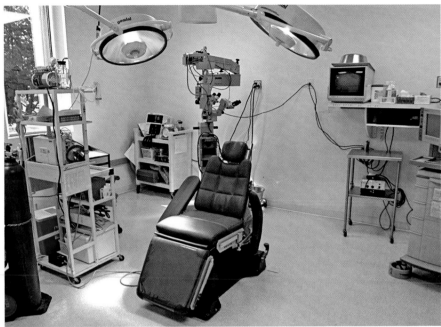

home of Maine's first Medicare certified Ambulatory Surgical Unit (ASU). This allows patients to undergo surgical treatments without having to go to a hospital.

In addition to their regular duties, many employees and physicians volunteer to take part in a nonprofit organization called Project Guatemala, of which Dr. Read is the head. Every year for the past eight years, several practitioners along with technicians have traveled to Guatemala to offer free eye care to some of the country's indigenous populations.

Pictured above is Maine Eye Center's Ambulatory Surgical Center. Patients can have their surgical procedures done in an office setting, making the experience much more comfortable and convenient.

This is a time when they give back to the world in thanks for the fortunate lives they have led in the United States.

Back home, they continue to provide the highest quality care available. They offer their services in nearly every ophthalmologic subspecialty to thousands of people each year. From traditional specialties such as routine eye exams to the latest techniques in laser vision correction, they focus on helping patients see better one at a time.

Luci Johnson Nugent, daughter of former president Lyndon Johnson, wrote, "The fact that we use the word 'see' to mean 'understand' indicates just how important vision is to our learning process." In a way, then, the staff of Maine Eye Center is protecting not only clients' ability to see, but their ability to understand and interact with their world. "We enjoy helping the people of our region see the world around them," they say. With continued focus on that simple goal, they plan to continue to do so for the next 100 years.

Fox Islands Thoroughfare near Vinalhaven.
Photograph by Rodd Collins

MAINE STATE CREDIT UNION (MSCU)

Maine State Credit Union (MSCU), which has a proud history of providing state employees excellent service for over seventy years, is situated in the state capital of Augusta. For the past twenty years, MSCU has been the largest credit union in the state of Maine. With its ongoing commitment to excellence and continued growth, MSCU seems unlikely to relinquish this honor any time soon.

While the core membership of MSCU remains state employees, in recent years its field of membership has expanded. Membership is now open to those who reside, work, worship or attend schools in Kennebec and Somerset counties. This change reflects the continual evolution of the credit union: its benefits now not only flow to state employees, but to other Maine residents as well. This allows MSCU to bring its trademark service to more members while creating a new niche in the community.

The credit union, now a thriving institution with nearly 21,000 members, was in fact born of financial despair. In the aftermath of the Great Depression, a distinct need arose for financial services for people of modest means. In 1935 a small group

The original Maine State Credit Union (MSCU) building.

of state employees came together to discuss how they might help one another in this regard. The relatively new concept of a membership-based cooperative was adopted, and soon state employees were pooling resources and making loans under the mantle of the Maine State Employees' Credit Union.

As in the past, the credit union's philosophy revolves around service for its members. The credit union, which was renamed Maine State Credit Union after its field of membership expanded, prides itself on offering the best range of services at the lowest cost. This includes not only basic banking functions, but also a host of other personal financial services. Whether a member needs a home loan or notary, Maine State Credit Union is ready to deliver.

Excellent service isn't just a meaningless marketing phrase at the credit union. Though many institutions claim to give the best service, the task is a mission at MSCU. Maine State Credit Union president

and CEO Normand Dubreuil believes that this commitment to members begins with his employees.

"I think that the staff will treat members like they should be treated," Dubreuil explained. "We truly believe in caring for our employees. That's reflected back to our members."

Mary Dolan, the credit union's Director of Training and Marketing, helps implement programs that support employee development and growth. Customer service evolves from giving employees the skills they need, then holding them to the highest standards. The Maine State Credit Union staff delivers in spades.

Dubreuil consistently hears positive feedback from members about how much they enjoy coming into the credit union. When asked what he is most proud of, he responded without hesitation. "My first thought is our staff. I am very pleased with the way they conduct themselves and how they treat our members."

Customer service may be crucial to the credit union's success, but so are the services it offers. The credit union has available a full array of financial

The first Maine State Credit Union facility at the State House building, 1948.

products and services. These range from deposit accounts to loans of all varieties, as well as IRAs and other long-term savings accounts. Many members may only take advantage of one of the credit union's many services, not realizing the resources available. Dubreuil is actively working to get the word out that the credit union is not just for basic account services. "We offer a multitude of products and services—at better prices."

The credit union offers amenities similar to any financial institution. Its online home banking is a big hit, especially since members live throughout the state of Maine. Members' needs are served with around-the-clock access to account information and bill paying.

ATM and debit cards have also taken off in the last few years, with members using them regularly for point of sale purchases. Dubreuil notes that ten years ago, debit card use was limited; most people preferred to pay by check.

The credit union has also found another way of serving consumer needs: providing indirect lending through local car dealerships. Car loans that are sought during off hours are reviewed via cell phone by an on-call credit union employee. This allows consumers who are shopping on Friday night or over the weekend to have their car loan application reviewed immediately.

This service has been a great boon to consumers. By facilitating off-hours car loans, the credit union helps consumers at the most convenient time for them. Indirect lending has led to a dramatic increase in the credit union's loans. It has also increased consumer awareness of the credit union, leading to 25 percent of MSCU's new members.

Those at Maine State Credit Union also feel a responsibility to help in

Normand Dubreuil, president and CEO.

their local community. The credit union is committed to helping in many ways, such as lending a hand to the local YMCA or contributing to Special Olympics events. The cause closest to the heart of the credit union staff, however, is the Ending Hunger Campaign. The campaign is spearheaded by the Maine Credit Union League, the state trade association. All credit unions throughout Maine

come together to contribute through various drives and events.

MSCU's most recent event was a highly successful walk-a-thon, which raised over $14,000. One hundred percent of the funds raised are distributed to those organizations that need it most: soup kitchens, food pantries and shelters. In this way the spirit of neighbor helping neighbor, the very ideal upon which the credit union was founded, is carried forward at MSCU.

What does the future hold for Maine State Credit Union? "Golden opportunity," responded Dubreuil. With goals to add more branches to the credit union family, Dubreuil feels MSCU will be even better suited to serve its members. In his twenty-one years of service at the credit union, he has seen its assets grow from $37 to $200 million. Maine State Credit Union will undoubtedly continue in this expansion by providing in-demand products and giving impeccable service to each and every member.

The new Maine State Credit Union facility at 200 Capitol Street, Augusta, Maine.

OCEAN NATIONAL BANK

Ocean National Bank was founded to meet the needs of Kennebunk mariners back in the mid-1800s. Though the shipping industry was blossoming, the town had no bank to serve the needs of the community. Ocean National Bank recently celebrated its sesquicentennial anniversary, but its primary goal has not changed in the past 150 years. Ocean National still stands to serve its customers and community, providing cutting-edge services and opening doors to financial possibilities.

Ocean National Bank opened on August 1, 1854. It became nationally chartered just eleven years later. The end of the 1800s saw the founding of other branches of the bank's family tree: First Savings of New Hampshire and Granite Bank. Little could the founders of these institutions know that these banks would merge more than a century later to become one of the largest commercial banks in New England.

Ocean National set up shop in the heart of town at 100 Main Street, in a building known as the "Old Brick." This building had previously been a general store but proved well suited to its new banking vocation. Unfortunately, the Old Brick was not destined to be Ocean National's permanent home. On December 3, 1869 the Old Brick was consumed by fire. The flames swept through the

This engraving, taken from a York County map printed in the 1850s, shows the "Old Brick," the first brick building in Kennebunk. The Ocean Bank sign, marking the bank's second floor offices, can be seen on the far left.

building with such speed and ferocity that rescuers were barely able to save vital documents housed in the bank's safe.

The following morning brought a sobering sight: the charred remains of the Old Brick. Though this tolled the end of the historic building, it did not signal the end of the bank by any means. Employees shifted operations, moving into temporary offices in the Warren Block, around the corner on Summer Street. A year later, the bank opened the doors to its new home at 100 Main Street, where its Kennebunk branch resides to this day.

Ocean National has continued building and growing throughout the years by providing the highest level of service. This means providing state-of-the-art products to serve customers' financial needs. Ocean National Bank has stayed on top of the changing technological landscape by developing comprehensive online banking for both personal and business customers. These services include

not only traditional banking, but also online investing and retirement plan management.

High-level service also means personal availability. Credit decisions are made on a local basis in order to help customers quickly and avoid corporate red tape. It also gives the bank the opportunity to get to know its customers instead of dealing with them at arm's length. In this way, the bank has the opportunity to review the needs of each customer as a whole. Ocean National currently offers "suite" products, which use this holistic assessment of individual customers to determine which products would be most beneficial and cost-effective. By looking at the big picture, the bank is better able to tailor its services to individuals, rather than expecting individuals to conform to cookie cutter products.

The bank also makes a concerted effort to avoid "nickel and diming" its

An obsolete bank note issued by Ocean Bank in the early 1860s under the authority of a state charter.

customers in regard to fees. For example, when many banks run debit card promotions, the savings come to individuals only on specific "signature" transactions. However, these types of transactions cost the merchants more than regular PIN transactions. Ocean National Bank has always refused to participate in these programs. The bank feels that they are inherently unfair to customers on several levels. First, all customers should benefit from promotions. Second, as a commercial bank, Ocean National is concerned that this type of promotion would negatively impact its business customers. Instead, it develops incentives and benefits for its entire customer base.

Providing great service means more than just understanding the financial end of the spectrum. To the bank, it means understanding, and giving back to, the communities it serves. Local GEO (Geographic) teams are ready to make decisions on requests for participation in community events, donations and sponsorship. This allows local employees with insight into the community to assess how Ocean National can best make a difference in the neighborhoods they call home.

Ocean National Bank takes its responsibility to the community seriously. The bank also believes in enabling others to make a difference. Teaming with New Hampshire, Ocean National offered discounted loan rates to businesses seeking to upgrade facilities and purchase materials to save energy. This took the form of Ocean National's Renewable Energy and Energy Efficiency Business Loan. This type of product represents the better of two ideals for Ocean National. Not only are energy-saving devices economical for the bank's customers, the end result of lowering overall energy consumption is environmentally friendly. This pragmatic approach typifies Ocean National

Ocean National Bank's first president, Joseph Titcomb (1854-1878).

Bank's commitment to its customers' best interests.

In the aftermath of the recent flooding that affected much of southern Maine, Ocean National Bank acted quickly to help local residents. With damage so severe that FEMA declared York County a national disaster area, assistance was needed to repair and rebuild. Ocean National immediately put in place a Flood Relief Loan, which was made available to renters, homeowners and small business owners.

Ocean National's contributions to the community hardly end there. The bank is involved with the Creative

Economy, which Maine Governor John Elias Baldacci called "a catalyst for the creation of new jobs in Maine communities." Ocean National provides scholarships at various local schools and also supports the York and Kittery historical societies. In addition, it is a major supporter of the United Way throughout York County, Maine and New Hampshire. These activities demonstrate the bank's commitment to contributing across the gamut and engaging with the many communities it calls home.

Ocean National Bank offers its customers "An Ocean of Possibilities." It has thrived by staying in touch with the needs of its customers and adapting to the changing tide of the times. Ocean National Bank has remained a steadfast beacon through the years, guiding both individual and commercial customers through ever-changing waters to financial wellness.

Today, when Ocean National customers walk into the Kennebunk branch (below), or any one of the thirty-six branches serving York County, Maine and southern New Hampshire, they open the door to a wealth of services coordinated by friends and neighbors living in their own community.

PARKVIEW ADVENTIST MEDICAL CENTER

Parkview Adventist Medical Center is located in Brunswick, Maine, twenty-five miles north of Portland and two miles from the Atlantic Ocean. The hospital opened its doors on July 12, 1959 and has since grown to a fifty-five-bed full service facility offering state-of-the-art services in the same warm and caring environment as the day it opened. Beyond treating the sick and injured, Parkview exists to treat the whole person—body, mind and spirit, while providing progressive healthcare and wellness education to help people both get well and stay well. Parkview's success can be attributed to the hospital's caring and expert staff, the use of state-of-the-art equipment and technology, the practice of evidence-based medicine and incorporating Adventist health principles into hospital care.

Adventist health is based on a philosophy of wellness. Wellness means being free from disease or injury and living in a state of total health and well being. Adventist health practitioners and organizations advocate

Adventist health practitioners strongly recommend whole grains as part of a healthy diet.

Parkview was founded by Dr. Marion Westermyer, Dr. Michael Weaver and Dr. Ronald Bettle.

eight principles of healthy living: eating a nutritious vegetarian diet, exercising to benefit the body's strength and immunity, drinking at least five glasses of water a day, absorbing the benefits of the sun, employing temperance, taking in fresh air and getting ample rest.

Parkview Adventist Medical Center is located near the birthplace of the Adventist health movement. Ellen G. White, one of the founders of the Seventh-day Adventist Church, grew up in Gorham, Maine, and lived for a time in Topsham, not far from the site where Parkview was developed. The Seventh-day Adventist Church was born out of the Millerite movements of the 1840s at a time and in a place where many Christians were searching for a greater understanding of the Bible. From its inception, the Church believed in the Biblical Sabbath, had an intense interest in the Second Coming of Jesus Christ and placed a strong emphasis on healthy living practices. Their approach to healthy living was especially important in the 1800s, as in retrospect

many medical practices seemed absurd. For example, the authoritative 1899 *Physician's Edition of the Merck Manual* recommended that asthmatics smoke tobacco. In the same era, Adventist health was among the first to assert that smoking was a harmful practice. In fact, in 1962 church health leaders developed the "Five Day Plan to Stop Smoking"— the first of its kind in the nation. In addition to awareness of the impact of smoking on the body, Adventist health was also at the forefront of healthy eating and living practices, before these concepts were popularized.

The first Adventist healthcare institution was the Battle Creek Sanitarium in Michigan which opened in 1876. At the facility, care would begin with a full physical examination, followed by treatments including water therapy, outdoor exercise and eating a simple, low calorie vegetarian diet. The sanitarium's medical superintendent was Dr. John Harvey Kellogg, one of the founders of what would become the Kellogg Company known for its grain cereals. As still recommended by Adventist health practitioners today, Kellogg advocated a diet rich in whole grains. One cold night, Dr. Kellogg and his brother, who also worked at Battle Creek, had forgotten a bowl of boiled wheat in the kitchen only to find it broken into flakes the next day, which they served as part of the morning meal. The toasted flakes, now a breakfast food of choice, were in fact a happy accident.

More than half a century later, in 1945, Marian Strickland in Canaan, Maine was the only known Seventh-day Adventist physician practicing in Northern New England. That would soon change. After serving in World War II, Dr. Ronald A. Bettle completed his residency at Maine General Hospital in Portland, and opened a practice in Brunswick. Brunswick was growing and ready to meet the needs

Parkview is located in Brunswick, Maine and only twenty-five miles from Portland.

of the rapidly growing community in every way, except medically. The privately owned town hospital was located in a wooden home and was twenty years behind the times. Soon, Dr. Bettle was appointed Medical Secretary for the Northern New England Conference of Seventh-day Adventists. Recruiting Adventist physicians for the conference, he met the challenge of filling the need for dedicated men and women to work in medicine in the Brunswick area. The first two to respond to his invitation were Dr. Marion Westermeyer and Dr. Michael Weaver who set up practices in the area and later helped found Parkview. The three doctors had successful practices and worked with two other Brunswick doctors to try to convince the town to build a modern hospital. They did not find success. Never giving up, the doctors and fellow Adventists formed a corporation, worked with the Association of Self-supporting Institutions and Adventist businessmen to make their dream a reality and build an Adventist hospital. The doctors spent five years acquainting

the community with the Adventist medical program; Parkview Memorial Hospital opened its doors with thirty-five available beds to the public in 1959.

By this time, the doctors had a support network that rallied around the hospital. A ladies auxiliary made necessary items for the hospital and collected Betty Crocker coupons to supply flatware. The hospital was also blessed with good fortune at crucial moments. For example, Dr. Bettle presented the book *Ministry of Healing*

to a wealthy patient and twelve days before the hospital opened, they received a gift of $25,000. Also, a fortuitous meeting on a plane between Carl Sundin of the General Conference of Seventh-day Adventists and Brunswick banker, Al Morell, led to the final approval of the loan for Parkview. The mission and philosophy as well as the work Adventists perform around the world swayed Morell to cancel his vacation and oversee the loan process. Funds in hand, the hospital was ready to fill staff positions.

Though small at first, physicians from across the country came to work at the hospital including specialists in obstetrics and gynecology, genitourinary, internal medicine, thoracic and vascular surgery, podiatry, oral surgery, orthopedics, pediatrics, ophthalmology and ENT. Less than four months after opening, Parkview was operating in the black.

In 1964, after five years of financial success, Parkview became a part of the Northern New England Conference of Seventh-day Adventists. After decades of growth, Parkview

Adventist health practitioners also recommend a vegetarian diet rich in vegetables and legumes.

Memorial Hospital became Parkview Adventist Medical Center in 2003 to better reflect its heritage.

From its humble beginnings, Parkview has become one the most technologically advanced hospitals in the state of Maine. In 2003 Parkview brought to southern Maine the first sixteen-slice CAT scanner and was the first hospital in that region to offer digital mammography in 2006. That same year, two local network news affiliates featured Parkview for the use of technology to help reduce medical errors. The news segments devoted special attention to the use of biometrics, a system that uses fingerprint technology in place of passwords to prevent unauthorized computer access to patient information. The reports also discussed Parkview's Bedside Medication Verification system, which safeguards patients from receiving the wrong medication using barcode technology on all drugs and patient ID bands.

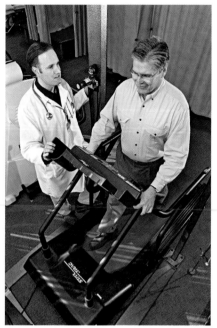

Parkview's Wellness Center offers progressive health education programs and classes.

Parkview brought the first multi-slice CAT Scan to southern Maine.

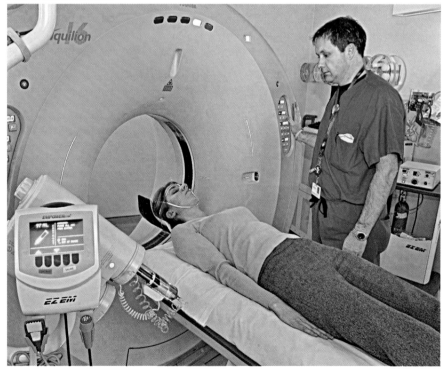

Parkview is also one of the most wired hospitals in Maine. In 2005 the hospital implemented an Electronic Medical Record system that links all hospital departments and physicians' offices with instantaneously updated patient records. Parkview was also one of the first small hospitals to successfully implement a Pictorial Archiving and Communication System (PACS), which keeps records electronically allowing for easy and comprehensive data retrieval which limits errors. These two systems allow even off-site physicians to log into the hospital network to retrieve reports, lab results, x-rays and other information on their patients.

The company that designed Parkview's Electronic Medical Records system noted that Parkview's fast and virtually problem-free installation defied typical implementation. Within six months the hospital brought a full suite of clinical, financial and administrative applications on board. To match these developments, Parkview doubled computer availability throughout the hospital. Having hospital and patient data in one place will improve patient care, reduce paperwork and lower healthcare costs.

In addition to using state-of-the-art equipment and medical technology to care for patients, Parkview continues its focus on wellness. With the rising cost of healthcare being a major concern in the United States, Parkview strives to reduce health costs with programs incorporating wellness principles to help people avoid the use of expensive medical interventions. The Lifestyle Choices Program, a two-week outpatient wellness program is designed to benefit anyone who has or is at risk for developing a chronic disease. Other programs from the hospital's Wellness Center include smoking cessation, stress management, nutritional counseling, hydrotherapy education, diabetes education, vegetarian cooking classes, business health, natural remedies and personal wellness profiling.

Parkview also participates in numerous community outreach programs. In 1995 the Community Health Information Partnership, or CHIP, started as a joint project between Parkview Adventist Medical Center and Curtis Memorial Library. After the library director noticed the lack of current health information, CHIP was formed as a consortium to provide health information and programs to both healthcare professionals and the general public in the Midcoast region. CHIP purchased over 2,000 educational materials in its first four years, has provided round-the-clock access to online health databases and three traveling collections of related material. It has conducted workshops and health fairs, co-sponsored Senior Passport, the lifelong learning project for seniors, and launched a program with the Jeremiah Cromwell Disabilities Center to distribute books on developmental disabilities to thirteen local sites.

In 1999 the Parkview Rehab and Wellness facility opened in partnership

Staff use computers at a patient's bedside to verify medications and access Parkview's electronic medical record system.

with the Highlands of Topsham, an assisted living facility. In 2006 Parkview Rehab expanded into Women's Fitness Studio and Spa, offering women's health physical therapy in the community.

The hospital also hosts free lectures and programs on topics such as heart disease, stroke, cancer, diabetes, hypertension, exercise, weight loss and more. These and other initiatives are part of a greater vision which calls for more community involvement and focuses also on health education and health improvement.

Parkview continues the tradition of international medical missionary work that Loma Linda Medical Center started more than 100 years ago. The world famous Loma Linda Medical Center on the outskirts of Los Angeles has a Parkview connection. Many of Parkview's Medical Staff are Loma Linda school graduates. In addition, both Loma Linda and Parkview are part of a network of Adventist medical facilities consisting of over seventy locations in the United States and more than 200

Parkview has been revered for its exceptional maternity care. Over 23,000 babies have been born at the hospital.

worldwide. Parkview is one of the many Adventist facilities that participate in humanitarian treks, international healing and education that continue today from Greece to Taiwan. Parkview annually participates in medical missionary clinics in underserved areas of Mexico.

Whether Parkview is reaching out to the world community or simply encouraging staff to drink more water, thereby lowering its healthcare cost, Parkview Adventist Medical Center demonstrates clearly that it cares. This small community hospital has delivered over 23,000 babies, provides care for more than 55,000 people every year and is nationally recognized as a leader in wellness and health education. Parkview Adventist Medical Center has the satisfaction of being involved with and leading a movement that fulfils what an early Christian apostle John hoped for Gaius: "I wish above all things that thou mayest prosper and be in health."

PENMOR LITHOGRAPHERS

Penmor Lithographers started as a buy and swap advertising publication in 1968. Bob Morton, a RCA microwave engineer, joined with Ray Pinette, a funeral director, and published *Bargain Ad* out of a former variety store on Pine Street in Lewiston, Maine using only a typewriter to type out pages.

Though *Bargain Ad* was initially printed elsewhere, Morton and Pinette decided expenses could be lowered if they did their own printing. They acquired a small eleven by seventeen-inch AB Dick press and hired one employee. To help offset costs, they began soliciting small print jobs, which soon turned into a profitable endeavor. By 1970 the Pine Street store front proved to be too small for the fledgling enterprise. *Bargain Ad* was still being published and distributed throughout Maine and New Hampshire, but Morton and Pinette began to focus more on printing.

With the aid of a Small Business Administration loan, Penmor Printers found larger quarters on Lisbon Street, a busy Lewiston main fare. Morton and Pinette shuffled the letters of their last names and created

Paul Fillion (rear left) and senior pressman Pete Poliquin check ink density on a press sheet.

Penmor Printers. They purchased a single color twenty-five-inch press and increased the staff to three full-time employees. Commercial printing had become the significant pursuit; ultimately *Bargain Ad*, though successful, ceased being produced.

Joe Fillion, an acquaintance of both Morton and Pinette, had over fifteen years of print experience when he agreed to join Penmor Printers in 1972. Fillion's expertise in all aspects of print production was well acknowledged and respected in the region.

The three partners agreed that four color printing was the prime avenue to choose and Penmor Printers exercised the means to make it possible. The pre-press department undertook color separation work, involving camera and negative composition as well as plate-making. When Penmor Printers purchased and moved into a 10,000 square-foot building on Park Street in 1976 it obtained a two-color Miehle press. The additional space also allowed them to expand their bindery operation.

The key ingredients which underscored all work produced at the plant was quality and customer assurance.

The Fillion family (clockwise from lower left): Karen Fillion Nicole, Glen Fillion, Joe Fillion, Wayne Fillion and Paul Fillion. As a family owned and operated business since 1968, Penmor believes they hold one another to a higher standard. Not only are they accountable to their clients, but also to each other.

To the three men who guided Penmor, client satisfaction was the most important facet. Morton, Pinette and Fillion believed success and growth depended on developing and maintaining a relationship with all its customers. Toward the end of the 1970s the Park Street plant had a workforce of thirty-five employees and ran two shifts. Penmor's client base had spread beyond Maine, into New Hampshire and Massachusetts. Penmor had turned into an established, sophisticated printer of note, the recipient of many awards from the graphics arts industry. The Small Business Administration presented Penmor Printers with the Person of the Year Award in 1979 "for exemplifying the imagination, initiative, independence and integrity" of the small businessman.

As the 1980s approached, continued growth in print sales compelled

Penmor to seek further expansion. The three partners had roots in Lewiston; they were also businessmen who had provided a process of manufacture involving employment, quality and dependability. Location and accessibility to distant clients was a must. With the economic shift in the area, could Lewiston continue to be their base of operations?

The Finance Authority of Maine helped Penmor acquire a four and a half acre site in the Lewiston Industrial Park at the corner of Mitchell and Lexington Streets, less than a mile from the Maine Turnpike. In 1985 Penmor constructed a 23,000 square-foot building and engaged forty-five employees. That same year Penmor Printers changed its name to Penmor Lithographers. The name change, Fillion says, "was to represent a statement in quality printing."

In 1986 the first six-color press in northern New England found floor space at Penmor Lithographers. "That opened a whole other segment of printing," Fillion admits. Penmor's name translated into high standards of multi-color printing and bindery production—and Penmor continued to garner more clients as well as awards. A new technology was just beginning to be heard from in the early 1980s: digital computerization.

Joe Fillion, oversees finishing on a job in the bindery.

The Penmor Lithographers facility at 8 Lexington Street, Lewiston, Maine.

In less than a decade desk top publishing had a pronounced impact on the print industry. "The Gutenberg movable type invention comes closest in comparison," Fillion states, adding that commercial printing had to be "completely overhauled."

Evolution of all key print production elements has always been a steady pattern for Penmor. The pre-press department underwent the first changeover to the new technology. A whole new format in preparing original art and layout for plate-making had to be developed and implemented. Eventually the film to plate process —the standard for many years— vanished as digital imposition took to form.

In addition to transforming the pre-press to state-of-the-art technology Penmor purchased forty-inch multi-color press units in 1992, 1998 and 2005 to remain competitive with industry demands and client criteria. It also expanded and augmented its bindery operation by incorporating progressive folding, saddle-stitch and perfect bind machinery. Penmor also integrated ink jet addressing and full service mailing capabilities in

its goal to provide one stop service for its customers.

By 1998 Penmor expanded its Lexington Street plant by another 22,000 feet, acquired Western Maine Graphics and had a work force of over eighty people. Fillion points out that in 1999 —the year following the company's major expansion—sales increased over 20 percent.

Bob Morton and Ray Pinette retired during the 1990s. Penmor's management team was reorganized under the leadership of the Fillion family. Joe is semi-retired but is chairman of the board. His eldest son, Paul, became president of the company in addition to supervising the sales force. Brothers Wayne and Glen direct pre-press and press operations while their sister Karen Fillion Nicole is the firm's treasurer and administers the estimating department.

In 2001 at an international graphic arts competition sponsored by The Printing Industries of America, Penmor received the prestigious Benny award, a bronze statue of Benjamin Franklin. This honor is bestowed on printers recognized for design and quality printing as well exemplary performance in the graphic arts community, local community and to serve as a model for others.

The Fillions sense the digital revolution is not even close to reaching its peak in the print industry. Whatever tools are required or personnel needed or education necessary, the Fillions are confident that the job will get done at Penmor, just as long as the most important aspects of the job—quality, service, craftsmanship and resolve—remain intact as it was in 1968 with two gentlemen who had an idea and a typewriter.

RTD ENTERPRISES

Like many other men in the late 1980s, Dan Emery had been faithful to his corporate employer for nearly two decades. He raised his family and had a comfortable life as a field manager for a New Hampshire landfill liner company. Then it happened. Emery found himself working for a financially struggling company and gave his employer two months notice. He was faced with two options: go to work in another environmental company or start his own business. Emery chose the latter.

Twenty years later, RTD Enterprises is helping to keep drinking water safe from coast to coast. Its primary service is installing heavy duty plastic liners to secure landfills that hold waste products. The goal is to avoid any water-related connection between the wastes and the surrounding environment, particularly the groundwater. The liners help prevent leachate, poisonous substance that forms when garbage mixes with groundwater. That hazardous waste can cause cancer, birth defects and other diseases.

Before the Clean Water Act of 1977, it was common for sewage to be dumped directly in the waters. Today, the Environmental Protection Agency

The 125 million gallon drinking water reservoir liner and floating cover contains drinking water for the city of Pittsburgh, Pennsylvania.

An aerial photograph of a landfill closure that measures approximately twenty-five acres.

imposes strict measures designed to keep water clean. One of those measures is to require a landfill liner to prevent the waste and water from mixing. It takes a crew of eight to twelve men six weeks to install the liner on a typical landfill. The cost of the job can range from thousands to millions. Hard work, determination and a focus on quality has made RTD a leader in the field.

It all began when Dan Emery, who is now a consultant for the company, saw the business opportunity in an environmental need. Environmentalists were generating media attention

in an era where recycling and "green" products were emerging as more than just a fad. Emery invested $40,000 he had saved over the years to start a landfill liner company called RTD Enterprises from his cellar in 1987. He enlisted his two sons, Robbie and Troy, to work alongside him. Having recently completed high school, they were ready, willing and able to tackle the challenge of building a business with their father.

The trio set out to become the premier installer of liners for landfills, as well as for drinking water reservoirs and waste treatment plants. However, the company was hardly an overnight success. In fact, the first three years were a struggle. The construction industry was not familiar with the RTD name. Despite the fact that Dan had been in the business for nearly two decades, contractors wanted to work with a company that had a proven track record.

The Emerys didn't give up easily. The trio continued to bid on small jobs and performed quality work. The simple strategy paid off. RTD's big break came in 1990, when a large New Hampshire general contractor gave them the opportunity they had been waiting for. That job led to additional work with the same contractor all over the Northeast. After just four years in business, RTD Enterprises moved from the cellar to a 3,000 square foot building in Madison. RTD owns the building, which it uses to house forty-five employees.

Troy Emery, co-president of the company with his brother Robbie, describes a strict four-part philosophy for operating RTD: be efficient, do it right the first time, adhere to industry standards and don't cut corners. General contractors appreciate RTD's philosophy because poor subcontractors cost them money, but good subcontractors make them money. Word of mouth led to growth of the company in the 1990s as RTD distinguished themselves with their quality and service in an industry where most major competitors use the same products to line landfills.

By 1993 RTD's name was known nationwide and opportunities were emerging on the West Coast. The family did not want to send one of the sons out West, so they hired a vice president locally to oversee a branch office in Gilroy, California. The warmer climate kept the company busy even during the traditionally slow winter months when weather often prevented installers from working. Two years after opening the California office, RTD was a major

A twenty acre landfill cell liner.

industry force on the West Coast. RTD has since closed its West Coast office, but still maintains crews of installers in the region and uses computer systems and CAD programs to manage the jobs remotely.

RTD has built a solid reputation in its industry. Now it strives to make that reputation a little bit better every day. The Emerys know that if their crews do substandard work, word will quickly spread among the general contractor community. RTD installers receive certification from liner manufacturers so they understand the proper techniques for working with the material. After all, if the liner leaks before its life span, the contractor will look to the installers. Also, if the groundwater becomes contaminated, it could lead to significant liabilities for the client and the company.

The Emerys do not have aspirations to take over the liner industry. They are satisfied with the slow and steady growth and the comfortable life it has offered the family. What they do have is trust for one another. The brothers don't always agree, but they tackle issues together to deter-

mine the best way to grow the business. The relationship has worked out so well that they started a separate roofing division, the largest in the region, with cousin Brian Emery, who brings twenty-five years of roofing experience to the company. The roofing division maintains the same mantra: "Do it right or don't do it."

RTD's reputation for quality and service has won it some significant bids over the years. The largest job RTD completed was a $1.5 million bid to line and cover a drinking reservoir for the City of Pittsburgh, Pennsylvania that took four months. While every job is different, Troy Emery insists that RTD pays the same attention to detail for million-dollar contracts as it does for smaller ones. For the Emerys, right is right and wrong is wrong. There is no grey area. They are most proud that they have maintained a reputation for quality and service over their nearly twenty year company history, and they plan to keep the RTD brand name among the leaders in its growing field.

TD BANKNORTH

Community is the heart and soul of TD Banknorth. The threads of that promise are woven throughout this Maine history that dates back to 1852 with the founding of the Portland Savings Bank; the same spirit continues at the company today.

The story begins in the days when Millard Fillmore was president of the United States. John Hubbard was governor of Maine; and Albion K. Parris, Portland's mayor and a former congressman, senator and governor, served as Portland Savings Bank's first president. The community bank soon had a large impact on economic development initiatives, investing in projects and employing members of the community much like TD Banknorth does today. One of Portland Savings Bank's first initiatives was a $100,000 loan to the Portland and Kennebec Railroad for the construction of a rail terminal at the corner of Commercial and Clark Streets. The bank continued to make investment loans, contributing to the development of the city of Portland.

Nearly a quarter century later, in 1875, People's Savings Bank was

Now professional office space, Bates Mill was originally one of the largest textile mills in the country. Civil War soldier uniforms were first made in the Mill. Later, in rooms such as this, skilled workers sewed curtains and made other fabrics for the home. Courtesy, Androscoggin Historical Society, Auburn, Maine

The front entrance to Lewiston's Bates Mill is little changed today from when it was first built. Courtesy, Androscoggin Historical Society, Auburn, Maine

established together with the Manufacturers National Bank in Lewiston, Maine. These local savings banks were dedicated to investing their deposits within the community. While the 1870s were marked by recession and a series of financial panics, Lewiston and Auburn rode out the decade well. At the end of the first year in business, People's reported $119,388.51 in total annual deposits.

TD Banknorth's roots originate in these and several other regional banks, such as Penobscot Savings and Waterville Savings, which were incorporated in 1869, and Rockland Savings Bank, founded in 1890, which later changed its name to Heritage Savings Bank. Nearly 100 years later, though, the thrift industry was struggling and survival meant consolidation. The five banks—Portland Savings, People's Savings, Heritage Savings, Penobscot Savings and Waterville Savings merged in the 1980s, forming Peoples Heritage Bank. The merger created the largest thrift institution in Maine. Peoples Heritage converted

from a mutual company and issued stock in 1986, a major turning point in the business, which in turn would pave the way for the bank becoming a powerhouse in a changing industry landscape.

William J. Ryan, joined the bank in 1989 as chairman, president and CEO, and since that time has grown the company into one of the twenty-five largest commercial banks in the United States. Beyond stellar customer service and competitive products, the bank accomplished its rapid growth through acquisitions. Between 1987 and 2006 the bank made twenty-six acquisitions—expanding its reach into Connecticut, Massachusetts, New Hampshire, New Jersey, New York, Pennsylvania and Vermont. It came as no surprise to the bank's many satisfied customers when, in 2004, *Forbes Magazine* named it "The Best Managed Bank in America" over much larger rivals.

Under Ryan's watch, TD Banknorth has also given back to the

cities of Lewiston and Auburn, as well as many other cities across Maine and the Northeast. The bank has invested tens of millions of dollars in infrastructure to help revitalize downtown Lewiston. The company was one of the first occupants of the restored Bates Mill complex when it located its major operations centers there, and it remains its largest occupant. Today, more than 800 employees work in the once abandoned buildings. TD Banknorth employs nearly 1,200 in the Lewiston region alone—with more than $40 million in annual payroll. Those investments helped stabilize the city's economy in the wake of high unemployment rates from textile manufacturing plant closings.

TD Banknorth executives consider its investment in Lewiston part of the bank's legacy and its future. It has provided financing for many of the region's new downtown buildings and apartment complexes, among the most significant being the Central Maine Medical Center, a 250-bed hospital that offers cardiac surgery,

comprehensive cancer care and houses a trauma center. TD Banknorth provided over $25 million in financing for the center, which has attracted some of the most talented heart surgeons in the Northeast.

In 2005 Peoples Heritage Bank, as the Maine retail division of TD Banknorth was then known, contributed over $2 million to support local communities and causes through charitable giving and sponsorships of events such as the Beach to Beacon 10K Road Race, which annually brings world-class runners to the state. Each year Maine employees contribute over 76,000 volunteer hours of service. Among the many organizations TD Banknorth helps support are United Way, March of Dimes, Boys & Girls Clubs and several of Maine's universities and hospitals and arts organizations, including the Portland Symphony Orchestra, Bangor Symphony, PCA Great Performances, Maine Center for the Arts, the Portland

The Storehouse No. 7 sign over the main entrance to TD Banknorth's operations center at Bates Mill is a historic link to the building's original use as a textile mill. Courtesy, Androscoggin Historical Society, Auburn, Maine

Museum of Art and the Farnsworth Museum.

Maine's nineteenth century bankers could never have foreseen the growth and consolidation in the industry, and probably never imagined that their community banks would one day grow into one of the largest banks in the Northeast and become part of an even larger international financial institution. In 2005 the Toronto-Dominion Bank in Canada became majority shareholder of Banknorth, and the company changed its name to TD Banknorth. Today, the bank has over $40 billion in assets with nearly 600 branches and more than 9,500 employees across eight northeastern states.

TD Banknorth executives are proud of the significant role the company has played in the region's economy. As Bill Ryan, CEO, says, "At TD Banknorth, community is at the heart of everything we do."

Space once cluttered with industrial materials is now an outdoor plaza with a fountain for the relaxation and enjoyment of the employees working in Bates Mill. Courtesy, Androscoggin Historical Society, Auburn, Maine

WBRC ARCHITECTS • ENGINEERS

Located at 44 Central Street in the historic Kirstein Building in Bangor is the corporate headquarters of WBRC Architects • Engineers, one of the most experienced and respected architectural and engineering firms in Maine. Many of the prominent buildings in Bangor are almost as aged as the century old firm, itself. After all, the founding fathers of the company built them. WBRC has a relationship with Bangor that dates back to around the turn of the century when the company filled a desperate need in the city. By doing so, the firm grew in experience, prominence and servitude to its community. The partnership entities have changed over its 104 years, but the philosophy of the firm has not. They aim to design buildings that reflect the vision of the owner, not the architect. The determination to practice this philosophy with innovation and excellence was inherent in the company's treasured founding fathers.

C. Parker Crowell and his partner, John F. Thomas, started their modest design firm in 1902 with only one

WBRC's founding principals at work. In the foreground, C. Parker Crowell (1902-1956) sits at his desk.

The Student Center at the University of Maine at Augusta won the Maine American School & University Interior Design Award.

other employee. Their connections in the northern part of the state coupled with their willingness to travel afforded many design opportunities from Houlton to Greenville to Patten, south to Hallowell and west of Foxcroft. The young firm had links with design schools, churches, hotels and individual residents. One of their most valued associations began in 1903 with Crowell's alma mater, the University of Maine. Thomas and Crowell were commissioned to design Lord Hall, the engineering building on the Orono campus. By the time Crowell retired many years later, the school had commissioned the firm time and time again. He completed forty-four buildings for the university as well as many renovations and additions. The strong working relationship between the university and WBRC still exists to this day.

The greatest growth opportunity for the company came ten years after it began and coincided with Bangor's greatest loss: the fire of 1911. Half the city burned to the

ground; its residents were devastated. The town needed to be rebuilt from the ground up— literally. Because of C. Parker Crowell's growing reputation, the city turned to his design firm. Now on his own and with more work than he could handle, he hired Walter Lancaster to assist him. Together, the two designed block after block of commercial buildings, and the company's business doubled.

Lancaster took a hiatus from the company, but then returned in the early 1920s and began a partnership with Crowell that lasted for thirty-seven years. In 1952 Ambrose Higgins joined the team, and this new partnership continued until 1956. By the end of the 1950s, the company's focus was exclusively on non-residential projects. The firm survived the Depression, the two World Wars and the retirement of the respected C. Parker Crowell.

During Crowell's fifty-four years in the firm, he helped erect more than one thousand buildings statewide. His exacting practices and attention to detail set the standard high for those who followed in the company. Crowell carried his "slipstick" on every job. He carried a stick with a mirror attached to the end so he could examine the tops of moldings, just to make sure they were correctly positioned and completely painted. In addition to his other prominent contributions to the city, Crowell is credited with the *River Drivers of Pierce* memorial which he designed in 1925. "The memorial is a timeless celebration of the men behind the growth, the wealth and the character of Bangor and the state of Maine," stated John Rohman, CEO of WBRC.

During the next half century the company evolved into eight additional partnership entities with changing names, until it became WBRC Architects • Engineers. The firm would also grow from twelve employees to sixty-five. One partner, whose name has been included in the title of the company from 1956 to present, is Edwin Webster.

Webster guided the company through the lean years of the late 1950s through the 1960s. In 1971 when Higgins passed away, Webster was left in the sole leadership position. He made decisions that held the company together and propelled it forward. He also was firmly established in the role of mentor. "He didn't have a problem with younger folks; he was open to sharing and mentoring. He was a team player. Because of that, the business got passed along," stated Mike Czarniecki, WBRC architect and principal.

Buchanan Alumni House at the University of Maine at Orono won the Maine American School & University Interior Design Award.

The Eastern Maine Medical Center Ambulatory Surgery Center (ABC Award to Wrenn Associates) in Bangor, Maine.

Among those who Webster mentored were young partners, Herb (Skip) Day, Alan Baldwin and John Rohman. During the 1970s the young partners represented a new era for the company. The new team operated more like a family. "The entire office might have worked on a job. We'd finish it, get it out to bid, and then all go out and celebrate," Rohman fondly remembered. "We were all about the same age; our wives knew each other. We played pool at Skip's house and always went out to lunch together."

Over the decades other principals honored the firm as top employees. Gertrud Ebbeson was one of them. The M.I.T. graduate was distinguished by being the first woman asked to take partnership in the firm. Alan Baldwin came to work for the company intent on spending a couple of years; he soon became partner and stayed for two decades. Dick Rollins and Mike Pullen began working for the firm in 1978 and 1979, respectively. Now there are nine principals in total: Mike Pullen, Rob Frank,

Dick Rollins, Al Bromley, Doug Whitney, John Rohman, Mike Czarniecki, Steve Rich and Richard Graves.

WBRC's buildings, renovations and additions are too numerous to list, but a few of the more recent accomplishments are EMMC Ambulatory Surgery Center, Buchanan Alumni House, University of Maine, Robert D. O'Donnell Commons at Husson College and The Jackson Lab Production Facility. The company serves the community but also strives to maintain the satisfaction of its existing talented employees. In 2002 a Sarasota office was opened to generate more business for the firm, but also to offer an option for the firm's people who desired a change of venue. Employees are also encouraged to explore additional creative skills. "We allow our people—we urge them—to go as far as possible in whatever direction they want. Mike Pullen started out in site engineering and ended up an architect; Dick Rollins began as a draftsman and is now an engineer. I was an engineer but was given the latitude to pursue my greatest interest: interior design," stated Rohman.

In addition to pursuing personal opportunities, WBRC's people also give back to their community. In the same tradition of C. Parker Crowell, employees are involved in fundraising for community events such as the National Folk Festival. In fact, the company's CEO is the chairman of this annual event. The strong reflection of the founding fathers' character not only remains in Bangor's buildings but also in the current employees of WBRC.

A TIMELINE OF MAINE'S HISTORY

11,200 years ago
Date ascribed to the oldest paleo Indian find in Maine: a caribou "killing ground" at Azicohos Lake in the southwest corner of the state. Some 10,000 artifacts were found there.

1497
John Cabot, (the Italian Giuseppe Caboto), sailing for England, reaches Canada and stakes out all future British claims to the eastern Atlantic coast.

1524
Giovanni Verrazano, another Italian, but sailing for France, lands in Maine and receives a hostile reception from the natives.

1568
David Ingram, an English sailor, claims to have walked from Mexico to Nova Scotia, passing through Maine. He spreads stories back home of *Norumbega*, a fabulous golden city, located ostensibly in Maine.

1583
Sir Humphrey Gilbert, half-brother of Sir Walter Raleigh, lands in Newfoundland and again claims the eastern Atlantic coast for England. He is lost at sea but his son Raleigh Gilbert will return and lead an expedition to settle in Maine.

1602
Bartholomew Gosnold stops in Maine—at Cape Elizabeth and York—before sailing on to the Cape Cod area. On Cuttyhunk Island, he built a small fort. Today, the only town there is called Gosnold.

1604
A French expedition led by the Sieur des Monts, a Protestant nobleman, and Samuel de Champlain, a Catholic navigator, spend a winter on an island in the St. Croix River, which is the present-day boundary between Maine and New Brunswick. Scurvy decimates the would-be settlers. After exploring as far south as Cape Cod, the French settle at Port Royal in Nova Scotia.

Fort Western on the Kennebec River in Augusta was built in 1754. It served as a fortified storehouse for the Kennebec Proprietors, speculators who had acquired land that was originally a part of the Plymouth Patent. During the American Revolution, Benedict Arnold provisioned his troops and prepared for the march to Quebec while at Fort Western. George French Collection, Maine State Archives

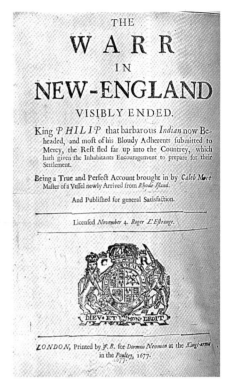

A 1677 publication announcing the end of King Philip's War. Instead of celebrating peace, however, the pamphlet revels in the death of King Philip. From A History of the American People by Woodrow Wilson, 1917

1605
The famous, or infamous, visit of Captain George Waymouth to Maine. He kidnapped five Indians and took them back to England, where they were boarded with two of the promoters of English overseas expansion, Sir Ferdinando Gorges and Sir John Popham, the Chief Justice of England. One of these Indians allegedly was Tisquantum, the famous Squanto, who befriended the Pilgrims. Another school of thought maintains instead that this was Samoset, also an English-speaking friend of the Pilgrims.

1606
Gorges, Popham and others persuade King James I to grant charters to companies they form for exploring and exploiting the eastern coast of North America.

1607

The two companies formed, the London Company and the Plymouth Company, send expeditions to North and South Virginia—the generic name for the whole coast having been derived in honor of the Virgin Queen, Elizabeth I. One expedition goes to Jamestown, the other to Maine.

1607–08

The Popham colony is established and its leaders are Raleigh Gilbert and George Popham. Sir John's nephew lasts through a winter, then abandons the site at a location in mid-coast Maine now known as Popham Beach.

1613

An attempted French settlement at Lamoine, opposite Mount Desert Island, is destroyed by an English warship out of Jamestown commanded by Captain Samuel Argall. The attack on the St. Sauveur colony helps lead to more than 100 years of warfare between France and England in North America.

1614

Captain John Smith coins the term "New England." He lands at Monhegan Island and extols the abundance of the Maine fisheries.

1618

Richard Vines, a servant of Sir Ferdinando Gorges, spends a winter at Biddeford Pool and calls it "Winter Harbor."

1620

The Plymouth Company, under Sir Ferdinando Gorges, becomes the Council of New England and grants lands to the Pilgrims and Puritans.

1622

Thirty English fishing vessels are at Damerill's Cove on Damariscove Island, off the coast of Boothbay.

1625

The Pilgrims send Edward Winslow up the Kennebec River, where he trades corn for fur with the Maine Indians.

The 400th anniversary of explorer George Waymouth's month-long visit in 1605 was marked in 2005. George Waymouth explored the midcoast region of Maine, making him the first European to visit the area. A woman is shown here visiting the Waymouth Monument in Thomaston in the 1940s. Courtesy, George French Collection, Maine State Archives

1628

Richmond's Island, off Cape Elizabeth, is first settled by "Great Walt" Bagnall, a giant of a man who mistreats the local Indians and is killed by them.

1629

The Pilgrims receive a grant of land in Maine at Cushnoc (present-day Augusta).

1634

First recorded murder in Maine. Shipmaster John Hocking, trespassing on Pilgrim territory, shoots and kills Moses Talbot and is fatally shot in return.

1638

First court established in Maine, which was then called New Somersetshire.

It is held at Captain Richard Bonython's house on the east bank of the Saco River.

1638

The earliest of John Josselyn's two trips to Maine. He has left highly readable accounts of these visits to see his brother, Squire Henry Josselyn.

1640s

George Cleeve creates a separate Province of Lygonia in the Portland area. The Province of Maine is reduced to today's southern York County. A third province called Sagadahoc includes the lands between the Kennebec and Penobscot Rivers.

1651

The Puritans of Massachusetts initiate the process by which they eventually take over all of Maine, sending a "loving letter and friendly" to Kittery.

1652

In November 1652 Kittery gives in and becomes part of the Massachusetts Bay colony. The town of York soon follows suit.

1653

Wells, Biddeford, Saco, Cape Porpoise and Kennebunk also submit to Massachusetts.

1658

The communities in the Province of Lygonia, comprised of present-day Scarborough and Portland, submit to Massachusetts.

1660

King Charles II imposes monarchical rule back on England, following the Oliver Cromwell-dominated interregnum.

1663

John Josselyn returns to Maine. He protests the actions of Massachusetts to thwart the government headed by his brother Henry, which Royal agents of Charles II had put in place in Massachusetts and its District of Maine.

1674

For a brief period Dutch pirates capture and hold Castine at the mouth of the Penobscot River.

1675

King Philip's War begins in southern Massachusetts and spreads to Maine. "King Philip" is actually Metacom, the son of Massasoit, the Pilgrims' benefactor.

1676–1677

Indian attacks continue throughout Maine, even after King Philip is killed in Rhode Island.

1677

Massachusetts authorities send King Charles II huge pine mast trees for the Royal Navy. They were trying to appease his anger after they bought the rights of the Gorges family to Maine without his permission.

1678

King Philip's War ends. Sir Edmund Andros, governor of New York, becomes governor of the Dominion of New England, stretching from New Jersey to Maine. The Sagadahoc area is made the property of the Duke of York, the future James II.

1688

Sir Edmund Andros attacks Castine, trashes the household of the Baron de St. Castin, the son-in-law of the Penobscot chief Madockawando, and

Burnham Tavern in Machias was built in 1770. Throughout the American Revolution it was a gathering place for local citizens to talk and strategize about the War. Locals met here in 1775 to decided how to deal with British demands that citizens swear allegiance to the Crown. Patriotic residents declined and Machias was the site of the first naval battle of the Revolution. From Maine: A History *by Louis C. Hatch, 1919*

starts a new conflict with the French and Indians.

1689

Sir Edmund Andros is overthrown by a popular revolt in Boston as soon as Massachusetts receives news of the "Glorious Revolution" in England, which replaces James II with William and Mary.

1690

Sir William Phips, the Maine-born adventurer, is appointed governor of Massachusetts, thanks to the influence of Increase and Cotton Mather, Boston's famous father and son Congregationalist ministers. Phips continues the struggle against France by capturing Port Royal in Nova Scotia. His attempt to capture Quebec City is easily defeated, however.

1692

"York massacre." Indians led by Madockawando raid this border town in southern Maine, kill forty settlers, including the Congregationalist minister, and carry more than 100 women and children off to Canada as captives.

1696

A combined French and Indian force captures Fort William Henry, the principal English fortification in mid-coast Maine.

1697 and 1699

Peace treaties at Ryswick in Holland and Casco Bay in Maine end what has been called "King William's War."

1701

The Massachusetts General Court (its legislature) promulgates an infamous law to prevent frontier inhabitants from leaving their homes due to Indian threats. Kittery, York and Wells are included.

1703

War parties from Quebec attack Wells, Saco and Casco Bay. Colonel Benjamin Church leads an English counterattack.

1710

Colonel Francis Nicholson and his Royal Marines capture the French stronghold of Port Royal in Nova Scotia.

1711

The English bungle a second attempt to capture Quebec City.

1713

Queen Anne's War is ended by the Treaty of Utrecht, bringing peace to Maine but only temporarily.

1724

When another more localized set of hostilities, Dummer's War, flares up in Maine, a group of Rangers, mostly from the York area, avenge the "massacre" of 1692 by destroying the Indian village of Norridgewock on the Kennebec River. They kill the resident Jesuit priest, Father Sebastian Rasle, and end the Kennebec Indians' existence as a tribal entity.

1725

The battle of Lovewell's Pond, near Fryeburg, ends in a draw but breaks the power of the Piquacket Indians.

1744

War again: started in Europe and accompanied by a French attack on Nova Scotia.

1745

William Pepperrell, a Maine merchant from Kittery Point, leads an expedition of New England volunteers (one-third from Maine) that captures the massive French fortress of Louisbourg on Cape Breton Island. Pepperrell becomes an overnight hero and is the first "American" to be ennobled by the English King.

1748

The Treaty of Aix-la-Chapelle ends the fighting in King George's War. The English government infuriates Mainers and other New Englanders by handing back their great conquest, the fortress of Louisbourg, in exchange for a French-captured fort in India.

1753

The Kennebec Proprietors are reorganized. This was one of several large land-owning groups that amassed property in Maine and brought in

General Henry Knox (1750–1806) was a self-taught military expert who rose from poverty to prominence during the American Revolution. His expertise in fort construction attracted the attention of George Washington and the two became life-long friends. After the war, Washington named Knox to his cabinet as the country's first secretary of war. George Washington's Cabinet, 1791. Courtesy, Library of Congress

settlers, despite the intervals of warfare. Samuel Waldo headed another such organization. Yet others included the Pejepscot Proprietors and the Pemaquid Proprietors.

1755

James Cargill, an Indian fighter from Newcastle, is arrested for "murdering" a peaceable Indian, his wife and baby son. But after two years in jail, Cargill is acquitted.

1756

At the town of New Marblehead, settled by "little proprietors" from Marblehead in Massachusetts proper, a battle with the local Indians kills Chief Polin. New Marblehead is now Windham, west of Portland.

1759

An expedition against the French and Indians led by Massachusetts Governor Thomas Pownall lays claim to the entire Penobscot watershed. A fort is built at the mouth of the river. The noted Maine landowner Samuel Waldo, one of Pownal's, dies of a sudden heart attack during this trip.

1762

Major grants are made by the Massachusetts General Court of land far downeast in Maine, in Hancock and Washington counties.

1763

Machias, previously under the French, is reoccupied by settlers from Scarborough.

1763

The Treaty of Paris gives all of Canada to England, ending the French threat forever to New England and especially to Maine.

1774

As relations with England worsen, patriots in Cumberland County hold a convention. They force the local sheriff to declare he will not enforce any of the laws of Parliament that Americans find intolerable.

1774

The first Massachusetts Provincial Congress is held at Salem. Delegates from Maine's Cumberland, York and Lincoln counties attend.

Colby College opened in 1813 as the Maine Literary and Theological Institution. Renamed Waterville College in 1821, Colby got its present name during the Civil War when Maine-native Gardner Colby gave money to keep the financially strapped school open. Colby moved its campus from downtown Waterville to Mayflower Hill because the intown location didn't allow room for expansion. The move was completed in 1952. Courtesy, George French Collection, Maine State Archives

1775
In June, two months after Concord and Lexington, the first "naval battle" of the revolution is fought off Machias. Local patriots capture the British cutter *Margaretta*.

1775
In October Captain Mowatt of the Royal Navy bombards Portland and destroys the city.

1775
In November Benedict Arnold, having led an expeditionary force through Maine, fails to capture Quebec City and brings French Canada into the fight for American independence.

1776
Another American invasion of Canada from Maine. Colonel Jonathan Eddy tries to take Fort Cumberland in Nova Scotia but has to retreat to Machias.

1777
A British attack on Machias is beaten back by Colonel John Allan with the help of his Maine Indian allies.

1779
The British capture Castine. An armada sent from Massachusetts to recapture the Maine outpost is destroyed in the Penobscot River: "the worst American naval defeat until Pearl Harbor."

1783
The Treaty of Paris grants independence to the United States. Benjamin Franklin, as a negotiator, is prevented by John Adams from giving up eastern Maine to the British.

1786
The first meeting in Maine of those wishing to separate from Massachusetts.

1791
Henry Knox buys 2 million acres of Maine land to add to his already large holdings, which his wife Lucy inherited from her grandfather, Samuel Waldo.

1792
Knox sells most of his land holdings to William Bingham of Philadelphia.

1792
The first referendum is held in Maine on separating from Massachusetts. The idea is rejected.

1794
The Passamaquoddy tribe signs a treaty with Massachusetts, handing over most of their land in return for minimal financial assistance. This treaty is never ratified by Congress, as a 1790 law requires, leading to litigation almost 200 years later.

1796
The Penobscots sign a similar treaty surrendering their land. It and a subsequent one in 1833 are not ratified by Congress.

1797
A referendum on separation passes but by such a narrow vote that Massachusetts refuses to recognize the results.

1797
Alexander Baring of the English banking house Baring Brothers buys half of William Bingham's land in Maine and marries his oldest daughter.

1802
Bowdoin College, named for Massachusetts Governor James Bowdoin and chartered in 1794, opens its doors in Brunswick.

1805
William King, who will lead Maine to statehood, is elected to the Massachusetts General Court as a Jeffersonian Democrat-Republican.

1807
Jefferson's embargo destroys the Maine shipping industry. Statehood for Maine loses by a three to one margin in another referendum.

1812
The War of 1812. Maine is again invaded by the British. Castine and Eastport are occupied and Bangor burned after an American defeat at Hampden.

1813
The founding of Colby College, originally called Waterville College.

1814
Maine's anger at Massachusetts Governor Caleb Strong for his refusal to help them against the British leads to new strength for the separation movement.

Maine poet Henry Wadsworth Longfellow (1807–1882) was the author of Evangeline, Hiawatha *and* The Midnight Ride of Paul Revere. *From* Maine: A History *by Louis C. Hatch, 1919*

1819
The final vote on Maine statehood. It passes overwhelmingly: 17,091 to 7,132.

1819
Maine holds a constitutional convention, defines its separate government and chooses the name Maine, instead of Columbia.

1820
Problems arise in Washington, D.C. The southern states balk at accepting Maine as a free state unless Missouri is accepted as a slave state.

1820
The Missouri Compromise allows Maine and Missouri to become the twenty-third and twenty-fourth states, respectively.

1823–1825
Bowdoin College graduates future illustrious Americans, including William Pitt Fessenden, U.S. senator and secretary of the treasury; Franklin Pierce, president of the United States; Nathaniel Hawthorne, writer, and Henry Wadsworth Longfellow, poet.

1824
The Reverend Jonathan Fisher paints his most famous picture, *A Morning View of Blue Hill.*

1827
The Maine Legislature finally agrees to accept land in Augusta on which to build a permanent capitol. Portland, site of the temporary capital, opposes the move.

1827
Arrest of John Baker by Canadian authorities on the land in the north claimed by Maine.

1829
The cornerstone for the new Bulfinch-designed Maine capitol building is laid in Augusta.

1831
The King of Holland tries to arbitrate the conflict between Maine and the Canadians over the location of Maine's northernmost border. Both sides reject his decision.

1832
The state capitol building is completed, and Augusta finally becomes the seat of Maine's government.

1839
"The Aroostook War." The U.S. and Great Britain almost go to war over the northeast boundary question. Troops from both countries face off, but no shots are fired.

1840
The Whigs win the governorship in Maine for the first time and also the presidency. Daniel Webster is named secretary of state. Webster and the British envoy Lord Ashburton settle the boundary dispute. Lord Ashburton is actually Alexander Baring, who owns hundreds of thousands of acres in northern Maine.

1843
Edward Kavanagh becomes governor of Maine, replacing John Fairfield, who is elected to the U.S. Senate. He is the first Roman Catholic to attain high office in New England.

1845
John A. Poor convinces Montreal businessmen to route the Grand Trunk Railroad to Portland instead of Boston.

1851
The first temperance law in the country is passed by the Maine Legislature. Prohibition becomes known in the U.S. as the "Maine Law."

1852
Harriet Beecher Stowe writes *Uncle Tom's Cabin* in Brunswick.

1853
The most famous Maine clipper ship, the *Red Jacket*, is launched at Rockland. Within two years, Maine is acknowledged to be the shipbuilding capital of the U.S.

1854
James G. Blaine, destined to be a major national political figure, migrates to Maine from Pennsylvania.

Alonzo Garcelon (1813–1906), a native of Lewiston, was elected mayor in 1871. In 1878 he was elected governor of Maine, the first Democrat to hold that office in more than twenty years. From Maine: A History *by Louis C. Hatch, 1919*

1854–1855

Anti-Catholic "Know Nothingism" peaks as a political force in Maine. A Jesuit priest, Father John Bapst, is tarred and feathered in Ellsworth; a Catholic church is burned in Bath and Anson P. Morrill is elected governor with Know Nothing help.

1855

A riot over liquor laws erupts in Portland, where the "father of Prohibition," Neal Dow, is the mayor. One man is shot to death.

1856

The "Maine Law" is repealed but is later reinstated. Maine stays legally dry from then on until 1933.

1857

Henry David Thoreau makes the last of his trips to the Maine woods, having come also in 1846 and 1853. His writings, particularly about Mount Katahdin, are today considered the inspiration for the "wilderness" movement in the U.S.

1860

Maine U.S. Senator Hannibal Hamlin runs as vice president with Lincoln. They are elected.

1862

The Maine Central Railroad goes into operation. Eventually it will incorporate fifty other railroad lines.

1863

Battle of Gettysburg. Its major hero is Maine's Joshua Chamberlain, Colonel of the 20th Maine Regiment. His defense of Little Round Top turns the tide for the Union forces.

1863–1864

Two Confederate attacks on Maine occur—an attempted bank robbery in Calais and a daring naval raid into Portland harbor.

1864

Hannibal Hamlin is replaced as vice president by Andrew Johnson.

1865

General Joshua Chamberlain is selected to receive General Robert E. Lee's surrender at Appamatox. He

Built in 1939 for the Aroostook War, the Fort Kent Blockhouse was named for Governor Edward Kent (1802–1877). Now an historic landmark on the National Register of Historic Places, the Blockhouse offers visitors local history and interpretive displays. Courtesy, George French Collection, Maine State Archives

orders his men to present arms when the defeated Confederates march by.

1865

Maine's U.S. Senator William Pitt Fessenden is made chairman of Congress's Joint Committee on Reconstruction.

1865

Maine native General Oliver Otis Howard is appointed head of the Freedmen's Bureau, in charge of aiding the emancipated slaves in the South.

1867

James G. Blaine is chosen Speaker of the U.S. House by the majority Republicans.

1870

Major immigration of French Canadians into Maine to work in the textile mills.

1871

John A. Poor's projected North American and European Railway reaches Vanceboro on the Canadian border. President Ulysses S. Grant travels to Maine for the ribbon cutting.

1871–1875

Growth of hotels in Bar Harbor and York Harbor, at both ends of the state, spurs Maine's summer tourist industry.

1876

James G. Blaine is favored to win the Republican nomination for president. His involvement in a railroad stock scandal hurts him politically; he is passed over for Rutherford B. Hayes, who wins the presidency in a highly disputed election.

1877

Sarah Orne Jewett, considered possibly Maine's finest writer of fiction, publishes her first book.

1878

The rise of the Greenback Party in Maine that favors cheap money. They are strong enough to combine with the Democrats and elect the first Democratic governor since 1854—Alonzo Garcelon.

1879

The infamous "Count Out" or "State Steal." Maine almost has a civil war over who will control the Legislature and the governorship. The Republicans, led by Blaine, prevail.

1880–1889

Maine legislators occupy key positions in Washington, D.C.

1880

Blaine loses the Republican nomination to James Garfield, his close friend, who appoints him secretary of state.

1880

Maine botanist Kate Furbish discovers the rare snapdragon plant (the Furbish lousewort) that is later used to help block the Dickey-Lincoln dam.

1881

Garfield is assassinated and Blaine leaves his job as secretary of state; then is elected by the Maine Legislature to the U.S. Senate.

1884

Blaine receives the GOP nomination for president. He loses New York by 1,020 votes and is defeated by Grover Cleveland.

1885

Maine lobstermen begin the practice of using color-coded buoys to mark their traps.

1888

Maine's Thomas Brackett Reed defeats William McKinley to become the Speaker of the House in Congress.

1890

Reed wins national recognition by overriding Democratic efforts to use the quorum call to stymie congressional action. He is nicknamed "Czar Reed" for his high-handedness.

1890

Aroostook County is a major U.S. potato producer, with 28,000 acres under cultivation.

1895–1899

Tom Reed seeks the Republican nomination for president, but it goes to McKinley who wins the White House in 1896. Opposed to McKinley's "imperialist" policies, Reed resigns from Congress in 1899.

1896

Maine shipbuilder Arthur Sewall is the Democratic candidate for vice president on the same losing ticket with William Jennings Bryan.

1898

International Paper, the giant company

Aerial view of the State House in Augusta, circa 1940. Courtesy,George French Collection, Maine State Archives

put together by Maine industrialist Hugh Chisholm by combining twenty small paper companies, begins operations.

1898

The battleship *Maine* blows up in Havana harbor. "Remember the Maine" becomes a rallying cry in the Spanish-American War.

1899

Walter Wyman begins the electric power business that turns into the Central Maine Power Company; the Maine Legislature charters the Great Northern Paper Company.

1901

The Great Northern Paper Company builds its paper mill complex in the Maine wilderness and creates the town of Millinocket.

1901

In Bar Harbor George Bucknam Dorr starts his two decade-long effort to create Acadia National Park.

1905

The Russo-Japanese Peace Treaty is signed on Maine soil at the Portsmouth

Naval Shipyard, which is physically located in Kittery.

1912

Governor Harris Plaisted leads the state-ordered eviction of a black and mixed-blood population on Malaga Island.

1913

Maine Congressman Charles Guernsey submits a bill in Congress to create a Katahdin National Park. It fails.

1917

Percival Baxter, as a candidate for State Senate, proposes that Maine buy Katahdin for a state park. He is unsuccessful.

1921

Percival Baxter, the president of the Maine State Senate, automatically becomes governor when the elected governor, Frederick Parkhurst, dies after a month in office.

1923

A battle royal develops over the control of water power in Maine between Governor Baxter and the paper and power companies. Baxter insists that the industries must pay for the use of it. He ultimately wins his point.

1924

Because of the Volstead Act, establishing national prohibition, Maine becomes a major target for rum runners bringing in liquor from Canada.

1925

The revived Ku Klux Klan movement in the U.S. reaches its Maine peak—an estimated 150,000 members. It is essentially aimed at Catholics. Within six years, the hooded secret order has dwindled to less than 200 souls.

1926

Engineer Dexter Cooper receives a preliminary permit from the Federal Power Commission to build the huge dam he conceived for harnessing the tides in Passamaquoddy Bay.

1926

After losing a Republican primary for U.S. Senate, Percival Baxter vows to spend the rest of his life and inherited money to buy Mount Katahdin and its surrounding area for a state park.

1932

Maine elects its first Democratic governor in two decades, Louis Brann.

1933

With the advent of the New Deal, Dexter Cooper's "Quoddy" dam project is revived. U.S. Army engineers proceed to build Quoddy Village to house the workers who will be needed. Congress then kills the project by withdrawing its funding.

1933

Civilian Conservation Corps (CCC) programs begin in Maine. Today, a statue in Augusta commemorates the achievements of these young men.

1935

Maine born and raised film director John Ford receives his first Oscar for *The Informer*. Other Oscars follow for this master of the cinematic art, especially known for his Westerns.

1937

The most violent strike in Maine history breaks out when the shoe workers of Lewiston and Auburn clash with state troopers and local police.

1940

Maine Congressman Clyde Smith dies

In 1987 the International Paperworkers Union Local 14 called a strike at the International Paper's (IP) Androscoggin Mill in Jay to combat the company's efforts to weaken their contract. The bitter sixteen-month strike divided the town and undermined the union. IP permanently replaced the striking workers, pitting townspeople who needed work against strikers standing up for a cause they believed in. This mural, located on the front of the PACE Local 1-0014 headquarters in Jay, memorializes the strikers and their efforts. Photo by Stephanie Philbrick

of a sudden heart attack. He is succeeded by his wife, Margaret Chase Smith.

1941

Even before the U.S. entered World War II, the Bath Iron Works begins building destroyers for the U.S. Navy and merchant ships that were sent to Great Britain.

1944

On January 27, 1944 the shipyard at Kittery launches four submarines of the eighty-five it built between 1939 and 1945. Later that year, two German spies from a U-boat land at Hancock Point. Observed by a high school student, they are tracked to New York City by federal authorities and apprehended.

1948

Congresswoman Margaret Chase Smith wins a four-way Republican primary for U.S. Senate and continues her distinguished career in Congress.

1950

Senator Margaret Chase Smith delivers her famous "Declaration of Conscience" speech, attacking her fellow Republican, Senator Joseph McCarthy, for his tactics.

1952

Rachel Carson writes *Silent Spring*, much of it at her summer home on Southport Island.

1954

Edmund S. Muskie, an obscure state representative, becomes the first Democratic governor of Maine since the Depression. He is also the first Catholic to be elected to the office.

1960

The election of John F. Kennedy leads to a revival of the Quoddy hydroelectric project, eventually to be tied in with a dam on the St. John River at the Dickey-Lincoln School location. Other hydro projects proposed for the St. John threaten the pristine Allagash River.

1964

The Maine Legislature creates the Allagash River Authority to plan for a "Wilderness Waterway."

1965

Maine Senators Margaret Chase Smith and Edmund Muskie push for the Dickey-Lincoln School power project.

1965

The 102nd Maine Legislature allows the Prestile Stream in Aroostook County to be polluted to facilitate a sugar beet refinery and a whole new agricultural industry—growing sugar beets—for northern Maine.

1966

Democrat Kenneth M. Curtis is elected as the youngest governor in the U.S., creating what some historians call a "revolution" in Maine politics.

Samantha Smith (1972–1985) was known as "America's Youngest Ambassador." She became famous after writing to Soviet Communist Party leader, Yuri Andropov, about the Cold War. Andropov sent a personal reply and invited Smith to Moscow. The result was a public relations event that helped thaw relations between the Soviet Union and the U.S. Smith translated her sudden fame into other opportunities, including a television series. In 1985 she and her father were returning from filming when their plan crashed, killing them both. Photo by Stephanie Philbrick

1968
Curtis successfully institutes a state income tax and achieves acclaim for two environmental bills, the first of their kind in the country.

1968
Maine's Ed Muskie is the Democratic candidate for vice president, on the same ticket with Hubert Humphrey.

1970
Ken Curtis is reelected by less than 500 votes, despite widespread anger over the income tax.

1971
An initiated referendum to repeal the state income tax is defeated by a three to one margin.

1972
Federal Judge Edward T. Gignoux rules that a federal law of 1790, the so-called Non-Intercourse Act, applies to Maine Indians, thus allowing a land claims case brought by the Penobscots and Passamaquoddies against Maine to go forward.

1973
Maine author Stephen King publishes his first novel, *Carrie*. It is an instant success and is made into a motion picture. A string of international best-sellers makes King one of the best known American writers of all time.

1974
James Longley, running as an Independent, is an upset winner for governor of Maine.

1980
President Jimmy Carter signs legislation incorporating the Maine Indian Land Claims Settlement.

1980
Ed Muskie is unexpectedly made U.S. secretary of state by Carter. Muskie's former aide, George J. Mitchell, is appointed to take his place.

1984
Maine runner, Joan Benoit wins the Olympic gold medal in the first women's marathon ever run in the Games.

1985
Samantha Smith, the Maine elementary schoolgirl who started an international peace exchange with a letter to Soviet leader Yuri Andropov, is killed in a plane crash in Lewiston. She was coming home from Hollywood, where she had been filming a TV series in which she was featured.

1988
Longtime Maine summer resident George H. W. Bush is elected president. Kennebunkport becomes the site of the summer White House.

1989
Senator George Mitchell is chosen by his fellow Democrats to be the majority leader in the U.S. Senate. He continues in that position until 1995.

1992
A bitter and prolonged strike occurs at the International Paper Company plant in January. It is the worst Maine labor dispute since the 1930s.

1993
The University of Maine hockey team wins the NCAA Division 1 national championship. Later they are accused of having used an ineligible player, but are allowed to keep the championship.

1995
Former Maine U.S. Senator George J. Mitchell accepts the invitation of the British and Irish governments to try to broker a peaceful accord between Catholic and Protestant antagonists in Northern Ireland. His efforts lead to the Good Friday Agreement. He is later asked by President Clinton to work on a similar accord in the Israeli-Palestinian conflict.

1999
The U-Maine hockey team again wins the national championship. Their extraordinary coach, Sean Walsh, dies of cancer two years later.

2002
Maine writer Richard Russo wins the Pulitzer Prize for his novel, *Empire Falls*.

2002
The all-time record catch of Maine lobsters: 57.2 million pounds, valued at $188.5 million.

2002
Controversy over Somali immigration into Lewiston. More than 4,000 Mainers turn out to protest against a handful of racists trying to stir up trouble in Maine's second largest city.

2003
A statewide referendum dooms the idea of an Indian gambling casino in Maine by a large margin. At the same time, Maine voters approve allowing slot machines at race tracks.

2005
A number of military bases in Maine are ordered closed by the U.S. Department of Defense under the Base Realignment legislation authorized by Congress. But the Commission (BRAC) established by the law keeps open and even expands facilities in northern Maine, as well as saving the Portsmouth Naval Shipyard, which is physically located in Kittery. Only the Naval Air Station at Brunswick remains on the closure list.

BIBLIOGRAPHY

Agger, Lee. *Women of Maine*. Portland, ME. Guy Gannett Books. 1982.

Ahlin, John Howard. *Maine Rubicon: Downeast, Settlers During the American Revolution* Camden, ME. Picton Press. 1966.

Albert, Thomas, l'abbe. *Histoire du Madawaska*. Quebec. Imprimerie Franciscaine Missionaire. 1920.

Arel, Jules J. *German Prisoners of War in Maine*. Portland, ME. *Maine Historical Society Quarterly*. "Maine History." Vol.34. Nos 3-4. Winter/Spring 1995.

Banks, Ronald. *Maine Becomes A State: The Movement To Separate Maine From Massachusetts, 1785-1820*. Somersworth, NH. New Hampshire Publishing Company. 1973.

_____(Editor). *A History of Maine*. Dubuque, IA. Kendall Hunt Publishing Company. 1969.

Barringer, Richard (Editor). *Changing Maine, 1960-2010*. Gardiner, ME. Tilbury House Publishers. 2004.

Barry, William David. *The Shameful Story of Malaga Island*. Camden, ME. 1980.

Beck, Horace P. *The Folklore of Maine*. Philadelphia, PA. J.B. Lippincott Company. 1957.

Beston, Henry (Editor). *White Pine and Blue Water: A State of Maine Reader*. Camden, ME. Down East Magazine Books. 1950.

Brain, Jeffrey. *The Popham Colony*. Salem, MA. The Peabody Essex Museum. 2000.

Brodeur, Paul. *Restitution: The Land Claims of the Mashpee, Passamaquoddy and Penobscot Indians of New England*. Boston, MA. Northeastern University Press. 1985.

Bunting, W.H. *A Day's Work: Part II*. Gardiner, ME. Tilbury House Publishers. 2000.

Burrage, Henry S. *The Beginnings of Colonial Maine*. Augusta, ME. State of Maine. 1914.

Callahan, North. *Henry Knox: General Washington's General*. South Brunswick, NJ and New York, NY. A.S. Barnes and Company. 1958.

Chase, Mary Ellen. *Jonathan Fisher: Maine Parson, 1768-1847*. New York, NY. The Macmillan Company. 1948.

Clark, Charles E. *The Eastern Frontier: The Settlement of Northern New England, 1610-1763*. New York, NY. Alfred A. Knopf, Inc. 1970.

Cleveland, Nehemiah. *History of Bowdoin College*. Boston, MA. James Ripley Osgood and Company. 1882.

Corson, Trevor. *The Secret Life of Lobsters*. New York, NY. Harper Collins. 2004.

Dorr, George B. *The Story of Acadia National Park*. Bar Harbor, ME. Acadia Publishing Company. 1942.

Eckstorm, Fannie Hardy. *Old John Neptune and Other Indian Shamans*. Orono, ME. University of Maine Press, reprint. 1980.

_____*The Penobscot Man*. Boston, MA. Houghton Mifflin. 1914.

Fischer, Jeff, (Director). *Maine Speaks: An Anthology of Maine Literature*. Brunswick, ME. Maine Writers and Publishers Alliance. 1989.

Gilpatrick, Gil. *Allagash: The Story of Maine's Legendary Wilderness*. Skowhegan, ME. Self-published. 1995.

Graham, Ada and Frank. *Kate Furbish and the Flora of Maine*. Gardiner, ME. Tilbury House Publishers. 1995.

Grant, W.L. (Editor). *Voyages of Samuel de Champlain*. New York, NY. Charles Scribner and Sons. 1907.

Hale, Richard Walden. *The Story of Bar Harbor*. New York, NY. Ives, Washburn, Inc. 1949.

Hatch, Louis. *Maine: A History*. New York, NY. American Historical Society. 1919.

Jewett, Sarah Orne. *The Country of the Pointed Firs*. New York, NY. Doubleday Anchor Books, reprint. 1956.

Josselyn, John. *An Account of Two Voyages in New England*. London. G. Widdows. 1674.

King, Stephen. *The Girl Who Loved Tom Gordon*. New York, NY. Charles Scribner and Sons. 1999.

Leamon, James S. *Revolution Downeast: The War For American Independence in Maine*. Amherst, MA. University of Massachusetts Press. 1993.

_____. *Historic Lewiston: A Textile City in Transition*. Auburn, ME. Central Maine Vocational Technical Institute. 1976.

McCann, Paul. *Timber! The Fall of Maine's Paper Giant [Great Northern Paper Company]*. Ellsworth, ME. The Ellsworth American. 1994.

Molloy, Anne. *Five Kidnapped Indians*. New York, NY. Hastings House. 1968.

Munson, Gorham Bert. *Penobscot: Down East Paradise*. Philadelphia, PA. J.B. Lippincott. 1959.

Niss, Bob. *Faces of Maine*. Portland, ME. Guy Gannett Books. 1981.

Pattangall, William. *The Maine Hall of Fame*. Waterville, ME. The Maine Democrat. 1909. 1910.

Peckham, Howard H. *The Colonial Wars, 1689-1762*. Chicago, IL. University of Chicago Press. 1964.

Reid, John G. *Maine, Charles II and Massachusetts*. Portland, ME. Maine Historical Society. 1977.

Ring, Elizabeth. *Maine in the Making of the Nation, 1783-1870*. Camden, ME. Picton Press. 1996.

Rolde, Neil. *Maine: A Narrative History*. Gardiner, ME. Tilbury House Publishers. 1990.

_____*The Interrupted Forest*. Gardiner, ME. Tilbury House Publishers. 2001.

_____*Unsettled Past, Unsettled Future*. Gardiner, ME. Tilbury House Publishers. 2004.

_____*The Baxters of Maine*. Gardiner, ME. Tilbury House Publishers. 1997.

_____*So You Think You Know Maine*. Gardiner, ME. Harpswell Press. 1984.

_____*York Is Living History*. Brunswick, ME. Harpswell Press. 1975.

_____*An Illustrated History of Maine*, Augusta, ME. Friends of the Maine State Museum. 1995.

Russell, Charles Edward. *Blaine of Maine*. New York, NY. Cosmopolitan Book Corp. 1931.

Scontras, Charles A. *Organized Labor in Maine: 20th Century Origins*. Orono, ME. University of Maine Press. 1985.

Skelton, William B. *Walter S. Wyman, 1874-1942: One of Maine's Great Pioneers*. Princeton, NJ. Newcomen Society. Princeton University Press. 1949.

Smith, David C. *History of Papermaking in the United States*. New York, NY. Lockwood Publishing Company. 1970.

Smith, David C. and Edward O. Shriver. *Maine: A History Through Selected Readings*. Dubuque, IA. Kendall Hunt Publishing Company. 1985.

Spencer, Wilbur D. *Pioneers on Maine Rivers*. Bowie, MD. Heritage Books, reprint. 1990.

Taylor, Alan. *Liberty Men and Great Proprietors*. Chapel Hill, NC. University of North Carolina Press. 1990.

Terrell, Carroll F. *Stephen King: Man and Artist*. Orono, ME. Northern Lights Publishing Company. 1990.

Thoreau, Henry David. *The Maine Woods*. New York, NY. Bramhall House, reprint. 1950.

Ulrich, Laura. *A Midwife's Tale: The Life of Martha Ballard, Based on Her Diary, 1785-1812*. New York, NY. Alfred A. Knopf. 1990.

Williamson, William Durkee. *The History of the State of Maine*. Two Volumes. Hallowell, ME. Glazier, Masters and Company. 1832.

Wing, Henry A. *Maine's War Upon the Liquor Traffic*. Portland, ME. *Portland Evening Express*. 1910.

INDEX